Beatriz Colomina
Domesticity at War

To my mother.
To my father, in memoriam.

Publisher
Actar
www.actar.com
info@actar.com

Author
Beatriz Colomina

Graphic designer
Reinhard Steger

Printing
Ingoprint SA

Distribution
Actar D
Roca i Batlle 2
08023 Barcelona
office@actar-d.com
www.actar-d.com
Tel +34 93 4174993
Fax +34 93 4186707

DL B-40984-06
ISBN 84-96540-11-1

© of the edition, Actar, Barcelona 2006
© of the texts, Beatriz Colomina
© of the photos, their authors

Printed and bound in the European Union

Every effort has been made to contact copyright holders of images published herein. The publisher would appreciate being informed of any omissions in order to make due acknowledgement in future editions of this book.

| 5 | Introduction
Built in the USA

| 21 | Chapter 1
1949

| 61 | Chapter 2
DDU at MoMA

| 83 | Chapter 3
The Eames House

| 111 | Chapter 4
The Lawn at War

| 145 | Chapter 5
X-Ray Architecture

| 193 | Chapter 6
Unbreathed Air

| 239 | Chapter 7
Enclosed by Images

| 275 | Chapter 8
The Underground House

| 295 | Epilogue

Introduction
Built in the USA

It was beautiful while it lasted. For a brief period, the span of about fifteen years following the end of World War II, America seemed to embrace modern architecture. It was not, as with the International Style exhibition of 1932 at the Museum of Modern Art, the importation of some European ideas repackaged as a style. It was the development of a whole new mode of operation, one that fascinated Europe in the same way that European models had once fascinated the United States. Indeed, it would seem that the Europeans were more fascinated by the new American models than Americans themselves were. As Alison and Peter Smithson put it:

> There has been much reflection in England on the Eames House. For the Eames House was a cultural gift parcel received here at a particularly useful time. The bright wrapper has made most people—especially Americans—throw the content away as not sustaining. But we have been brooding on it—working on it—feeding on it.[1]

Feeding on it? British architects were absorbing American architecture through the pages of architectural magazines, in the same way that they were absorbing other products of postwar America through advertisements in popular journals. Modern architecture was part of a general fascination, as attractive and colorful as the other products of the Good Life: the cars, the appliances, the food, the toys, the furniture, the dresses, and the lawns. It was yet another well-packaged, consumable object—a desirable image, good enough to eat. Can we forget that rationing did not end in the UK until the 1950s? And that Alison Smithson's grandmother used to receive food parcels from a second cousin who was a college librarian in America? Included in those parcels were copies of *Ladies' Home Journal* and the *Woman's Home Companion*, considered in retrospect by the Smithsons as "cultural gift parcels." Clippings from these journals became raw material for the Smithsons' work as part of the Independent Group.² **6** If the IG came together as collectors of images, architecture was part of that collection and food one of its dominant themes. The Eames House became another cultural gift parcel fed to a hungry audience.

In their decisive 1956 article "But Today We Collect Ads," the Smithsons write about postwar American advertisements as "good images": "Ads which do not try to sell you the product except as a natural accessory of a way of life." Likewise, it could be said that modern architecture in the US presented itself as a "good image," a part of an overall package, a way of life rather than an isolated artistic or technical object. When European architects turned to the US for inspiration in the immediate postwar years, they were presented with modern architecture as a happy, mass-consumable environment. The buildings were simply a frame for attractive objects, a kind of shelf, a storage and display system so overflowing with objects that the architecture itself dissolved.

Images in the 1950s were the new architecture, "the unclassified background material against which we pass our lives," as the Smithsons put it. **7 8 9 23** This represents a fundamental transformation of the urban condition of even just the previous fifty years. If early in the twentieth century Walter Benjamin described architecture as that art form which is perceived only unconsciously, in a state of distraction, that role was now being taken over by images. An endless flow of images now constituted the environment. Buildings had become images, and images had become a kind of building, occupied like any other architectural space.

---

1 Alison and Peter Smithson, "Eames Celebration," *Architectural Design*, September 1966, 432.
2 *The Independent Group* (IG) was a group of about fifteen young artists, architects, and intellectuals who frequented the Institute of Contemporary Arts in London and organized themselves into a discussion group committed to exploring what they called the "aesthetics of plenty." See *The Independent Group: Postwar Britain and the Aesthetics of Plenty*, ed. David Robbins (Cambridge, MA: MIT Press, 1990).

The significance of architects like the Eameses lies in their particular sensitivity to this transformation. But they were not alone. A number of postwar American architects were innovative in making this transition. They understood that to be an architect in the 1950s meant something completely different than what it had for the previous generation. Images had become the raw material of their craft. **10** **11** **22**

How are we to understand this phenomenon? What precise role was played by the institutions that supported it? The Eames House was part of the Case Study Program of exhibition houses in Los Angeles, sponsored by the magazine *Arts & Architecture* under John Entenza and supported by the manufacturers of consumer products.[3] **12** **13** Meanwhile on the East Coast, the Museum of Modern Art played a crucial role by commissioning a series of exhibition houses to be built in the garden of the museum in collaboration with department stores and popular magazines. **14** **80** **82** **84** **85** These programs redefined the role of architecture, positioning it within a new consumer culture and a new cult of domesticity. As exhibition houses became indistinguishable from the array of products they displayed, domestic architecture was absorbed into the flow of images, and a new form of domesticity was found within images.

Both programs were related to war. Just as manufacturers were turning wartime industry to peacetime, missiles to washing machines, cultural institutions were turning wartime strategies to new ends. The Museum of Modern Art program of exhibition houses was a direct extension of the institution's wartime operations. The Case Study Houses likewise emerged out of wartime activities on the part of the journal, the architects, and the industries involved. **15** Both institutions

---

[3] *Blueprints for Modern Living: History and Legacy of the Case Study Houses*, ed. Elizabeth A. T. Smith (Los Angeles: Museum of Contemporary Art; Cambridge, MA: MIT Press, 1989).

targeted the middle-class consumer, understood as a completely new figure, a "modern man," as Entenza put it, who on returning from the war would rather live in a modern environment utilizing the most advanced technologies than in "old fashioned houses with enclosed rooms." The war had, as it were, educated the taste, the aesthetic sensibility of the public.

It was the engagement with World War II that finally created the conditions for the development of modern architecture in the US. This late arrival has to be carefully reconsidered in terms of the architecture of the historical avant-garde that was itself produced explicitly in response to World War I. Modern architecture is inseparable from war, not simply because it emerged and was developed in the years around World War I, as we could say of the artistic avant-garde, but in a much more intimate sense: modern architecture borrowed—or perhaps "recycled" is a more accurate word—the techniques, materials, and ways of doing that were developed for the military. Postwar architecture was not simply the bright architecture that came after the darkness of the war. It was the aggressively happy architecture that came out of the war, a war that anyway was ongoing as the cold war. The new form of domesticity turned out to be a powerful weapon. Expertly designed images of domestic bliss were launched to the entire world as part of a carefully orchestrated propaganda campaign.

Architects and institutions participated in this campaign. The figure of the architect changed from the heroic one of the modern movement—serious, masculine, austere, formally dressed, earnest, in public—to the domesticated agent of the postwar years: happy, pleasure seeking, sensual, casually dressed, relaxed, at home. Even the most strict architects of the modern movement who had emigrated to the USA before or during the war transformed themselves in the postwar years.

Take the image of Ise and Walter Gropius at breakfast on the screened porch of their house in Lincoln, Massachusetts. **17** The photograph was published as a full-page image in a 1950 issue of *L'architecture d'aujourd'hui* edited by Paul Rudolph and dedicated to the Gropius school at Harvard. The table is set for four, but only the couple is seated. Gropius, with his back to the camera and a toaster by his side, is wearing an all-American plaid shirt, with what appears to be a soft sweater hanging from the empty chair next to him. Diagonally across from him sits Ise, in an embroidered white blouse, her head sharply turned to show her striking profile. They are both looking in toward the house rather than out to the landscape. What comes across is an attractive scene of domestic bliss in a modern environment. Gropius had arrived in the USA in 1937 to assume the position of chair of architecture at the Graduate School of Design, and the house was his first realized building in this country. But why was such a domestic image so prominently displayed in an issue of an architectural journal dedicated to a school of architecture? Why is Gropius at home rather than at work? Why is Ise rather than Gropius or the house itself the center of the photograph? Why has the house evaporated into a sparse frame for a lifestyle? Selling the school of architecture at Harvard meant selling such a lifestyle, not so different from selling any other product in postwar America. If the school had reoriented itself to teach modern architecture, the first need was to establish that modern was livable, glamorous, desirable. A professionally shot full-page photograph of the domestic life of the chairman becomes an advertisement for the new direction of a very public school of architecture.

Roll back to 1923, to the famous press photograph, reprinted on the back of the Smithsons' book *The Heroic Period of Modern Architecture*, of Gropius and Le Corbusier sitting at a small round table at the Café des Deux Magots in Paris. **18** Both architects are formally dressed, with suits, ties, long coats, and even hats,

while having an intense conversation—in Gropius's recollection—about Le Corbusier's plans for a city for three million and their ideas for the standardization and prefabrication of homes. Behind them, sitting at an adjacent table but clearly cut from the scene, Alma Gropius appears as if another anonymous customer of the café. Her hand to her chest, she has the look of concern—as Alan Colquhoun once told me—of somebody who has just found a cockroach on her plate, but the men are oblivious. What comes across in this slightly blurry documentary photograph is a public display of heroic figures, two edgy manifesto writers detached from their domestic lives, a world away from the breakfast table in Lincoln.

This book is a study of the space between these photographs, the space within which American architecture would rapidly arise and flourish for a time. In a sense, it is a continuation of my previous book *Privacy and Publicity: Modern Architecture as Mass Media*. Yet the difference between these two photographs marks such a radical shift that new forms of research and interpretation are needed. Even the character of the archives fundamentally changes.

In the last few years, while working on this project, I have been going through boxes of documents belonging to the archives (now in the Library of Congress) of Charles and Ray Eames, shuffling through their papers, peeking into their correspondence, going through their so-called publicity file (where they kept track of every notice of their work in the press, in professional journals, in catalogs, in advertisements), and so on. I thought, having spent so much time at the Fondation Le Corbusier in Paris, that Le Corbusier was the most compulsive filer one could find, that only he could keep track of "everything." That was before I met the Eameses. With them, all the stuff of everyday life enters the archive. [20] They kept track of such mundane things as what they ate at the office on a particular week (menus, with two choices for each course, are typed and are now kept in the archives) or the clothes they were taking on a trip (lists of items to take are first scribbled on a scrap of paper, then typed, then filed away); even the memos of who called on what day, at what hour, with what message, are filed away. It is a kind of obsessive domesticity documented in fetishistic detail and requiring a new kind of architecture. Buildings were seamlessly blurred into the wider visual field. This mentality organizes *House: After Five Years of Living*, the Eameses' 1955 film about their own house, a kaleidoscopic array of slides of domestic details in which the house itself dissolves into images, exemplifying the redefinition of architecture that was occurring on many fronts. **21** **176** **407** Cold-war anxieties about global threats were masked by endlessly multiplied images of the absolute control of domestic details and permanent smiles.

This sense of obsessive, embattled domesticity is the trademark of the immediate postwar years and the focus of this archaeological study. A set of interlocking case studies explores the unique phenomenon from different angles to build up a multifaceted picture of the period. Architectural culture, military culture, and mass culture are tightly woven together in a way that defined a unique historical moment.

Chapter 1
1949

Was postwar American architecture the next stage of the historical avant-garde in architecture, the beginning of a new avant-garde, or the loss of the avant-garde as a useful category for architecture?

There still seems to be quite a bit of confusion about whether there ever was an architectural avant-garde in North America. A symposium in New York in 1996, celebrating the ninetieth birthday of Philip Johnson, addressed the "American architectural avant-garde between 1923 and 1949," as if the very idea of an American architectural avant-garde and those particular dates were unproblematic. Yet they are very problematic.

Nineteen twenty-three was an important year for the historical avant-garde. It was the year of, among other things, the publication of Le Corbusier's *Vers une architecture*; the first issue of the Berlin magazine *G* (edited by El Lissitzky, Hans Richter, and Werner Gräff), where Mies van der Rohe's projects for a Glass Skyscraper and a Concrete Office Building were published; the exhibition of El Lissitkzy's Proun rooms at the Grosse Berliner Kunstausstellung; the de Stijl exhibition of architectural models at the Galerie Léonce Rosenberg in Paris; the first Bauhaus exhibition in Weimar; Mies van der Rohe's project for the Concrete Country House; and so on. **24** But the US was quite slow, if not hostile, to the reception of the ideas of modern architecture; it would seem that there was no climate for their reception. Despite Le Corbusier and Ozenfant's serious efforts to come up with an American version of *L'Esprit nouveau* (the journal where Le Corbusier first published the material later collected in *Vers une architecture*), the project did not take off. **25 26** *Vers une architecture* was not translated into English until 1927 (and then only in England!). Only a handful of architects in the USA would have known about it in 1923. There was no notice of the book in any American architectural journal. In fact, if one is to take publications seriously, and one should,

South Africans knew about Le Corbusier before Americans did: in 1925, the *South African Architectural Record* published an article entitled "The Modern Movement in Architecture," while it would take three more years for the American *Architectural Record* to acknowledge Le Corbusier, with the article "Modern Architecture: the New Pioneers," written by Henry-Russell Hitchcock.

Even lesser known must have been Mies van der Rohe's projects for the Brick and the Concrete Country Houses. Indeed, they seem to have passed totally unnoticed, unlike his earlier projects for the Friedrichstrasse Skyscraper (1921) and the Glass Skyscraper (1922), which received some attention, albeit derisive, in the professional journals in America. **230** **231** Their plans appeared in a 1923 issue of the *Journal of the American Institute of Architects* devoted entirely to the skyscraper. While Mies is not mentioned by name in the text (perhaps because the journal did not consider skyscraper architecture high art), this constitutes the first publication of Mies's polemical work in the USA.[1] In one article, William Stanley Parker writes that if he were to caption the plan of the Glass Skyscraper it would be "Nude Building Falling Downstairs,"[2] unintentionally becoming the first to present Mies's work publicly as avant-garde.[3] Still, in 1930, in an issue of *Architectural Record* devoted to glass architecture, where Mies's Glass Skyscraper and the Glass Industry Exhibit of Stuttgart, designed with Lilly Reich in 1927, are featured, neither Mies nor Reich is mentioned by name in the text. As far as I can determine, architects in the USA did not have any idea who Mies was until the exhibition Modern

---

1 *Journal of the American Institute of Architects*, September 1923, includes articles by George C. Nimmons, "Skyscrapers in America," and Walter Curt Behrendt, "Skyscrapers in Germany." George Nimmons dismisses the plans of the Glass Skyscraper as "too fantastic and unuseable for offices or apartments."

2 William Stanley Parker, "Skyscrapers Anywhere," *Journal of the American Institute of Architects*, September 1923, 372.

3 In the late 1980s and early 1990s the question of whether Mies's work qualified as avant-garde still occupied historians and theorists of architecture. See Michael Hays, *Modernism and the Posthumanist Subject: The Architecture of Hannes Meyer and Ludwig Hilberseimer* (Cambridge, MA: MIT Press, 1992), and Detlef Mertins, ed., *The Presence of Mies* (New York: Princeton Architectural Press, 1994).

Architecture: International Style, organized by Philip Johnson and Henry-Russell Hitchcock for the Museum of Modern Art in 1932, which incidentally included the Brick Country House in the catalog.[4]

I could not make sense of the "1923" in the title of the symposium about avant-garde architecture in North America until I read the transcript of a lecture given by Johnson at Barnard College in 1955 entitled "Style and International Style," where, after going on and on about how 1923 was the year in which everything had happened ("there was no style in our times until the year 1923"; 1923 was the "magic year"), Johnson says, "I could not, even if I would, tell you just what happened, but I am at home from that year on."[5] Paradoxically, since all the events of 1923 that he cites are European—Mies's Brick Country House, Le Corbusier's Ozenfant House, and so on, Johnson is at home away from home, a metaphor itself of the modern house.

Nineteen forty-nine, on the other hand, is a far more promising date for a consideration of the American context, even if we may still have to leave the "avant-garde" issue suspended. It was, arguably, the year things really started to happen, the "magic year" of modern architecture in the USA—the year of Johnson's Glass House in New Canaan, Connecticut, of Mies's Farnsworth House in Plano, Illinois, and of the Eames House in Santa Monica, California. **28 29 30** More significant, 1949 was the year the eyes of the architectural world shifted direction. It was no longer America looking at Europe but the other way around. And not just Europe, but the rest of the world. Countries on the edges of the map—Australia, New Zealand, South Africa—were suddenly looking in this direction. It was as if the war had broken barriers between countries, opening up new frontiers. The postwar years saw an extraordinary outburst of innovative design in the USA, an experimental form of modern architecture that commanded world attention. As Johnson was able to declare in 1955: "No magazine publishes, no school teaches anything but modern, and modern architecture gets more and more beautiful every year. And without being chauvinistic, it can be said that architecture in this country is the best in the world."[6] The USA swung from innocence about the most radical work to producing the most advanced experiments. If this is what we mean by avant-garde, then it could be argued that 1949—or, in any case, the immediate postwar years—coincide with the beginning of an American architectural avant-garde. Or perhaps it is the beginning and the end: 1949 will simply be emblematic of what had happened in architecture in the USA in the immediate postwar years, and that will soon move into a completely different direction.

Take, for example, the July 1950 issue of *L'architecture d'aujourd'hui* (one of the most—if not the most—widely read of the architectural journals in Europe). The issue is dedicated to the house, and while practically every country listed has one architect represented, France, naturally, has four, and the USA a total of nine! **32** Moreover, the cover goes to an American house, Marcel Breuer's own house in Connecticut. Breuer got several of his houses published in this issue, including the 1949 House in the Garden at the Museum of Modern Art. **60** Philip Johnson's Glass House was included, as were Pierre Chareau's Motherwell House, Richard Neutra's Case Study House in Santa Monica and the Tremaine Residence in Santa Barbara, Paul Laszlo's residence at Brentwood, several houses by

---

4 It was Hitchcock who also introduced Mies to the readers of *Hound and Horn* in December 1931, with an article on the Berlin Building Exhibition. He notes the collaboration of Mies and Lilly Reich on the exhibition of materials and states that "the work of Mies van der Rohe stands out like that of Schinkel in old Berlin." "Architectural Chronicle-Berlin; Paris: 1931," *Hound and Horn* 5, no.1 (December 1931): 94–97. While Hitchcock refers to Mies as one of the "New Pioneers" in his *Modern Architecture: Romanticism and Reintegration* (New York: Payson & Clarke, 1929), the only illustration of his work that appears in the book is the House at Guben of 1926.

5 Philip Johnson, "Style and International Style" (speech, Barnard College, New York, April 30, 1955), *Writings* (New York: Oxford University Press, 1979), 75.

6 Ibid., 73–74.

Ralph Twitchel and Paul Rudolph (which is understandable, since Rudolph had in February of the same year edited the issue dedicated to the Gropius school at Harvard), and so on.[7] **33** **34** **35** It is a big list, but one dominated by European émigrés. This is consistent with the standard view that if there is an architectural avant-garde in post-1945 USA it is because of the influx of émigrés. Symptomatically, *L'architecture d'aujourd'hui* missed the Eames House of 1949, perhaps because, as the editorial announces, the issue was interested in the house as a work of art and not in the question of the mass-produced house. "Such documentation," the editors ask themselves rather rhetorically (if not defensively), "could it be of interest today? . . . We think so. . . . The work of art is gratuitous by definition, but necessary to man."[8] The Eames House would not be covered by *L'architecture d'aujourd'hui* until December 1953.

It is interesting to note that while the old center, France, missed out on the Eames House, for the margins it had an immediate appeal. Reyner Banham wrote:

> For most Europeans—and some Africans, Australians, and Japanese to whom I have spoken—the Case Study era began around Christmas 1949. By that time the magazine *Arts & Architecture* had achieved a sufficient degree of penetration into specialized bookstores and architectural libraries for the impact of the first of the steel-frame Case Study houses to trigger—as British architect Peter Smithson said—"a wholly different kind of conversation."[9]

That first steel-frame house that Banham refers to as having triggered, in Peter Smithson's words, a "wholly different kind of conversation" was, of course, the Eames House, number 8 of the Case Study House program in California, into which the Eameses moved precisely on Christmas Eve 1949. **36** The Case Study House program was, as Banham noted, "overwhelmingly Charles and Ray

Eames in foreign perception."[10] That explains why foreigners thought of the program as starting in 1949, even if had actually been initiated in January 1945, a few months before the end of the war. **37**

Note that the significance of the house for the Smithsons, in Banham's account, seemed to lie less on itself, its particular form, its innovative organization, than on its capacity to provoke a discussion. The history of architecture is not simply the history of buildings but of what we make of these buildings: the theories we have about them, the photographs we take, the conversations we have. Good institutions (publications, museums, schools, and so on) are those that do not simply report such conversations or teach already established principles but, rather, instigate new conversations. Good architecture is always a provocation.

In that sense, the Case Study House program, sponsored by *Arts & Architecture* magazine under John Entenza, was exemplary.[11] The journal commissioned a number of architects to design houses as prototypes for a new way of living—the postwar way of living. The twenty-six houses resulting from this program were not only published in *Arts & Architecture* but, for the most part, built. It was a requirement to have a "real client" and to open the house to the public for six to eight weeks. Each house was to be completely furnished under an arrangement with the manufacturers participating in the program. The program was enormously successful, both professionally and among the wider public: the first six houses to be opened received almost four hundred thousand visitors.

---

7 Gordon Drake, Ralph Rapson, and John van der Meulen are the other American architects included in this issue. *L'architecture d'aujourd'hui*, July 1950.

8 *L'architecture d'aujourd'hui*, July 1950, 1.

9 Reyner Banham, "Klarheit, Ehrlichkeit, Einfachkeit . . . and Wit Too! The Case Study Houses in the World's Eyes," in *Blueprints for Modern Living: History and Legacy of the Case Study Houses*, ed. Elizabeth A. T. Smith (Los Angeles: Museum of Contemporary Art; Cambridge, MA: MIT Press, 1989), 183.

10 Ibid.

11 About the Case Study House program see Esther McCoy, *Modern California Houses* (1962), reprinted as *Case Study Houses 1945–1962* (Los Angeles: Hennessey & Ingalls, 1977); and Smith, *Blueprints for Modern Living*.

The program was preceded by two other competitions organized by *Arts & Architecture:* the 1943 Design for Postwar Living and a second such competition in 1944, sponsored by the US Plywood Association. **38** These competitions encouraged participants to arrive at a "pattern of living for the American worker" and his family. "This American worker," says the call for entries, "conditioned by the war-time years (including the members of the armed forces who will become a part of the working population) . . . is likely to have an enormous respect for the machine both as creator and as a weapon of destruction . . . and it is very likely that he will not only accept but demand simple, direct, and honest efficiency in the material aspects of the means by which he lives."[12] World War II, the magazine implied, provided the context for the acceptance of modern architecture.

A historical reference for the Case Study Houses can be found in Le Corbusier's fascination with the technologies developed during World War I and his dream of an architecture that would "recycle" these materials and techniques into the mass production of houses. This was most obvious in his relationship with Gabriel Voisin, who after the war was looking to transform his war-aircraft factories by breaking into the building industry.[13] **39** The Case Study program likewise exemplified the impact of the war on both architectural discourse and the specific techniques and materials employed in the production of housing. On the one hand, the industry was recycling the products and techniques that it had developed and tested at war. On the other hand—and this is what is new—the architects themselves had been involved in the development of these military products. If European architects during World War I found themselves either on the front or at home, unemployed or painting (like Le Corbusier), American architects during World War II were working for the military.

Charles and Ray Eames, for example, formed a company with John Entenza during the war to mass-produce plywood military products. In 1941–42 they developed a molded plywood splint for the United States Navy to replace a metal leg splint used in the field that did not sufficiently secure the leg and led to gangrene. **40** The navy accepted the Eames prototype and, with the financial support of Entenza and the help of other architects such as Gregory Ain (who later also became involved in the Case Study Program), designed the equipment needed for mass production, eventually putting 150,000 units into service. **42** The splint performed very well in the field and was praised for its lifesaving features. In addition, the company designed and developed a plywood body litter and an arm splint, molded plywood aircraft parts, and so on. By 1945, the Eameses were producing lightweight plywood cabinets and molded plywood chairs and tables with the technology they had developed for the military. **43** A photograph of the plywood lounge chair of 1946 shows Charles Eames reclined on it, the straightened position of his leg indicating that he has not forgotten where it comes from. **44 45** In addition, the Eameses produced molded plywood children's furniture, molded plywood animals, and even plywood Christmas decorations from leftover splints. **46 47 161 163 405** Military equipment had become the basis of domestic equipment.

This obvious displacement from war to architecture can be found throughout the Case Study House program in more subtle forms. The very idea of standardization, for example, was a major part of the program's agenda. Every component of the Eames House was selected from a steel manufacturer's catalog and bolted together like a Meccano set. It took a day and a half to get the structure of the

12 John Entenza, "Competition: Designs for Postwar Living," *California Arts & Architecture*, April 1943.

13 Beatriz Colomina, *Privacy and Publicity: Modern Architecture as Mass Media* (Cambridge, MA: MIT Press, 1994), 159.

Eames House up. The house for John Entenza, designed by Eames and Eero Saarinen on an adjacent site, was built from the same standardized elements but was very different architecturally. A simple set of lightweight components allows different houses to be quickly assembled, taking the logic, speed, and efficiency of the factory to the site itself. One is reminded again of Le Corbusier, who, in relation to his potential collaboration with Voisin, had written (with Ozenfant) in *L'Esprit nouveau*:

> Houses must go up all of a piece, made by machine tools in factory. . . . It is in aircraft factories that the soldier-architects have decided to build the houses; they decided to build this house like an aircraft, with the same structural methods, lightweight framing, metal braces, tubular supports.[14] **39**

The Eames House thus represents the realization of Le Corbusier's dreams. While Le Corbusier theorized the factory-made house, or at least new materials and building techniques, the houses he managed to build in the meantime used the most conventional methods. Like Le Corbusier, Charles Eames was an avid reader of catalogs on marine and aviation equipment. He later said that he regretted having "stuck so close to the building industry" with the house, neglecting several offers from outside quarters, and that if he were to do it all over again "he might treat this house more as a job of 'product design,' less architecture in the traditional sense."[15]

But how could the house be less architecture in the traditional sense? It seems to be one of the Eameses' plywood cabinets blown up in scale. **404** **405** It was built from off-the-shelf components, assembled off the back of a truck, in just over one day. **122** It is hard to imagine a more radical gesture, and it was precisely its radicality that attracted worldwide attention.

The Eameses' displacement of architecture from a stable enclosing form to a lightweight, demountable, infinitely rearrangeable storage system acting as the stage set for a relentless domesticity, a displacement that fascinated the world, was but the first step in an even more radical displacement into product design and the consumable image. Even the superlightness of the Eames House undermines the figure of the heroic architect. Its delicacy, even indeterminacy, facilitates the slippage from solid object to flickering ephemeral image. Architecture as building gives way to architecture as crafted image. This does not mean leaving material construction behind; on the contrary, the Eameses were expert craftspeople, shaping the structure into an image and images into structure.

It is worth remembering that, arriving in California in 1941, Charles Eames had worked as a stage designer for the MGM movie studio. Under Billy Wilder he used to put together, often in just one night, structures whose sole purpose was to produce an image. Eames later said that "he had learned more about design by watching Billy Wilder than from working with any architect."[16] To think about the Eameses' architecture is to think about this extraordinary intimacy with film, an intimacy that marks a distinct shift from the productions of the historical avant-garde. Modern architects like Robert Mallet-Stevens had produced stage sets for avant-garde films, and many architects, such as Le Corbusier, experimented with film as a form of representation, **175** but only with the Eameses do we encounter an architecture that comes straight out of the logic of Hollywood. The austere polemics of the '20s give way in the '50s to the Technicolor representation of everyday life. Life itself is seen as a continuous advertisement for itself, with every citizen acting as if being filmed or about to be filmed. **22**

---

14 Le Corbusier–Saugnier, "Les Maisons 'Voisin,'" *L'Esprit nouveau* 2 (November 1920): 214. Saugnier is a pseudonym for Ozenfant.

15 Charles Eames quoted in "Life in a Chinese Kit," *Architectural Forum*, September 1950, 96.

16 Quoted in James A. Moore, "From Idea to Place: An Interpretation of the Role of Technology in the Architectural Development of the Post-War Single-Family House" (PhD diss., University of Pennsylvania, 1986).

Everything about the Eameses had this quality, from their carefully chosen clothes to the ecstatic smiles they wore in every image of themselves alongside their latest inventions. A photograph from around 1945 shows them happy, smiling, looking adoringly at the model of the first version of the Eames House as if it were a newborn baby they are about to kiss. **50** In contrast, there is a photograph of Mies during the MoMA exhibition of his work in 1947 that shows the architect gravely scrutinizing the model of his Farnsworth House as if he had never seen it before. **51** Despite the similarities between the two projects, these photographs already speak of the abyss that opened up between the two generations and that would become evident in the second Technicolor version of the Eames House, where the detached analytical gaze of Mies was replaced by an emotional family scene.

I have always been fascinated by a picture of Billy Wilder and his wife, Audrey, taken from the backseat of a convertible car. **52** They were on their honeymoon. And the photographer? Charles Eames. Believe it or not, the Eameses accompanied the Wilders on their honeymoon trip to Lake Tahoe in June–July 1948, photographing, they said, Virginia City and Lake Tahoe. It is a voyeuristic image of a domestic scene, capturing not merely the Eameses' intimacy with the filmmaker and with film but also the intimacy of film itself, its closeness to everything, its construction of an endless, relentless domesticity. The Eameses used this domesticity of the image as the basis for a new kind of architecture, as exemplified in the house they designed for the Wilders in 1950. The movement from film to architecture comes full circle with this project. The house, which was modular in plan and assembled out of prefabricated off-the-shelf parts, resembled a lightweight stage set. **56** Even photographed against a backdrop of clouds, the model looks like it is about to be filmed. **54** In other photographs, the Eameses and the Wilders can be seen staring into the model as if trying to catch the angle of a possible shot. **57**

Unfortunately the Wilder House was not built. Indeed, it was one of the last architectural commissions that the Eameses would undertake. When asked in a 1972 interview why he turned away from the practice of architecture, Charles said:

> That's partially the result of my chickening out. Architecture is a frustrating business. You work on an idea, but standing between you and the event are many traps. The finance committee, the contractor, the subcontractor, the engineer, even politicians—all of them can really cause the concept to degenerate. Going into furniture or film is a deviation of a sort, but at least we had a more direct relationship with the end product—a better chance to keep the project from degenerating.[17]

Though leaving building behind, the Eameses continued to think of themselves as architects, insisting that film and even graphic design were forms of architecture. As Charles put it: "I think of myself functionally as an architect. I can't help but look at the problems around us as problems of structure—and structure is architecture. A good film needs structure as much as a good front page does."[18] The Eameses became architects who no longer built. The historical figure of the avant-garde architect as heroic constructor gave way to a new kind of avant-garde figure operating somewhere between product design and image design. If the architects of the 1920s were already expert with images and had started to absorb the logic of image culture into their architectural work, the Eameses went one step farther, into the flow of images.

[17] Digby Diehl, "Q&A: Charles Eames," *Los Angeles Times WEST Magazine*, October 8, 1972, 16, reprinted in Digby Diehl, *Supertalk* (New York: Doubleday, 1974). In the transcript of this interview, now in the Library of Congress, Eames elaborates: "The architect really does have a tough time. When Eero [Saarinen] was still alive, I naturally thought that he was really accomplishing something in architecture, but then he'd come out to our home and bemoan the fact that he wasn't able to give that kind of attention to detail in the studio. Even he was interested in doing furniture, because at least if he did a chair, he would have the opportunity for one minute to do a small piece of architecture, which wasn't quite so apt to get out of hand."
[18] Diehl, "Q&A," 14.

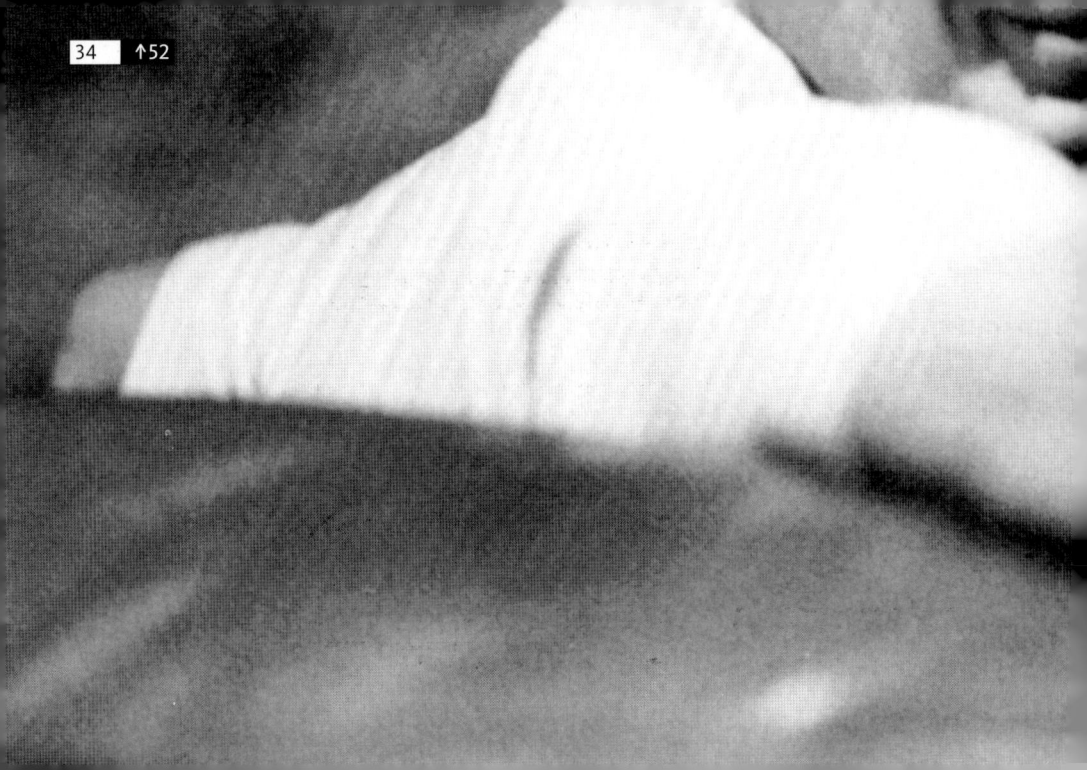

36 ↑54

MoMA's House

But 1949 was not exclusively a West Coast phenomenon, and this radical shift from war to domesticity to product design and the consumable image, this shift from mass production to mass consumption, was not unique to the Eameses. Nineteen forty-nine was also the year MoMA built a house by Marcel Breuer in the museum's first sculpture garden (designed by John McAndrew in 1939). **14** **58** **59** **60** It is important to note that the house had an independent entrance: the visitor was provided with the address, 4 West Fifty-fourth Street, and was charged a separate admission fee, reflecting perhaps the ambiguous role of architecture in the museum. The house was in the museum and yet separate from it, its status as an art object put into question. The arrangement reflects the new understanding of architecture as a good-life environment, a kind of display case for consumable objects rather than an art form.

The House in the Garden was intended for the commuter, MoMA said, a middle-class man in his thirties, employed in the city but living in the suburbs with his wife and two children.[19] Was this middle-class family likely to own modern art? Not really. But it was nevertheless already tied to the museum through programs such as the Good Design products introduced by Edgar Kaufmann in 1950 and preceded by John McAndrew's series of Useful Objects exhibitions.[20] **62** **63** **64** **65** Among the many consumptive needs of these postwar figures was a house—a suburban house, not a work of art. In fact, the museum went out of its way to solicit bids from construction companies to build the house in different versions in the suburbs of Connecticut, New Jersey, and New York State.[21] The plans of the house were made available. **66** This house was not a unique art object. It was a prototype.

To some extent, the museum addressing the commuter in this way was the museum undoing itself. While there was some art in the house,[22] the television set, which was designed by Breuer and featured a proto–remote control, was clearly more interesting to most reporters and visitors,[23] of which there were plenty. **67 68** Seventy thousand people went through the house, and the event received enormous publicity from the press, popular and professional, national and foreign.

The museum had reaimed itself at the middle class immediately after the war.[24] It would be important to assess the influence of the programs of the war years in the museum. Breuer's house was not "the first architectural structure built for public exhibition in the Museum's first sculpture garden," as the official history of the museum claims.[25] In 1941, Buckminster Fuller had his Dymaxion Deployment Unit (developed from a standard metal grain-storage bin and completely

---

19 Breuer described the house as "the house for the commuter who has personal views in selecting his land, probably at least an acre." The house was designed for building in two stages: "The first phase . . . contains a living-dining room, two bedrooms, children's playroom, bath, kitchen and utility room. . . . Later on, when the children are older, the garage will be added, with a new master bedroom, bath and sun deck above it, giving the parents complete privacy." "Museum Builds Expandable House," *Architectural Record*, February 1949, 24.

20 On these exhibitions see Terence Riley and Edward Eigen, "Between the Museum and the Marketplace: Selling Good Design," in *The Museum of Modern Art at Mid-Century at Home and Abroad*, Studies in Modern Art 4 (New York: Museum of Modern Art, 1994), 150–79.

21 The following prices were listed: "Three-bedroom house. Similar to the House in the Museum Garden $27,475. Same three-bedroom house. Wall, ceiling and floor finished of alternate materials $25,110. Two-bedroom house; without garage and third bedroom. Wall ceiling and floor finishes similar to the House in the Museum Garden $21,960. Same two-bedroom house. Wall, ceiling and floor finishes of alternate materials $19,975." *Bulletin of the Museum of Modern Art*, vol. xvi, no. 1, 1949. This issue of the *Bulletin* served as the exhibition catalog for The House in the Museum Garden, organized by the Department of Architecture and Design, April 14–October 30, 1949.

22 There was not much art in the Breuer house. Most journalists did not even remark on it, except for an isolated complaint: "Nothing in the art world these days is where you expect to find it. In a museum we find pots and pans. In a commercial movie we find art. [The house in the garden of the Museum of Modern Art] is shown complete with knives, forks, pots and pans and even art books on the book shelves. But on the walls there are only two small pictures. In one bedroom is a small, modest, chaste, Juan Gris abstraction. In another, is a similar work by Leger. A wooden abstract relief by Hans Arp on a stairway wall, an African negro fetish on the fireplace and a Calder metal construction clinging like a huge and fascinating bug to one outside wall. . . . Here is the MoMA presenting a model home almost devoid of fine arts." *New York World Telegraph*, May 2, 1949.

23 Breuer designed for this house a "radio-television-phonograph" in two units: "A table height unit supported on metal legs houses the screen, radio and phonograph mechanisms, as well as the storage place for records. A completely separate coffee table in front of the sofa is fitted with remote control panels so the viewer can switch programs and mediums without moving from his seat. At the back of the coffee table are shelves for books. Both pieces are lacquered black with polished metal supports." The units were produced in sample form by Philco. "Ultramodern House Will Open in New York," *Retailing Daily*, April 8, 1949.

24 John Elderfield, preface to *The Museum of Modern Art at Mid-Century at Home and Abroad*, Studies in Modern Art 4 (New York: Museum of Modern Art, 1994), 6–11.

25 Sam Hunter, introduction to *The Museum of Modern Art: The History and the Collection* (New York: Harry N. Abrams and Museum of Modern Art, 1984), 28.

prefabricated) set up in the museum garden. The museum called it Defense House. 69 116 117 In September 1941, the *Bulletin of the Museum of Modern Art* attributes the delay in the opening of "Buckminster Fuller's Demountable Defense House," which had originally been scheduled for July of the same year, to "Navy priorities."[26] The *Bulletin* of the following month shows Fuller's house, renamed the Dymaxion Deployment Unit, installed in the museum garden. 103 118

The Defense House was made up of two deployment units whose interior had been reorganized to accommodate a family of six. The units that were serving as military barracks, furnishing sleeping space for twenty-four soldiers on double-decker cots could, the museum insisted, be manufactured at the rate of a thousand per day at $1,500 each.[27] Barracks had been turned into mass-produced, infinitely rearrangeable modular housing units. 106

Another precedent of a structure to be built in the museum garden, even if it did not ultimately materialize, also comes from the war years. According to Peter Galassi, Edward Steichen (director of the Department of Photography 1947 on), who had worked as a photographer for the army in World War I and for the navy in World War II and who had organized important war exhibitions at MoMA such as Road to Victory (1942) and Power in the Pacific (1945), brought a Quonset hut to the museum to be placed in the garden and used for exhibition space. 70 71

Demountable, prefabricated Quonset huts, which had served during the war as military barracks, were, of course, readily available in the immediate postwar years. About 170,000 had been produced and erected around the world, many to return to the home front after the war.[28] Already in 1944, *Architectural Record* was

---

26 *Bulletin of the Museum of Modern Art*, September 1941, 9.
27 *Bulletin of the Museum of Modern Art*, October 1941, 17.
28 Cf. Peter S. Reed, "Enlisting Modernism," in *World War II and the American Dream: How Wartime Building Changed a Nation*, ed. Donald Albrecht (Washington, DC: National Building Museum; Cambridge, MA: MIT Press, 1995), 25.

printing advertisements announcing a "Peacetime use for the Quonset Hut." **72** And Pierre Chareau used a Quonset hut to build the studio-house for Robert Motherwell in East Hampton in 1948 (a house that, symptomatically, appeared in the July 1950 issue of *L'architecture d'aujourd'hui*). **73** But the planned expansion at MoMA did not work out. The Quonset hut was in the museum, but in the end it had to be sold at a loss.[29]

In fact, the museum garden was occupied by the military in different ways. During the war the garden was used as entertainment center for troops of all Allied nations.[30] **74** **75** They occupied the garden and the front covers of museum *Bulletin*s at the same time that they occupied theaters of war in Europe. The postwar houses in the garden have to be understood in this context.

The transition from military to domestic is unambiguous in the museum's collaboration with *Ladies' Home Journal* for the exhibition Tomorrow's Small House, organized by Elizabeth B. Mock, curator of architecture, immediately after the war. The kind of thinking evident in the exhibition War Time Housing of 1942 slides into the private construction of suburban houses. The Spring and Summer 1945 issues of the *Bulletin of the Museum of Modern Art* mark this transition from war to peace very starkly. As the issues appear today in a bound volume, we see, on the left, the last images of war (as represented in the exhibition Power in the Pacific) and, on the right, the first images of domestic bliss (Tomorrow's Small House). Not by chance are the new images for the first time in color. **76**

War Time Housing, an exhibition organized in collaboration with the National Committee on the Housing Emergency (April–June 1942), was a multimedia event. As one reporter described it, there were "movies, photographs, models, recorded voices that appear to come from nowhere, sound effects."[31] A recording of President Roosevelt greeted the visitor at the entrance. The message emphasized that "homes for workers in war industries are an essential element in the whole program of making the weapons of war."[32] The National Housing Administration "spoke with some pride of 'the housing sector of the war front.'"[33] A point brought out again and again is that "wartime housing facilities can be converted to peacetime."[34]

Tomorrow's Small House was an exhibition of models, or as they were called, "postwar houses in miniature," which visitors were encouraged to imagine themselves inside. As the museum's *Bulletin* puts it: "The danger of realistic models is the easy magic of the medium. The delight of tiny bentwood chairs, workable four-inch lawnmowers and real greenery . . . you must put your eyes just a little above the ground level of the model, then imagine yourself five or six inches tall and walk about each house until you feel quite at home, inside and out."[35] The arrangement of models in the space of the exhibition reinforces that way of reading them. They were installed on high platforms, which brought the floor to eye level. **77**

But to whom was the museum addressing itself with this exhibition, with this easy-to-absorb language? Definitely not to architects or to the cultivated public that may have seen the International Style show, but to the most general public. Reporters speak of "crowds packing" the exhibition. It opened with eight small houses built to the scale of an inch to a foot completely landscaped and furnished, all adaptable to prefabrication (except Frank Lloyd Wright's). The architects were Wright, George Fred Keck, Carl Koch, Philip Johnson, Mario Corbett, Hugh Stubbins, Plan-Tech Associates, and Vernon DeMars. Two more models

---

29 Peter Galassi, "Two Stories," in *American Photography 1890–1965: From the Museum of Modern Art, New York* (New York: Museum of Modern Art, 1995), 34.

30 The Museum of Modern Art held fourteen fortnightly parties in the museum garden for "fighting men": "sailors, soldiers, marines, merchant marine, and airmen of the United nations." They were attended by 4,115 men. "They arrived at seven o'clock for a buffet supper in the Museum's penthouse or garden and went on until 11pm with games, sing-songs, dancing, motion pictures from the Museum's Film Library collection, or were entertained by professionals such as Ruth Draper, Gracie Fields and many others." "A Museum's War Program: An Editorial," *American Artist*, November 1942, 30.

were to be added later: a house by John Funk and one by Wurster & Bernardi. The original site plan by DeMars was developed by Serge Chermayeff and Susanne Wasson-Tucker. The exhibition traveled to some department stores such as Gimbel's in Philadelphia.

Are the houses in this exhibition high art? On the one hand, one finds here architects such as Wright and Johnson: nothing would seem more high art. But then, in the only reference I have been able to find to Johnson's project, Kenneth Frampton accuses the project of being "banal."[36] This could, of course, pass as a compliment these days, but the point is that while there are seemingly high-art architects in the exhibition, they do not produce high-art architecture. Proof: they do not include these projects in the heroic accounts of their careers.

This may help to answer a question about the house in the garden: Why Breuer? Why did Johnson, who had just taken up, again, the direction of the Department of Architecture and Design at the museum, choose Breuer to do this house? Why not Mies or Le Corbusier? Breuer had been Johnson's teacher at Harvard, and Johnson was always sentimental about him. In a 1995 issue of the *GSD News,* he still goes on about how Breuer "was simply the best teacher of architecture [he] ever worked with," about how Breuer was really an "artist in the field of architecture."[37] But he certainly was not Mies or Le Corbusier; nor was the house admired as a work of art. Indeed, it has always been looked down on, even by Breuer himself, who recognized that it was not his best project. What is radical about the house is not the form but its context: the very idea of an exhibition house in the garden of the museum designed for a commuter rather than for an art collector (the traditional client of high-modern architecture), according to a militarized logic of mass production, for a generic upper-middle-class suburb—a house that could be reproduced by anybody, anywhere.

While the plan of the house "assumed a suburban location on at least an acre of land," Breuer insisted that "with minor changes it could be adapted to a lot in a suburban development."[38] As if to reinforce that point, many articles in newspapers and magazines airbrushed out the context of the museum. [78] [79]

There was a second house in the garden of the Museum of Modern Art: Gregory Ain's house of 1950, sometimes referred to as the Woman's Home Companion House because of the collaboration of the museum with the journal *Woman's Home Companion*. [80] In many ways this lesser-known house is closer to the logic of the exhibition Tomorrow's Small House than Breuer's. As with Tomorrow's Small House, the museum collaborated on this project with a women's magazine. Also, Ain's house was smaller and less expensive than Breuer's, which had been criticized even by Eleanor Roosevelt for being "too expensive."[39] [83] We should remember this was the age of the prefabricated house. As Lewis Mumford put it: "Today almost any vacant corner lot in midtown Manhattan is apt to burgeon with a cozy bit of prefabricated domesticity."[40] In that context, Breuer's house was seen as too exclusive. A few copies were made—one in Chappaqua, another one in Princeton—but the house was not for the masses. The one built in the museum's garden was in the end bought by John Rockefeller, not exactly your typical middle-class commuter, who installed it on his estate as a guesthouse.[41]

---

31 *New York Times*, April 22, 1942.
32 *New York Times*, April 23, 1942.
33 *New York Times*, April 22, 1942.
34 *New York Times*, April 22, 1942.
35 *Bulletin of the Museum of Modern Art*, Summer 1945, 5.
36 Kenneth Frampton, "The Glass House Revisited," *Philip Johnson: Processes*, catalogue 9 (New York: Institute for Architecture and Urban Studies, 1978), 51.
37 Philip Johnson, "Breuer: An Artist in Architecture," *GSD News*, Fall 1995, 33.
38 While the plan of the house "assumed a suburban location on at least an acre of land," Breuer insisted that "with minor changes it could be adapted to a lot in a suburban development." Antoinette Donelly, "Chatter," *News*, January 15, 1949. As if to reinforce that point, many articles in newspapers and magazines airbrushed the context of the museum.
39 "Museum Model House Is New but Expensive," *New York World Telegraph*, June 24, 1949. The headline of this article is a direct quotation from Eleanor Roosevelt, who had visited the house the day before.
40 Lewis Mumford, "The Sky Line: Design for Living," *New Yorker*, June 25, 1949, 72–76.
41 Incidentally, the Deployment Unit of Fuller was also advertised by the museum as a bomb shelter now, a guesthouse during peacetime.

Nearly three hundred thousand people visited Ain's house. They found the house furnished down to a black Jeepster in the garage (a Jeepster, Peter Blake, then curator of architecture and design, said, was "a happy adaptation of the wartime Jeep"[42]), grocery bills on the kitchen bulletin board, towels in the bathroom, hangers in the hall closets, and so on.[43] An issue of *Retailing* writes, "This architecture affects your sales."[44] Indeed, sales at Bloomingdale's of various brand-name kitchen products used in the house doubled,[45] and the house was extensively used as a background for advertisements. **84** **85** Newspaper and magazine articles gave complete lists of furnishings with prices and retail stores where the pieces could be purchased.[46]

The first color images of Ain's house were presented in the June 1950 issue of *Woman's Home Companion*. The context of the museum was airbrushed to make look like a regular suburban home. As one reads the article, it becomes clear that it was the museum that had approached the journal and not the other way around. The journal, which calls Ain's house "our house," doesn't push very hard to have readers visit it at the Museum of Modern Art: "Even without a visit to New York, you can go through our house on these pages by means of the pictures."[47] **82**

The Museum at War

The program of houses in the garden constitutes a shift in the policies of MoMA's Department of Architecture from those of the prewar years, a shift that is perhaps reflected in Johnson's introduction to *Built in USA: Post-war Architecture,* a book accompanying a 1952 exhibition at the museum, where he proclaims, "The battle of modern architecture has long been won. Twenty years ago the Museum was in the thick of the fight, but now our exhibitions and catalogues take part in that unending campaign described by Alfred Barr as 'simply the continuous, conscientious, resolute distinction of quality from mediocrity—the discovery and proclamation of excellence.'"[48] [86] The Department of Architecture, in other words, was no longer at war, no longer compelled to present an avant-garde architecture. It had become a referee. In the tradition of the so-called (by the museum) service exhibitions, initiated in 1938 by John McAndrew and expanded by Edgar Kaufmann in 1950 with the Good Design programs, its role was simply to point out what was good and what was bad. This pot is good; this one is not. This house is good; this house is not. Can one talk about avant-garde here? Not really. The house in the museum garden is as avant-garde as the pots MoMA was endorsing in collaboration with the Merchandise Mart in Chicago.

Johnson was quoting Barr, who had made the point that "the battle of modern architecture is won" in the earlier *Built in the USA: Since 1932*, published in 1944.[49] Understanding the museum's programs as military campaigns was not new. Already in 1931, in his preface to *The International Style*, Barr had identified the project of Johnson and Hitchcock as a military campaign to introduce modern architecture in this country. And when in 1948 Barr opens the symposium "What Is Happening to Modern Architecture?"—a symposium of major figures organized by the Museum

42 "In announcing selection of the Jeepster, Peter Blake, museum curator of architecture and design, explained: 'When we were looking for a small car to use with the MoMA-Woman's Home Companion Exhibition house, we sought a car that was handsome, in addition to having good performance. We have long felt that the original war-time Jeep was probably the best looking, mass-produced American car of the past eight or ten years. We like its clean, unpretentious lines; we like its honest proportion; we like its rugged and serviceable look; and we think all its elements combine to make it a first-rate piece of industrial design.' Referring to the Willys Sports phaeton, Mr. Blake said that 'The Jeepster, which is a happy adaptation of the war-time Jeep, has retained all these features without adding to them the ‹juke box› treatment with which we are becoming increasingly familiar.'" *Morning Sun*, May 29, 1950.
43 *Herald Tribune*, May 19, 1950.
44 "This Architecture Affects Your Sales," *Retailing Daily*, June 27, 1950.
45 *Brooklyn Heights Press*, June 22, 1950.
46 *New Yorker*, July 22, 1950.
47 "Our House: With a View to the Future," *Woman's Home Companion*, June 1950, 65–72.
48 Philip C. Johnson, preface to *Built in USA: Post-war Architecture*, ed. Henry-Russell Hitchcock and Arthur Drexler (New York: Museum of Modern Art, 1952), 8.
49 "As Alfred Barr has said: 'The battle of modern architecture in this country is won but there are other problems with which the Department has concerned itself. . . . Above [all] is the one unending campaign which involves not merely the Department of Architecture but the Museum as a whole. This is simply the continuous, conscientious, resolute distinction of quality from mediocrity—the discovery and proclamation of excellence.'" Philip L. Goodwin, preface to *Built in USA: 1932–1944*,

of Modern Art in response to a Lewis Mumford article in the *New Yorker*—he says: "I have read with care Mr. Mumford's piece in *The New Yorker*, which is the basis of tonight's discussion. If we differ this evening, lay it to the fact that it is hard for two old soldiers to remember a campaign in exactly the same way."[50]

While this rhetoric is part of a widespread tendency among art historians to use such expressions as "battle of the styles," it takes on a particular resonance when we consider the fact that the so-called modern movement in architecture was born around World War I and is inseparable from that episode and, second, that in 1944, the year that Barr proclaims victory, the country was at war. MoMA was at war in more than one sense. The museum was not only deeply engaged in military programs but also at war with itself. Barr had been fired as the museum's director in 1943. He did not leave, however; he became director of research and in 1947 was rehabilitated as director of museum collections.[51]

The idea of victory pervaded the mid-1940s. From 1942 on, all sorts of advertisements appeared in journals using V's, from rugs with a big V, three dots, and a dash inscribed on them advertising rugs by Klearflax in *Arts & Architecture* to dresses for victory. **87** **88** And suddenly, looking at the catalog of the 1944 exhibition Art in Progress, an exhibition commemorating the fifteenth anniversary of MoMA, I can see only that V, which I never saw before. **89** Could it be unintentional? And back to the Breuer house—what are we to make of that V-shaped roof, particularly when we realize that the first time he introduced this feature (clearly indebted to Le Corbusier's 1930 Errazuris House in Chile[52]) was in his project for

50 Alfred H. Barr, "What Is Happening to Modern Architecture?" *Bulletin of the Museum of Modern Art,* Spring 1948, 5. An excerpt from Lewis Mumford's October 11, 1947, article in the *New Yorker* is published in this *Bulletin*, p. 2. Speakers included, among others, Barr, Mumford, Henry-Russell Hitchcock, Walter Gropius, George Nelson, Marcel Breuer, Peter Blake, Eero Saarinen, Vincent Scully, Philip Johnson, and Edgar Kaufmann Jr.

51 Galassi, *American Photography*, 33.

52 For a comparison of Le Corbusier's project for the Errazuris House and Breuer's House in the Museum Garden see Klaus Herdeg, *The Decorated Diagram: Harvard Architecture and the Failure of the Bauhaus Legacy* (Cambridge, MA: MIT Press, 1983), 5–11.

the competition Design for Postwar Living, organized by *Arts & Architecture* in 1943? 90 38 Unintentional it may be. But that does not mean that the unconscious is not playing a role.

The way the museum design program emerged out of World War II echoes the relationship between modern architecture and World War I. Architects like Le Corbusier conceived of their architecture as a surrogate military campaign. Architecture is war by other (and preferable) means. The necessary equipment of modern life is, for Le Corbusier, that of the soldier. His rearrangement in the space of a page in *L'Esprit nouveau* of Hermès bags echoes an image that appeared in the illustrated newspaper *L'Illustration* in 1919 showing the equipment of a French soldier during the war.[53] 91 In 1943, the Museum of Modern Art organized Useful Objects in Wartime, a variation on the series of Useful Objects exhibitions where members of the armed forces provided recommendations on what objects of everyday life were needed in the army.

This mentality of the soldier as client, the civilian as soldier, quickly passes from the wartime exhibitions to the peacetime ones. It runs through Useful Objects in Wartime, to the Wartime Housing exhibition, to Fuller's Defense House, to Tomorrow's Small House, to Breuer's House in the Museum Garden, to Ain's house, and so on. Tomorrow's Small House was the turning point from war to peace. War does not go away. Rather, it is carried out in the consumption of mass-produced spin-offs of military technology and efficiency. The museum's sustained attempt to produce an idealized image of postwar domesticity was, in a way, a military campaign.

This idealized image quickly become a national issue. Indeed, it would become the very issue of the nation, of national identity, as became clear in the Kitchen Debates of 1959. In July of that year, at the peak of the cold war, vice president Richard Nixon traveled to Moscow to open the American National Exhibition in

Moscow, where he engaged in a heated debate with premier Nikita Khrushchev about the virtues of American life.[54] [92] [360] [361] [362] For Nixon, superiority rested on the ideal of the suburban home, complete with modern appliances. The exhibition was a showcase of American consumer goods, but the main attraction was a full-scale model house, cut in half to allow viewing. [93] [94] In the department-store tradition, appropriated by MoMA, it had been erected by a Long Island builder and furnished by Macy's. It was in the Ramond Lowey–designed kitchen of this fourteen-thousand-dollar, six-room ranch-style house filled with appliances that the debates began, with an argument over automatic washers. Nixon proclaimed that this "model" suburban home represented nothing less than American freedom: "To us, diversity, the right to choose, is the most important thing. . . . We don't have one decision made at the top by one government official. . . . We have many different manufacturers and many different kinds of washing machines so that the housewife has a choice."[55]

The house that resulted from the war was itself deployed as a weapon in the cold war. After Moscow, the model house was redesigned by Lowey as the Leisurama house and exhibited full scale on the ninth floor of Macy's in New York. By 1964, 250 $9,999 Leisuramas had been built as vacation houses in Montauk, at the tip of Long Island, and fully stocked by Macy's with all the furniture, appliances, dishes, linen, towels, and even toothbrushes. The weapon house had become a beach house, a diversion from the pressures of the cold war. [95]

---

53 Colomina, *Privacy and Publicity*, 168–69.
54 Elaine Tyler May, *Homeward Bound: American Families in the Cold War Era* (New York: Basic Books, 1988), 16. See also Karal Ann Marling, *As Seen on TV: The Visual Culture of Everyday Life in the 1950s* (Cambridge, MA: Harvard University Press, 1994).
55 Quoted by May in *Homeward Bound*, 17. For transcripts of the debate see "The Two Worlds: A Day-Long Debate," *New York Times*, July 25, 1959, 1–3; "When Nixon Took On Khrushchev," a report of the meeting and the text of Nixon's address at the opening of the American National Exhibition in Moscow on July 24, 1959, printed in "Setting Russia Straight On Facts about U.S.," *U.S. News and World Report*, August 3, 1959, 36–39, 70–72; "Encounter," *Newsweek*, August 3, 1959, 15–19; and "Better to See Once," *Time*, August 3, 1959, 12–14.

The issue of the Kitchen Debates was the nuclear house: the house for the nuclear family in the nuclear age. Not by accident does the same issue of *Life* magazine devoted to the kitchen debates also include an article on a couple who spent their two-week honeymoon in a Miami fallout shelter.[56] **96 97** A couple of years later, *Life* would present the iconic photograph of a cold-war family in their fallout shelter, surrounded by their supplies of canned food, water, games, blankets, and so on.[57] **98** Images of domesticity in the face of possible annihilation.

The bright experiments of postwar American architecture are covertly organized by the trauma of war—the trauma of the war that just finished and the trauma of the fact that it had not really finished after all. To understand this extraordinary blurring of military culture, image culture, and architectural culture, the condition of the postwar house needs to be dissected. A haunted picture emerges, domesticity at war.

---

56 "Their Sheltered Honeymoon," *Life*, August 10, 1959, 51–52.
57 "Fallout shelters: You could be among the 97% who survive if you follow the advice in this article. An urgent letter to all Americans from President Kennedy." *Life*, September 15, 1961, 104–105.

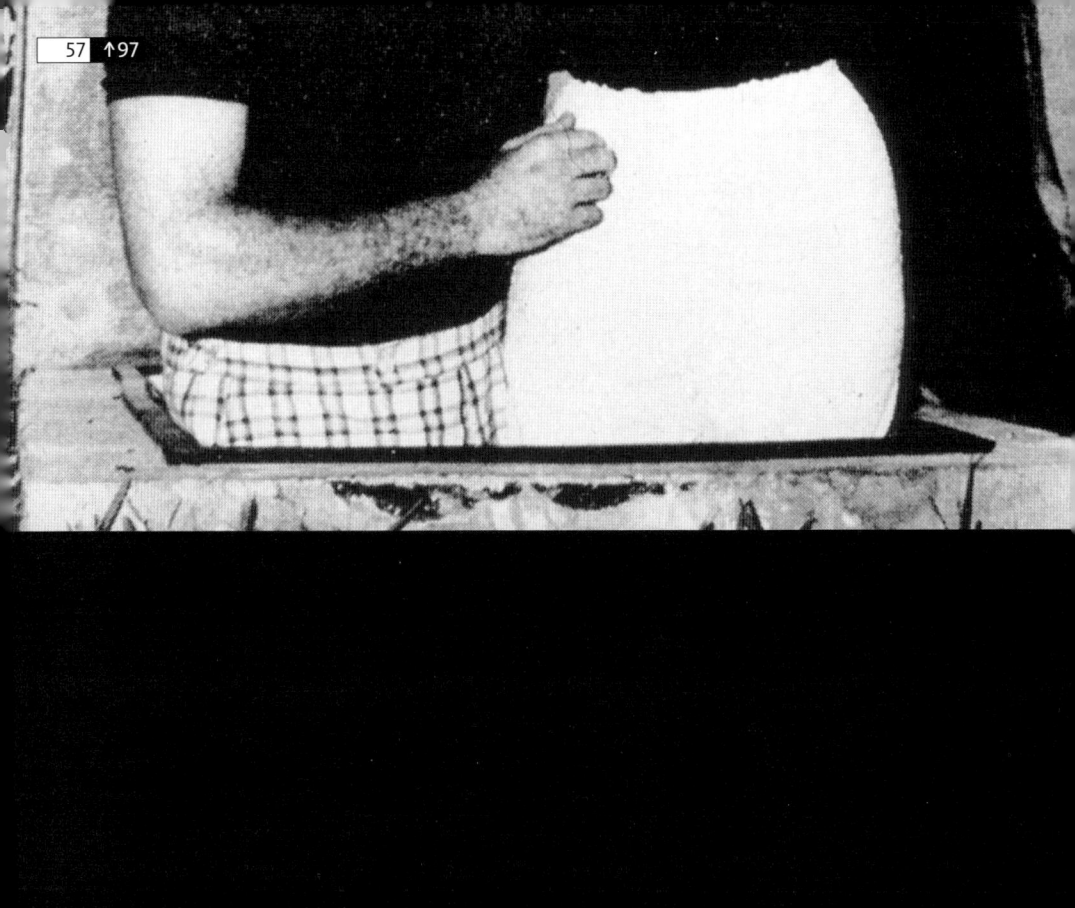

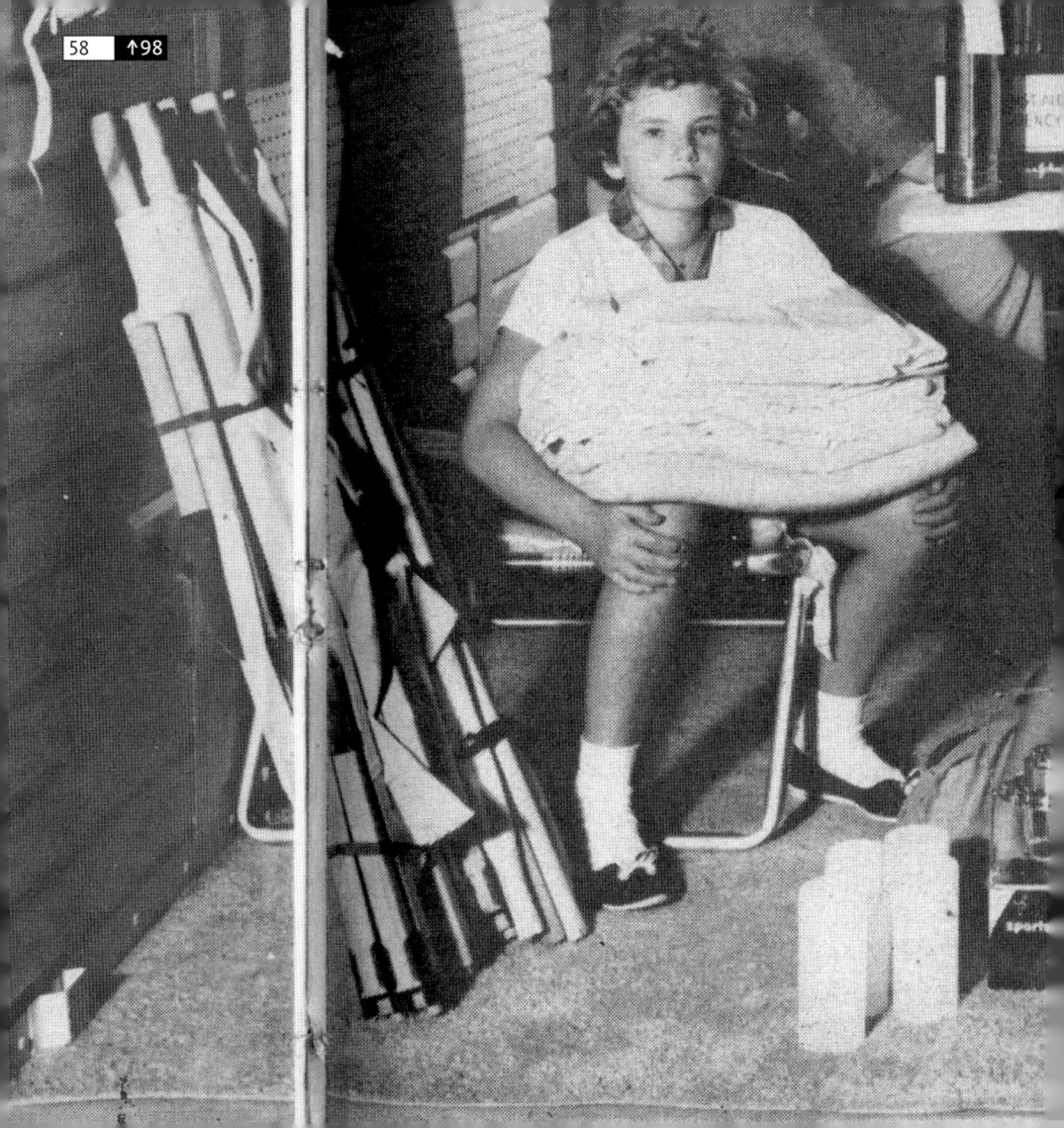

Chapter 2
DDU at MoMA

In 1939, MGM released a film featuring a flying house. *The Wizard of Oz* broke every record at the box office and has since been seen by more than a billion people, one of the largest audiences in the history of entertainment. A year after the film's release, Buckminster Fuller, who had always dreamed of flying houses, came across some sitting in the middle of wheat fields in Missouri. They had been built in Kansas.

This is how Fuller recounts the story:

> In the summer of 1940, Chris Morley and I were driving through Missouri—Hannibal, Missouri, where Mark Twain lived—and I noticed in the wheat fields, a row of glistening, galvanized, corrugated-steel grain bins. I told Chris that there were the most efficient engineering unit for a small prefabricated house now on inventory in mass-production industry.
>
> "That grain bin would provide enough room to house a small family at a cost of less than $1 per square foot of floor space with fireproof construction," I said, "and that's 80% below construction costs in the building industry. Those bins could easily be converted to dwelling machines." But I was broke of course, and couldn't do anything about it.[1]

These cheap, corrugated-steel bins were designed to protect grain from rats and weather. Produced by the Butler Manufacturing Company of Kansas with support from the second New Deal public spending program, they were part of the US Department of Agriculture's Ever Normal Grainery program. A farmer would fill a grain bin, and the government would pay a fixed price for it, seal the bin, and sell the grain when and wherever it was needed. **100 101** Fuller immediately saw the bins as a device to house people, not grain: emergency housing units that could be airlifted anywhere in the world. But he did not have enough money to pursue the idea. His traveling companion was writing a novel and promised to finance the project if the book was a success. It was. According to Fuller, Morley called one day to relay a message from the novel's protagonist: "Bucky, Kitty wants you to go out and see the Butler grain-bin people and get the thing going."[2] Fuller quickly drafted up the plans and, with Morley's financial support, flew to Kansas City to present his proposal to the Butler company. They were convinced and entered into a joint venture with Fuller's recently formed Dymaxion Company to develop mass-production housing units, called Dymaxion Deployment Units, or DDUs. 102 104

Fuller's first proposal for the DDU involved, as he put it, "few basic manufacturing changes," a "little adaptation" like that which transforms a truck into a station wagon, an industrial tool into a piece of domestic equipment: "With steel flooring this container is proof against fire, rodents and moisture. . . . Bins such as this thirty years old are still in good condition. But the bin looks pretty crude as a house? Let us see what a little adaptation such as that which converts a truck into a station wagon may do."[3] In fact, the changes were even less than that. Fuller made very few concessions to the traditional house. There were no windows, and the house was half buried. 107 108 Translucent plastic panels let light in from above. All Fuller did was replace the original top of the grain bin with a compound roof system of radial panels that "open up like petals—and are snap-locked to a flying ring."[4] He lined the inside of the bin with 3/16-inch plywood panels snapped into place and suggested that hay and crumpled newspapers be stuffed between the ply and the metal for insulation. The floor was a layer of steel coated with Masonite. The interior was organized to accommodate a family

---

1 Buckminster Fuller, *Autobiographical Monologue/Scenario*, ed. Robert Snyder (New York: St. Martin's Press, 1980), 78–79.
2 Ibid.

3 Buckminster Fuller, *The Artifacts of R. Buckminster Fuller: A Comprehensive Collection of His Designs and Drawings*, ed. James Ward (New York: Garland, 1985), 66.
4 Ibid., 67.

of four, with fireproof curtains able to divide the space into three pie-shaped sections. All shelving, equipment, plumbing fixtures, and furniture were attached to the circular walls, with only a tiny stool and a small circular coffee table floating in the space. The whole house was so simple that Fuller was able to boast that it could "be bolted together or unbolted by two men in three hours."[5]

Before the unit went into production, Fuller developed a second version. A series of small circular portholes glazed by acrylic plastic were added (the first time this material had been used for windows, other than in airplanes), and the shape of the roof was changed to give more headroom. The folding petals were replaced by a streamlined roof with a series of small circular acrylic skylights, and the inside of the bin was lined with fiberglass-backed wallboard. **104** **112** **113**

The story of Fuller's infatuation with grain bins recalls the fascination of European avant-garde architects with American grain silos in the first decades of the century. First was Gropius, who had a bunch of photographs of American grain elevators and factories published in the 1913 *Jahrbuch des Deutschen Werkbundes*. But he had not seen the silos. The photos had been sent to him from various sources in America and Canada. In the 1920s, Le Corbusier borrowed these same images for publication in *L'Esprit nouveau*. He wanted them to support his argument that architecture was a play of volumes in the light and that the clean and virile engineers were on the right side of things. But since the photographs were, on close inspection, not sufficiently "clean," he proceeded to purify them of every bit of extra ornament and decoration before their republication. The retouched images then traveled through many avant-garde journals and publications such as *De Stijl*, *MA*, and *Buch neuer Künstler*. Nobody seemed aware that what they were publishing did not actually exist.

---

[5] Ibid., 70.

Like his European colleagues, Fuller traced the origins of his architecture to an encounter with an ordinary object, an anonymous industrial design. Unlike them, he was interested not so much in the aesthetics of this object (although one can hardly miss the image of the "glistening" metal bins sitting in the middle of the fields like some kind of recently landed spacecraft) as in its practicality. He saw the grain bin as an already-made object that could be used as a prefabricated house, flown anywhere and built by anyone in a matter of hours. Smack in the middle of America, Fuller came up with a ready-made house, a mass-produced object, a generic metal grain bin. But is this a "readymade"? Can there be such a thing as an architectural readymade?

Marcel Duchamp's criteria for readymades are quite specific. In fact, he wrote the "Specifications for Readymades" as a manuscript included in his *Green Box* of 1934. The first requirement of the readymade is that it be "a kind of *rendez-vous*."[6] As Thierry de Duve puts it, the readymade is "born of the encounter of an object and an author. Object and author are nothing but the conditions of their encounter. The object is given; it exists somewhere. . . . Given an object and an author, it is sufficient that they have a *rendezvous* for a readymade to be *inscribed*."[7]

Inscription is the second of Duchamp's criteria. He writes: "Naturally inscribe that date, hour, minute, on the readymade as *information*."[8] The object has to be marked, named, dated. The artist becomes a marker rather than a maker or, rather, makes by marking. For Duchamp, to make is to choose. It is the choice that is marked. The only act is to mark the choice. Even the choice is made by the object.

---

6 "*The important thing then is just* this matter of timing, the snapshot effect, like a speech delivered on no matter what occasion but *at such and such an hour.*" See Marcel Duchamp, "Specifications for 'Readymades,'" in *Salt Seller: The Writings of Marcel Duchamp*, ed. Michel Sanouillet and Elmer Peterson (New York: Oxford University Press), 32.
7 Thierry de Duve, "Echoes of the Readymade: Critique of Pure Modernism," *October* 70 (Fall 1994): 71.
8 Duchamp, "Specifications for 'Readymades,'" 32.

When asked in a 1968 interview how he chose a readymade, Duchamp responded, "It chooses you, so to speak."[9] It is precisely not an aesthetic choice, as he insisted in a 1961 lecture at MoMA entitled "Apropos of 'Readymades'":

> A point which I want very much to establish is that the choice of these "readymades" was never dictated by esthetic delectation. This choice was based on a reaction of visual indifference with at the same time a total absence of good or bad taste . . . in fact a complete anesthesia.[10]

Furthermore, the object that chooses you is not unique in any way. On the contrary, Duchamp's specifications conclude by noting the "serial characteristic of the readymade." The readymade is never an isolated object. It is always exemplary of an endless succession of identical objects.

These specifications fit the DDU. First, the rendezvous in the wheat fields of Missouri, on a particular day in the summer of 1940, a story that has been repeated many times, with almost no variations, by Fuller and his acolytes. Then, the inscription. The object is named, dated, registered, and even patented (on March 21, 1941, Fuller filed for the patent of the Dymaxion Deployment Unit, which was granted on March 7, 1944). Even the endless retelling of the story is part of that inscription. As for the absence of aesthetic taste, Fuller is adamant about his disregard for taste in architecture. For him, the grain bin is simply a mechanism for efficient housing. That it "looks pretty crude as a house" does not bother him. He just lines it with plywood and adds a more streamlined roof. And on the question of the "serial characteristic of the readymade," the grain bin is, of course, exemplary. Not only it is the product of serial production, but Fuller appropriates it only to accelerate its mass production further. From the very first encounter, all that Fuller thinks about is how many can be produced and delivered in what time.

In his 1940 "Deployment" manual, a manuscript written "preparatory to inception of the Dymaxion Deployment Unit activity with the Butler Mfg. Co.," he predicts that one hundred thousand units can be delivered every month.[11]

But above all what makes a readymade a readymade is its placement within the gallery. The anonymous object is thereby registered as an artwork. What is remarkable about the DDU is that, despite Fuller's disinterest in the idea of architecture as art and his contempt for the Museum of Modern Art's curatorial policies, he placed it within its walls. In November of 1941, the same year he applied for the patent, Fuller put the DDU on display in the sculpture garden of the Museum of Modern Art. The museum called it Defense House. **116** **117**

The house was made up of two coupled deployment units whose interior was reorganized to accommodate a family of six. **106** The original twenty-foot-diameter unit could, as the museum put it, "serve as a spacious living room but may also be divided into three rooms by means of curtains,"[12] while the adjoining fifteen-foot unit contained kitchen, bath, and a separate bedroom. For the first time, MoMA had a whole house on display. Domestic life was reframed as an artwork.

The November *Bulletin of the Museum of Modern Art* shows the house installed in the sculpture garden.[13] The ground is covered with snow. In the background we see the Rockefeller apartment building on West Fifty-fourth Street, where Alfred J. Barr and other museum officials lived. **103** The humble grain bin has become the

---

9   Marcel Duchamp, "I Propose to Strain the Laws of Physics," interview by Francis Roberts, *Art News*, December 1968, 62. Cited by de Duve.
10 Duchamp, "Apropos of 'Readymades,'" in *Salt Seller*, 141.
11 Fuller, *Artifacts*, 65.
12 *Bulletin of the Museum of Modern Art*, October 1941, 17.
13 "Museum Notes: BUCKMINSTER FULLER'S DYMAXION DEPLOYMENT UNIT: Mr. Fuller's demountable defense house is now open in the Museum garden. Completely prefabricated, the two adjoining cylindrical metal units as shown at the Museum are arranged and furnished to supply complete living facilities for a family of six. The original unit, twenty feet in diameter, may serve as a spacious living room but may also be divided into three rooms by means of curtains. The adjoining fifteen foot unit contains kitchen, bath and a separate bedroom. Shelves, lighting equipment, plumbing and closets are built in. The units could serve as barracks, furnishing living space for 24 persons on doubledecker cots, or could be adapted to a number of other defense needs such as field laboratories. They can be manufactured at the rate of 1,000 per day at $1,500 each." *Bulletin of the Museum of Modern Art*, November 1941, 17.

center of attention. But with its door facing away from the museum, it is as if the house had turned its back to the institution, setting up a domestic, if not suburban, relationship to the house across the street. The DDU's relationship to the world of art—its status as an art object—remains unclear.

The event was preceded by a notice in the September *Bulletin of the Museum of Modern Art* announcing a delay: "Navy priorities have prevented delivery of the house," originally scheduled for July. The exhibition of "this ingenious defence shelter developed from a standard metal grain storage bin" is postponed until late September.[14] And when the house finally arrived in November, it had been renamed the Dymaxion Deployment Unit. It had swung from domestic defense to military attack. The museum spoke of the ease with which the same unit that was being exhibited as a private house could be converted into military barracks sleeping twenty-four soldiers.

This slippage between domestic and military was built into the project from the beginning. The original "Deployment" manual of 1940 proposed a different arrangement of the same unit as a "sleeping shelter" for encampments of soldiers or for civilians who, Fuller said, could be evacuated from the city to dispersed country sites "to reduce national vulnerability to air attack." Drawings show the unit completely filled with cots. **106** In the "Deployment" manual, representations of domestic life alternate with images of military life. We see the house nestled between two trees, with children's toys beside the path leading to the door, and photographs of the model with bombers in the sky overhead at night. **107 108** The first line of the manual insists that the house is "the initial tactic of a winning defensive department in overhead combat." Even the specific design of the house is promoted in these terms. The house was half underground for insulation efficiency but also for camouflage and as protection against bombs. The manual says that the ring holding the roof panels can also support "camouflage netting" and that "all panels could be closed for blackout without interrupting air circulation." It even includes a sketch labeled "camouflage" showing that a half-buried house is harder to see from the air and another sketch labeled "ballistics" showing the trajectory of missiles and arguing that a circular form presents fewer right angles to an incoming projectile than any other shape. **109** Fuller presents a list of nine performance characteristics of a successful housing program, which includes "air protection" and "concussion resistance." The shape of the house is meant to deflect the impact of bombs. When windows are added in the second version of the unit, their little covers are said to be for protection against flying shrapnel.

This militarization of the house is consistent with Fuller's idea of the house as "shelter." He repeatedly referred to the etymological meaning of the word as "SHELL<scyld (shield) TER<trum (firm): That which covers or shields from exposure or danger; a place of safety, refuge or retreat."[15] When describing the mass-producible condition of the Wichita House in 1946, he describes the routine functions of the house in terms of defense: **110** **111**

> The house is to be conceived of scientifically as man's *initial* advantage relative to the forces of the environment. . . . The house can be considered as his first line of defense against the large category of elements which seek constantly to destroy him, such as fire, earthquake, tornado, flood, pestilence, politics, selfishness. Then . . . the elements which seek to destroy him inside his house as well . . . : bacteria, accident, laziness and habits (which have to be severely inspected) and

---

14 "Museum Notes: BUCKMINSTER FULLER'S DEMOUNTABLE DEFENSE HOUSE: Exhibition in the Museum garden of this ingenious defense shelter, developed from a standard metal grain storage bin, was announced as scheduled for July. Navy priorities have prevented delivery of the house, but Mr. Fuller now promises its arrival in New York in time to be exhibited late in September. The completely prefabricated circular unit, twenty feet in diameter, will be set up in the Museum garden with complete living facilities for a family of four. Supplementary material will explain its possible adaptations to other defense needs such as barracks, storage units, stores, schoolrooms, etc." *Bulletin of the Museum of Modern Art*, September 1941, 9.

15 Buckminster Fuller, *Nine Chains to the Moon* (New York: J. B. Lippincott, 1938), 34.

the routine inevitable functions of man as a process, that is eating, sleeping, being clean, refusing [sic], etc., which if you did not help him with . . . might readily get the better of him."[16]

The house is always at war; the DDU simply makes this explicit. The basis of many of the innovations of the famous Wichita House, the DDU was in fact Fuller's most successful attempt to integrate military and domestic ambitions. The house became a significant part of the war effort.

The first prototype of the DDU, fully furnished as a house, was erected outside the Butler factory in August 1940. But before the production run of domestic units could take off, wartime restrictions on materials limited access to steel to the military. The British army became interested in the units. They placed a large order for troop housing, then canceled it because they needed the shipping space for weapons. The breakthrough came when the United States escalated its support of the Allied forces. The DDU seemed ideal for quickly housing troops and protecting equipment. The military asked the Butler Company to produce a model and install it in Haynes Point Park in Washington for study by government and military housing agencies. The fully furnished house went up in April 1941. The head of the Department of Architecture at the University of Michigan and his wife "test-dwelt" the unit, and Butler photographed the couple for the company's publicity brochures presenting them alongside images of models acting out stereotypical domestic rules. **112** **113** **114** The military thought the unit was ideal for airlifting into isolated sites like radar installations on the Pacific Islands, where people and equipment had to be housed, and placed a big order. Butler received the highest priority for steel and promptly started mass production. Thousands of the units were sent to the Persian Gulf and assembled into a small city for American pilots and mechanics assembling and testing war planes. 115 But with the Pearl Harbor attack in December 1941, the production of DDUs stopped. Weapon production required all the available steel.

It is in this military context that the Defense House appeared in the museum and was understood. The slippage between domestic and military life and back again that organized all of Fuller's design work was then gripping the whole country. The house received extensive coverage in newspapers across the country. The similar reports ("War Inspired," "Comfortable though Bombed," and "A Shelter in War—A Beach House in Peacetime" are some of the repeated headlines in newspapers) point to one source, MoMA's press release. 116 117 The museum presented the house as a bomb shelter of sorts. Not totally safe in case of a direct hit but definitely an improvement over traditional building. "Its circulate, corrugated, surfaces, deflect bomb fragments or flying debris," one newspaper recounted. "Its steel structure is entirely fireproof and its shape and anchor foundation render it non-collapsible. A nearby bomb hit might cause it to bounce a few inches."[17] But the biggest advantage by far is that it would be unrecognizable as a building by a bomber. Buildings are square. This house, according to another newspaper, "could be made to look like a tree, or even a hole in the ground."[18] The DDU is therefore a house in camouflage. Not by chance, the house was itself camouflaged in the museum garden, covered with shrubbery that disguised it from the traditional galleries. 103 117 The following year the museum would hold an exhibition titled Camouflage for Civilian Defense (1942).[19] The *Bulletin* of October–November

---

16 Buckminster Fuller, "Designing a New Industry" (from a talk given at the Beechcraft Co., Wichita, KS, January 26, 1946), in *The Buckminster Fuller Reader*, ed. James Meyer (London: Jonathan Cape, 1970), 169.
17 "Buckminster Fuller Invents a Dymaxion Deployment Unit," *Eagle* (Pittsfield, MA), October 18, 1941.
18 "The Totem Pole," Herald Express (Los Angeles), February 21, 1941. An article in the *Philadelphia Inquirer*, November 23, 1941, entitled "Sheltering Art from Bombs" showed Buckminster Fuller's "shelter" as it would look to a bomber.
19 The museum's first exhibition of camouflage was prepared in connection with the exhibition Britain at War (1941). Camouflage for Civilian Defense of 1942 emphasized civilian and industrial defense. "The Museum and the War," *Bulletin of the Museum of Modern Art*, October–November 1942, 8.

1942, "a record in tabloid form of the special wartime activities of the Museum" entitled *The Museum and the War*, shows a photograph of the DDU being assembled in the garden. The caption describes the house as "comparatively bomb-proof and easily camouflaged." **118** A panel from the camouflage exhibition on the facing page reads: "Camouflage must deceive both the eye and the camera." **120**

The exhibition of the DDU at MoMA was part of the reprogramming of the museum during the war years. A few months before the installation, Alfred Barr had written in his annual report: "What good is art in a time of war? What good are art museums during a national emergency? Why maintain our cultural interests and activities when the air hums with bombers and the news of the battle?"[20] To the question of whether the museum should "ignore the crisis and get on with its normal activities" or "devote itself explicitly, exclusively to the defense effort,"[21] Barr favored doing a bit of both. Already programmed exhibitions went ahead while the museum organized special wartime activities and exhibitions. The museum's war program began in May 1941 with the exhibition Britain at War, followed by two exhibitions of the winning posters from its National Defense Poster Competitions, three camouflage exhibitions, the Wartime Housing show, and the very important Road to Victory, a procession of photographs of the nation at war, curated by Lieutenant Commander Edward Steichen (later director of the Department of Photography) and installed by Herbert Bayer. **70 71** The exhibition was seen by eighty thousand people. In fact, attendance to the museum increased dramatically—almost 50 percent—during the war years.[22]

In addition, the museum organized many activities for troops of all Allied nations, including a series of parties in the museum garden. Attended by more than four thousand soldiers, the parties started with a buffet supper and went on until 11 p.m. with games, sing-alongs, dancing, motion pictures, and so on.[23] **74 75**

A museum photograph shows a couple using one of the sculptures in the garden as a prop for intimacy. Likewise, the DDU was used as the site of intimate exchanges. An exhibition review noted, "It seems that very young lovers found it a lovely place to carry on. This produced a number of embarrassments so the museum people turned off the heat to discourage the lovers."[24]

The attraction of the house extended far beyond the domains of art and the military. Not only was the house extremely popular with visitors, but it was featured in mass-circulation magazines as background for fashion shots. The caption of a spread in *Vogue* reads: "Dark Fur, Pale Dress: The glistening black of Persian lamb photographed against the pale, modern shape of Buckminster Fuller's 'Defense House,' at the Museum of Modern Art." **121** The pale dress matches the pale house with the black fur as accent.[25] An old form of camouflage.

The use of the house as background for fashion shots follows a long tradition in the history of modern architecture. But is the DDU modern architecture for the museum?

Not really. If anything, the museum understood the DDU as a "design" product, a piece of equipment. When describing the house, the museum did not mobilize the rhetoric it had used to promote modern architecture as an art form. It simply talked about the usefulness of the house, its cost, the ease of its innovative construction system, its ability to be moved, reprogrammed, and so on. Fuller's installation raised issues about the status of the design object in the museum. Just as the Useful Objects under $10 exhibition, which was on display at the same time as the DDU, produced the headline "Potato Peeler Gets a Place of Honor at the Museum of Modern Art," newspaper reports treated the Defense House and its presence in the

---

20 Alfred H. Barr Jr., "Report of the Director," *Annual Report*, Museum of Modern Art, New York, 1940–41.
21 Ibid.
22 "A Museum's War Program: An Editorial," *American Artist*, November 1942, 24.
23 Ibid., 30.
24 Quoted in a review of the exhibition, "The Totem Pole," *Herald Express* (Los Angeles), February 21, 1941. Author unknown.
25 "Dark Fur, Pale Dress, " *Vogue*, November 15, 1941.

museum humorously: "Yesterday," one journalist wrote, "I played house in a steel something that looks like an open parachute from above, like a silo from the outside and like an orange inside. This is a house in which to brave bombs."[26]

While the unit was understood primarily as a bomb shelter, all reporters picked up on Fuller's suggestion that it could easily be turned into a guesthouse or summer cottage after the war: "You can put one in your backyard, for instance, dive into it if any dive bombers come over and maybe next year (provided there is no direct hit) turn it into a guest house or cart it to the beach for a summer cottage."[27]

The house moves from the battlefields to the backyard of a museum to a suburban backyard and beyond. But it is not simply a supplementary piece of equipment. Fuller insisted that everybody should live in such a house: "After the war hundreds of thousands of people will live in round houses and if they do not like their neighbors they can call the truck and move somewhere else." The house completely redefines tactics in the suburban battlefield.

Once again, the DDU slides backward and forward between military and domestic realms. It binds them together.

Interestingly, the exhibition of the DDU at MoMA seems to have been forgotten, even by the museum itself. The monumental book *The Museum of Modern Art: The History and the Collection* (1984), which constitutes the museum's official history, not only ignores Fuller's house but claims that Marcel Breuer's House in the Garden of 1949 was "the first architectural structure built for public exhibition in the Museum's first sculpture garden."[28] Was the DDU so radical that it had to be blocked from the museum's memory?

While Fuller is a figure traditionally neglected from accounts of the American architectural avant-garde, he did exhibit several times at MoMA. In a letter to Charles Eames, Fuller refers to the museum as the MMA, only to correct himself immediately by saying "MOMA, I suppose we should say now, which is rather touching if you think about it." MoMA, the mother of all American architecture, had invited Buckminster Fuller like the unwanted child for whom space is always made in the house, no matter how reluctantly.

When Fuller landed his DDU in the garden of the museum, he may have hoped to kill the Wicked Witch of the East Coast establishment: the International Style. He repeatedly criticizes it for misusing the European's first liberating encounter with "giant silos, warehouses, and factories in the cleanly emergent United States—structures which had been disembarrassed in unique degree, in the space-rich American scene, of economically unessential aesthetics."[29]

It was precisely by treating the grain silo as an unembellished readymade that Fuller transgressed the institution of architecture. Like Duchamp, he was admitted into MoMA late. Unlike Duchamp, he was never rehabilitated. The difference between what Fuller did and the institutionalized view of modern architecture was simply too great. As George Nelson pointed out in the symposium "What Is Happening to Modern Architecture?" held at MoMA on February 11, 1948, "The difference between the Tugendhat house and a dwelling in the 'Bay Region Style' is almost invisible by comparison with the gap between the Tugendhat house and Buckminster Fuller's Dymaxion house. It is here that we will find the No Man's Land of future Professional battles."[30] While the museum continued to be engaged in the battle of the styles, Fuller attempted to completely redefine the battlefield.

He lost. But the war continues in the margins of institutions. Different margins, different tactics.

26 Margaret Kernnodle, "How to Be Comfortable in Spite of Bombers," *Herald* (Grand Rapids, MI).
27 CC Charlotte, *News*, October 17, 1941.
28 Sam Hunter, introduction to *The Museum of Modern Art: The History and the Collection* (New York: Harry N. Abrams, Inc., and Museum of Modern Art, 1984), 28.
29 Buckminster Fuller, "Influences on My Work" (1955), *Buckminster Fuller Reader*, 61.
30 "What Is Happening to Modern Architecture?" *Bulletin of the Museum of Modern Art*, Spring 1948, 12–13.

Chapter 3
The Eames House

So, somehow through Mies, through a rejection of much of Mies, but still through Mies, or so it seems to me, we get the 1949 house—something wholly original, wholly American.
—Peter Smithson[1]

The oldest published photograph of the house shows a truck on the site, occupying the place of the house, taking its place, anticipating it. The windshield happens to lie exactly where a glass facade will terminate the building. The steel frame of the house is being assembled from a crane on the back of the truck as it steadily moves down the narrow site carved out between a steep hillside and a row of eucalyptus trees. It is said that this process took only a day and a half.[2] 122 123

The Eameses immediately celebrated. A sequence of photographs shows the ecstatic couple holding hands under the frame, then stepping off the retaining wall onto a thin beam suspended like a tightrope across the space, and finally posing in the middle of the beam, still holding hands. Ray has a white bird in her raised hand.[3] 124 125 126

The Eameses liked to celebrate things. Anything. Everything. This was not just whimsy, a distraction from the work: it was part of the work itself. Walking along the beam of the house under construction was the beginning of the occupation of the house. They were literally moving in, even if the crafting of the basic fabric of the building was to take almost a year. The house became an endless process of celebration over the course of their lives. Not by chance, they moved in on Christmas Eve 1949: they wanted the house to be a Christmas gift. When they walked across the steel tightrope before the tent had even been pulled up over the frame, they were launching an intense program of construction through festive play. Every stage of the play was recorded, photographed, and disseminated to an international audience.

At first glance, the image of the Eameses poised on the frame echoes the long American vernacular tradition of workers photographed on top of their new structures. From riveters on steel-frame skyscrapers high above New York to midwestern farmers perched on their wooden frames over the prairie, to climb up on the structure and be photographed is a way to celebrate it, to claim it and the land below. **128** But there is something else going on with the Eames image. While workers are usually posed in relatively stable positions, sitting on the frame or holding on to it, and all the women definitely remain on the ground, Ray and Charles are right in the middle of the beam, only just balanced, wobbling even. And they are not the workers. Just what are the architects doing up there?

Circus, it turns out, was one of their fascinations. When Charles was asked in 1970 to give the prestigious Charles Eliot Norton Lectures at Harvard University, he concluded the first of his six lectures by presenting a three-screen slide show of circus photographs he had been shooting since the 1940s. The 180 images were accompanied by a sound track featuring music and other sounds recorded at the circus. **129** The theme of the lectures was that "the rewarding experiences and aesthetic pleasures of our lives should not be dependent solely upon the classic fine arts, but should be, rather, a natural product of the business of life itself."[4]

---

1 Alison and Peter Smithson, "Phenomenon in Parallel: Eames House, Patio and Pavilion," *Places: A Quarterly Journal of Environmental Design* 7, no. 3 (Spring 1991): 20.

2 The Eameses said that the structural shell of the house was raised by five men in sixteen hours. "Life in a Chinese Kit: Standard Industrial Products Assembled in a Spacious Wonderland," *Architectural Forum*, September 1950, 94.

3 The first photograph was published in Elizabeth A. T. Smith, ed., *Blueprints for Modern Living: History and Legacy of the Case Study Houses* (Los Angeles: Museum of Contemporary Art; Cambridge, MA: MIT Press, 1989), 182, and credited to the Eames Office. The second, in "Steel in the Meadow," *Interiors*, November 1959, 109, is attributed to Jay Connor. The third, reproduced here, was printed in John Neuhart, Marilyn Neuhart, and Ray Eames, *Eames Design: The Work of the Office of Charles and Ray Eames* (New York: Harry N. Abrams, 1989), 108; it is attributed to John Entenza.

4 Digby Diehl, "Q&A: Charles Eames," *Los Angeles Times WEST Magazine*, October 8, 1972, 14, reprinted in Digby Diehl, *Supertalk* (New York: Doubleday, 1974). Original transcript in box 24, folders 4–5, The Work of Charles and Ray Eames, Manuscript Division, Library of Congress, Washington, DC.

Eames turned to the circus because what "seems to be a freewheeling exchange in self-expression, is instead a tightly knit and masterfully disciplined organic accumulation of people, energies and details."[5] In a talk given before the American Academy of Arts and Sciences in 1974, he elaborates on the point:

> The circus is a nomadic society which is very rich and colorful but which shows apparent license on the surface. . . . Everything in the circus is pushing the possible beyond the limit. . . . Yet, within this apparent freewheeling license, we find a discipline which is almost unbelievable. There is a strict hierarchy of events and an elimination of choice under stress, so that one event can automatically follow another. The layout of the circus under canvas is more like the plan of the Acropolis than anything else.[6]

In many ways, this is what Eames thought architecture was—the ongoing theatrical spectacle of everyday life, understood as an exercise in restrictions rather than self-expression. The endless photographs of the almost ridiculously happy Eameses displaying their latest inventions are part of an extraordinarily precise and professional design practice. We see them on top of the frame of their house, "pinned" by metal chair frames, holding Christmas decorations, waving to us from inside a Christmas ball, wearing Easter hats or masks, photographing their own reflections in the house, and so on. **47 50 131 132 159** In almost all of the early photographs, they wear matching outfits, as if to emphasize the performative aspect of their work. The Eameses were very precise about their clothes, commissioning their dress from Dorothy Jenkins, the Oscar-winning designer who created the costumes for films including *South Pacific*, *The Ten Commandments*, *Night of the Iguana*, and *The Sound of Music* (Ray Eames's distinctive pinafore dresses are even reminiscent of Julie Andrews's dresses in the latter film). **133 134** The effect of the Eames costume was that of the professional couple as a matching set, carefully positioned like any other object in the layout. The uniform clothes transformed the couple into a designer object that could be moved around the frame or from picture to picture. It was always the layout that was the statement, not the objects. And the layout was constantly reworked, rearranged.

If design was not the self-expression of the designer, it was the occupant's daily life that left its mark on the house. Eames houses used "industrial technology to provide . . . an 'unselfconscious' enclosure that would satisfy the essentials for comfortable living. Such a structure could then be made into a personal statement by the occupant, who could fill it with the accessories of his or her own life."[7] All the ephemera of daily living were to take over and define the space.

For the Eameses, everything was architecture, from the setting of a table for breakfast to a circus performance. **135** Everybody was a designer. Charles trusted, sometimes to later disappointment, the choices craftsmen would make.[8] If they knew their trade, he believed, they would know what a good solution was. The capacity of an individual, even one without experience, to choose well was respected: "I don't believe in this 'gifted few' concept, just in people doing things they are really interested in doing. They have a way of getting good at whatever it is."[9] Employees arriving at the Eames Office were routinely assigned tasks for which they had no previous training.[10] It was thought that anyone who applied his or her attention totally, obsessively, to a problem would come up with a good

---

5 "1970, Charles Eliot Norton Lectures: Lecture 1," in Neuhart, Neuhart, and Eames, *Eames Design*, 356.

6 Charles Eames, "Language of Vision: The Nuts and Bolts," *Bulletin of the American Academy of Arts and Sciences*, October 1974, 13–25. Quoted in Neuhart, Neuhart, and Eames, *Eames Design*, 91.

7 Neuhart, Neuhart, and Eames, *Eames Design*, 137.

8 Charles decided to leave the design of a door handle and lock for their home in the hands of a locksmith, "who, he felt, would handle the problem with a degree of sensitivity born of his own training and craftsmanship. He was later horrified to find a large and clumsy fitting placed in an awkward position on the door." John Neuhart and Marilyn Neuhart, *Eames House* (Berlin: Ernst & Sohn; London: Academy Editions, 1994), 56.

9 Charles Eames quoted in Bill N. Lacy, "Warehouse Full of Ideas," *Horizon*, September 1980, 27.

10 Pat Kirkham, *Charles and Ray Eames: Designers of the Twentieth Century* (Cambridge, MA: MIT Press, 1995), 89.

solution, especially if there were many restrictions, such as limited time, materials, or money. Charles spoke nostalgically of his days at the MGM studios, where he would often have only one night to design a whole new set out of a limited range of available props.

This idea of design as the rearrangement of a limited set of parts was constant in the Eameses' work. Everything they produced could be rearranged; no layout was ever fixed. Even the formal lectures were sometimes rearranged in midstream. Kits of parts, movable partitions, "The Toy," the plywood cabinets, the House of Cards, the Revell Toy House, the Kwikset House are all infinitely rearrangable. **43 136 137 138 139 140 141 405**

The Eames House is a good example. Not only was it produced out of the same structural components as the utterly different Entenza House (designed by Charles Eames with Eero Saarinen), but the Eames House was itself a rearrangement of an earlier version. **48 49 142 143 144** After the steel had already been delivered to the site, Eames decided to redesign the house, putting the same set of steel parts together in a completely new way.[11]

The structure exhibited the same logic of rearrangement that would soon dominate its interior. The Eames House blurred the distinction between designer and occupant, accommodating structure and mobile accessories. Where did the work of the designer end and that of the occupant begin in this house? Were the famous colored panels on the facade ephemera (picked up from the history of modern art like the pieces of driftwood the Eameses were always picking up and rearranging) or "unselfconscious structure"? **145 146**
In fact, the color of the panels was meant to change. Ray said that they chose the cheapest kind of paint from Sears, Roebuck so that they could experiment, but the original colors remain.[12] Eventually the panels became fixed in the mind

of the architectural community and taken to be the architecture. But for the Eameses, the real architecture of the house was to be found in their endless rearrangement of collectibles within it. The real space was to be found in the details of their daily life. **147** **148**

Charles constantly reflected on what "quality" made a good architect. In an interview with Digby Diehl, Eames recalls a conversation he had with Saarinen on the subject: "One of the things we hit upon was the quality of a host. That is, the role of the architect, or the designer, is that of a very good, thoughtful host, all of whose energy goes into trying to anticipate the needs of his guests—those who enter the building and use the objects in it. We decided that this was an essential ingredient in the design of a building or a useful object."[13] The house has to efface itself in favor of the creative choices made by its occupants. Its only role is that of the "shock absorber" that protects a unique and ever-changing lifestyle: "The house," Eames says, "must make no insistent demands for itself, but rather aid as a background for life in work . . . and as re-orientator and 'shock absorber.'"[14] It is difficult not to think of the war. **149** Domestic life could no longer be taken for granted. It became an art form carefully constructed and marketed by a whole new industry: a form of art therapy for a traumatized nation, a reassuring image of the "good life" to be bought like any other product. Instead of offering a complete environment to the postwar consumer,

---

11 While many sources insist, following the Eameses, that the new version used only those parts already delivered to the site, with the exception of one additional beam, Marilyn and John Neuhart question this: "A count of the seventeen-foot vertical girders needed for both house and studio yields a total of twenty-two for the first and sixteen for the latter, considerably more than would have been needed for the first version of each. In addition, there do not appear to have been any seventeen-foot girders in the original house. Additional trusses would also have been required to accommodate the reworked plan." Neuhart and Neuhart, *Eames House*, 38.

12 Ray Eames, interview by Pat Kirkham, July 1983, transcript, box 61, The Work of Charles and Ray Eames, Manuscript Division, Library of Congress, Washington, DC. See also Kirkham, *Charles and Ray Eames*, 115–16.

13 Diehl, "Q&A," 16.

14 "Case Study Houses 8 and 9 by Charles Eames and Eero Saarinen, Architects," *Arts & Architecture*, December 1945, 43. Also quoted in *Portfolio Magazine*, Summer 1950, unpag.

the Eameses offered a variety of components that individuals could construct and rearrange themselves. The Eameses insisted that life consisted of making choices. They left most of them to the occupants, rejecting the role of the artist in favor of that of the industrial designer and catalog distributor. **43** **150**

The idea of the house as shock absorber was also literal. The Eameses devoted considerable research to perfecting the rubber shock absorbers in their furniture. In the 1946 exhibition of their plywood furniture at the Museum of Modern Art, New York, a rotary device was used to show the strength and flexibility of the rubber shock mount, and a tumbling drum containing the plywood "Eames chair" demonstrated its durability. **151** **152** A house was likewise meant to absorb the eccentric movements of everyday life. In the Eames House, panels shift; furniture moves in and out. It became a kind of testing ground for all the work of the office. Everything moved in the end. Only the basic frame stayed still, and this frame was meant to be almost invisible. A necessary prop—no more than that. As Esther McCoy wrote as a caption for an image of trees reflected on the glass walls of the Eames House, "After thirteen years of living in a house with exposed steel frame, Ray Eames said, 'The structure long ago ceased to exist. I am not aware of it.' They lived in nature and its reflections—and reflections of reflections."[15] **154** The house dissolved in a play of reflections, restless images that immediately caught the eye of the world. The Eames House was published everywhere, exposed, scrutinized.[16] **156** The images multiplied and became the objects of reflection. Their appeal was part of the general fascination with postwar America that extended from pop-up toasters to buildings.

Perhaps nobody was so captivated by the Eameses, and more lucid about their work, than their buddies the British architects Alison and Peter Smithson.

In "Eames Celebration," a 1966 issue of *Architectural Design* that the Smithsons prepared devoted exclusively to the Eameses, they wrote: 157 158 159

> There has been much reflection in England on the Eames House. For the Eames House was a cultural gift parcel received here at a particularly useful time. The bright wrapper has made most people—especially Americans—throw the content away as not sustaining. But we have been brooding on it—working on it—feeding on it.[17]

The house as an object, a gift all wrapped up in colored paper. 158 This comment reflects so much of the Smithsons' obsessions, so much of what they saw as new in the Eameses: the attention to seemingly marginal objects (which the Smithsons perceptively understood as "remnants of identity"), the love of ephemera and of colored wrapping paper, and so on.

For the Eameses, gifts were all important. They maintained that the reason they began to design and make toys (such as the House of Cards, the Toy, the masks) was to give them to their grandchildren and the children of staff members and friends. 136 137 138 160 161 But the concept of gift extends far beyond the toys. Not only were the Eameses extremely generous with their friends (they once paid for the Smithsons' airline tickets so the couple could visit them in California), but they understood all their work as a gift. In an interview, Charles said: "The motivation behind most of the things we've done was either that we wanted them ourselves, or we wanted to give them to someone else. And the way to make that

---

15 Esther Mc Coy, *Modern California Houses* (1962), reprinted as *Case Study Houses 1945–1962* (Los Angeles: Hennessey & Ingalls, 1977), 54.
16 In addition to *Arts & Architecture*, the Eames House was published in *Architectural Forum*, September 1950; *Architectural Review*, October 1951; *Arquitectura* (Mexico), June 1952; *L'architecture d'aujourd'hui*, December 1953; *Interiors*, November 1959; *Domus*, May 1963; *Architectural Design*, September 1966; etc.
17 Alison and Peter Smithson, untitled, in "Eames Celebration," ed. Alison and Peter Smithson, special issue, *Architectural Design*, September 1966, 432.

practical is to have the gifts manufactured.... The lounge chair, for example, was really done as a present to a friend, Billy Wilder, and has since been reproduced." Wilder wanted "something he could take a nap on in his office, but that wouldn't be mistaken for a casting couch."[18] In addition to the "nap" chaise, the Eameses designed a "TV chair" for Wilder. An article in a 1950 issue of *Life* magazine shows a multiple-exposure photograph of the director moving back and forth on the plywood lounge chair of 1946, claiming that it was designed so that the "restless Wilder can easily jump around while watching television."[19] **162**

From the toys to the furniture to the houses (which were either designed for their closest friends, John Entenza and Billy Wilder, or as toys, like the Revell House **139** and the Birthday House designed for Hallmark Cards in 1959) to the major productions (such as the film *Glimpses of the USA*, which they conceived as a token of friendship to the Russians) **372** **374** **382** **384** to their most complex exhibitions, the Eameses always concentrated on what they were giving and how it should be presented. Everything was thought of as a gift. Design was gift giving.

No one has understood this aspect of the Eameses' work better than the Smithsons. They took it all personally, seeing the Eames House as a colorfully wrapped gift, the Eames chair as "a message of hope from another planet,"[20] and the Eames cards as giving them "the courage to collect whatever pleases us."[21] These gifts transformed their own practice:

> The prettiness of our lives now I attribute to Ray even more than Charles; we would not be buying flower-patterned ties but for the Eames card game.... I like to think it is to Ray and Charles Eames we owe the debt of the extravagance of the new purchase. The penny whistle, the Woolworth's plastic Christmas decoration and toy, on to the German pressed metal toy and the walking robots: fresh, pretty, colorful ephemera.[22]

The Smithsons were eager to return the favor. "Eames Celebration" was a gift given in return for so many others. **159** They write: "The essays on the work of Charles and Ray Eames which make up this issue are very personal, and the impulse behind them was to repay the debt the authors felt they owed to the Eames in a way that would be both pleasurable and useful to the Eames themselves."[23]

The sense of the Eames House as a gift also points to the constant shift in scale in their work: from house to cabinets to children's furniture to toys to miniatures. **161** **163** **404** **405** Even the architectural models were treated like toys, played with by excited architects and clients acting like curious children. **57** Eames once said that in the "world of toys he saw an ideal attitude for approaching the problems of design, because the world of the child lacks self-consciousness and embarrassment."[24] **164** In the Eameses' architecture everything was a toy; everybody is a child. Perhaps this accounts for the constant presence of children in the photographs of their work. Since when have we seen so many children in architecture? **165**

Charles and Ray saw everything through the camera, which explains the astonishing continuity between their work in so many different scales: if the eye is the eye of a camera, size is not fixed but continuously shifting. The Eameses used to shoot everything. This was surely not just an obsession with recording; there is that, no doubt, but they also made decisions on the basis of what they saw

---

18 Diehl, "Q&A," 17. The Wilder-inspired aluminum-frame chaise was first manufactured by Herman Miller in 1968.

19 "A Designer's Home of His Own: Charles Eames Builds a House of Steel and Glass," *Life*, September 11, 1950, 152.

20 Alison Smithson, "And Now Dhamas Are Dying Out in Japan," in "Eames Celebration," 448.

21 Alison Smithson, "Eames Dreams" (paper delivered on the occasion of the opening of an Eames exhibition in Berlin, September 1979), in Alison and Peter Smithson, *Changing the Art of Inhabitation* (London: Artemis, 1994), 84.

22 Alison Smithson, "And Now Dhamas," 447.

23 Alison and Peter Smithson, untitled, in "Eames Celebration," 432.

24 *Current Biography*, 1965 ed., s.v. "Eames, Charles."

through the lens, as is evident in Ray's description of the process of decision making in the Eames House:

> We used to use photographs. We would cut out pieces from photographs and put them onto a photograph of the house to see how different things would look. For instance—there was a space in the studio we wanted filled. It was between the depth of the floor where it opens for the stairs (this is not so in the house where there is a balcony rail). We wondered what to do. We had some pier pylons from Venice pier (we had wanted to keep something of it to remember it by). Well, we had pictures of it, glued them onto a photo and decided it worked so we went ahead and did it.[25]

To remember the Venice pier, they took a piece of it with them. This was characteristic of the Eameses, who over the years accumulated an astonishing quantity of objects. The pylons could be seen standing outside the house. But to see if they could keep a memory of the object inside the house, they used photographs and collage. Indeed, a photograph of the Venice pier ended up filling the space in the house they had tested using collage. **167**

The photo-collage method had already been important to architects of the early European avant-garde. Mies van der Rohe photo-collaged pictures of the models of his glass skyscrapers onto a photograph of the Friedrichstrasse; glued photographs of landscape, materials, and Paul Klee's painting *Bunte Mahlzeit* to the Resor House drawings of 1938; and glued together pictures of water, trees, sculptures, and Picasso's mural *Guernica* in the collage of the Museum for a Small City of 1942. The structure of the building gave way to a juxtaposition of photographic images.

---

25 Ray Eames, interview by Pat Kirkham.

But it would be important to understand in what sense the Eameses transformed the strategies of the avant-garde. How was the Eames House able to "trigger," in Peter Smithson's words, "a wholly different kind of conversation"?

The Smithsons wrote:

> In the 1950s the Eames moved design away from the machine aesthetic and bicycle technology, on which it had lived since the 1920s, into the world of the cinema-eye and the technology of the production aircraft; from the world of the painters into the world of the lay-out men. . . . The Eames-aesthetic, made definitive in the House at Santa Monica Canyon, California (as the machine aesthetic was given canonical form in the 'dwelling unit' in the Esprit Nouveau Pavilion, Decorative Arts Exhibition, in Paris, 1925), is based on an equally careful selection, but with extra-cultural surprise, rather than harmony of profile, as its criteria. A kind of wide-eyed wonder of seeing the culturally disparate together and so happy with each other. This sounds like whimsy, but the basic vehicle—the steel lattice frame and in the case of the house, the colour film and colour processing in the graphics work, the pressing and mouldings in the case of the furniture—are ordinary to the culture. . . . Charles Eames is a natural Californian Man, using his native resources and know-how—of the film-making, the aircraft and the advertising industries—as others drink water; that is almost without thinking.[26]

This shift from the machine aesthetic to color film, from the world of painting to that of the layout men, from Europe to California, can be traced in the shift between the first and second versions of the Eames House. The first version, the so-called Bridge House, published in *Arts & Architecture* in 1945, seems to have been based on Mies's 1934 sketch of a glass house on a hillside. **144** **168** **169**

The scheme was rejected in 1947, after Charles went to MoMA to photograph the Mies exhibition, in which the sketch was first made public. Charles must have already known of the drawing before 1947. In fact, he said that he didn't see anything new in the projects that were exhibited but that he was inspired by Mies's design of the exhibition itself. Shortly after his visit to the exhibition, the Eameses came up with a new scheme for their house.

The first version, which Charles designed with Eero Saarinen, faithfully followed the Miesian paradigm in every detail. The house is elevated off the ground as a kind of viewing platform. The sheer glass walls are aimed at the landscape, lined up with the horizon. In the original drawings, we see the occupant of the house standing behind the glass, an isolated figure looking out at the world that is now framed by the horizontal structure. **12** The interior is almost empty. In the model of the house published in March 1948, the only things occupying the house are the reflections of the surrounding trees, which the Eameses went to considerable trouble to photograph by placing the model on the actual site and carefully superimposing an image of the trees in the foreground. **169** The effect is classic Mies. As in the Farnsworth House, there is a stark elevated interior with at most a few isolated pieces of furniture floating near the glass in a fixed pattern prescribed by the architect.

In the second version, the house drops to the ground and swings around to hug the hillside. It no longer faces the ocean. The view is now oblique and filtered by the row of eucalyptus trees in front of the long east face. **170** A low wall wraps around the patio on the south facade, partially blocking the ocean from the view of someone sitting in the space and focusing attention on the patio as an extension of the house, as an interior. **172** The dominant focus

[26] Peter Smithson, "Just a Few Chairs and a House: An Essay on the Eames-Aesthetic," in "Eames Celebration," 443.

is now in rather than out. The house abandons the Miesian sandwich, where floating slabs of floor and ceiling define a strictly horizontal view. The floor is treated like a wall with a series of frames defined by rugs, tiles, trays, and low tables on which objects are carefully arranged. **173** In fact, floor, wall, and ceiling are treated in a similar way. Not only are they now given the same dimensions (the sandwich being replaced by a box), but they start to share roles. Paintings by Hans Hofmann used to hang horizontally from the ceiling—Ray had said that it was necessary to protect them from the strong light and that one "would be able to see them well from that position."[27] **172** So where are they? Many photographs of the house are taken from a very low angle, and we often see the Eameses sitting on the floor surrounded by their objects. The west wall is clothed in birch because they needed something they could hang objects on. On the east wall, much of the glass has become translucent or is wired ("to make people realize it is there"[28]) or replaced with opaque colored panels. The sheer surface is broken up with louvers. **174** The occupants can see only fragments of the outside, fragments that have the same status as the objects that now take over the interior. The view is there but restricted to a few of the many frames. Everything overlaps, moves, and changes. The singular unmediated view is replaced by a kaleidoscopic excess of objects.

The eye that organized the architecture of the historical avant-garde has been displaced by a multiplicity of zooming eyes. Not by chance, the Eameses' 1955 film *House: After Five Years of Living* is made up entirely of thousands of slides. **21** **176** **407** Every aspect of the house is scrutinized by these all-too-intimate eyes. The camera moves up close to every surface, every detail. But these are not the details of the building as such: they are the details of the everyday life that the building makes possible.

Le Corbusier had also considered film the best medium to represent his architecture. In his movie *L'architecture d'aujourd'hui*, made with Pierre Chenal in 1929, he moves through the space of his houses (the Villa Savoye, the Villa Stein in Garches, the Villa d'Avray) without taking his jacket off. **175** In *House: After Five Years of Living*, the Eameses take the opposite approach. Everything, as the title indicates, is about living in the house. The focus is extremely close: flowers, bugs, eggs, pots and pans, crockery. While Le Corbusier had included figures to provide the scale and, perhaps, to insist that he was just visiting, in the Eames film there are no figures, only traces of ongoing life. And while Le Corbusier's film is all horizontal panning—like the modern house, which frames a horizontal view—the Eames film is just a collection of slides. This is consistent with the house itself: it is impossible to focus in the Eames House in the same way that we do in a house of the 1920s. Here the eye is that of a television viewer, not the one of the 1950s, but closer to the one of today, looking at multiple screens, some with captions, all simultaneously. It helps to follow more than one story at once.

To some extent the Eameses pioneered this mode of viewing. They were experts in communication. In 1959 they brought *Glimpses of the USA* to Moscow, projecting it on the seven screens suspended within Buckminster Fuller's geodesic dome. **368** **372** **382** Twenty-two hundred still and moving images presented the theme of "A Day in the Life of the United States." Fuller said that nobody had done it before and predicted that advertisers and filmmakers would soon follow.[29]

---

[27] "We hung them off the ceiling for two reasons—one was because they needed to be kept away from strong light and the second was because we thought we would be able to see them well from that position." Ray Eames, interview with Pat Kirkham.

[28] Charles Eames quoted in "Life in a Chinese Kit," 94.

[29] R. Buckminster Fuller to Ms. Camp, November 7, 1973, box 30, The Work of Charles and Ray Eames, Manuscript Division, Library of Congress, Washington, DC.

The Eameses used the technique repeatedly:

> Having come upon the use of multiple images, we exhibited a tendency to find new uses for it. If you give a young boy a hammer, he'll find that everything he encounters needs hammering. We found that everything we encountered needed the multiple-image technique. . . . I used the process with triple slides in the Norton lectures at Harvard, in order to give a depth of view. In each lecture I would talk for five minutes and then show three minutes of imagery, and then talk seven minutes more.[30]

The Eames House is also a multiscreen performance. **402** **403** But Mies is not simply abandoned. Indeed, the house takes an aspect of Mies's work to its extreme. When Charles Eames gave up on the first scheme after seeing the Mies exhibition at MoMA, he did so because he saw something else there. Eames was impressed by the zooming and overlapping of scales: a huge photographic mural of a small pencil sketch alongside a chair towering over a model next to a twice-life-size photograph, and so on. He also noted the interaction between the perspective of the room and that of the life-size photographs. The visitor experienced Mies's architecture rather than a representation of it, by walking through the display and watching others move. It was a sensual encounter: "The exhibition itself provides the smell and feel of what makes it, and Mies van der Rohe great."[31] **178** **179** **180** **181**

What Eames learned from Mies, then, was less about buildings and more about arrangement of objects in space. Exhibition design, layout, and architecture were indistinguishable, as Mies had demonstrated in his layout for the magazine *G*, his numerous exhibitions with Lilly Reich, the Silk Cafe, the Barcelona Pavilion, and so on. Eames picked up on the idea that architecture was exhibition and developed it.

Once again, the Eames House took something from history and transformed it. The house was an exhibition, a showroom, but a different kind of showroom from those of the modern movement. The multiple eye belonged to a completely different kind of consumer. It was the eye of the postwar acquisitive society. While Mies is famous for his comment "Less is more," the Eameses said that their "objective is the simple thing of getting the most of the best to the greatest number of people for the least."[32] The glass box gives way to such a density of objects that even the limits of the box blur. The role of the glass changes. With Mies, reflections consolidate the plane of the wall, and the complex lines of trees become like the veins in marble. With the Eames House, the plane is broken. The reflections of the eucalyptus tree endlessly multiply and relocate. **182** The Eameses even replaced a panel on the south facade with a photograph of a reflection of the trees, confirming that every panel should be understood as a photographic frame. **183** Furthermore, they took photographs of the reflections on the exterior glass, switched some from positive to negative, and reassembled them into a panel. Apparently intended for the house, the panel ended up in the Herman Miller showroom in Los Angeles. **184**

Just as the house was a showroom, the showroom was a house. The Eames House and the showroom for Herman Miller, built at the same time, were in fact the same project, employing the same principles. A light, unselfconscious enclosure, a minimum of architecture, provided a flexible frame for multiple interior arrangements. A wall-size photo-mural was used to construct the sense of an

---

30 Charles Eames quoted in Diehl, "Q&A," 14.
31 Ibid.
32 Charles Eames quoted in "A Designer's Home," 152.

exterior, complete with patio, garden, trees, outdoor furniture and a neighboring house. 185 A complete lifestyle was laid out down to the smallest detail of cutlery and table settings. The space was even filled with personal objects: an African leopard and an early American weather vane loaned by Billy Wilder, a Herbert Matter photograph and a Hofmann painting loaned by John Entenza, and so on—gifts from friends.[33]

The showroom quality of the Eames House was exemplified by its repeated use as the site of fashion photographs. Magazines such as *Life* and *Vogue* inserted their models into the building, lining them up with the architecture, even merging them into the interior elements.[34] 11 186 In this, the house participated in another long tradition of the historical avant-garde. Ever since the turn of the century, modern architecture had been used as a setting to market fashion. 186 In fact, the history of modern architecture is the history of the showroom, the history of a blending of architecture and exhibition. But the Eames House was not just a uniform backdrop for fashion designs as discrete innovations. The garments blended into the fabric of the house, mingling with the objects. The accompanying text bounced backward and forward between the "California bold look" of the architecture and the fashion. What was on display in the showroom was the equal status of all kinds of objects. The announcement of Case Study Houses #8 and #9 in the December 1945 issue of *Arts & Architecture* shows the silhouettes of both the Eameses and Entenza surrounded by the galaxy of objects that define their respective lifestyles. 12 The role of the architect is simply that of happily accommodating these objects.

Nowhere are the differences between Mies and the Eameses more clear than in the photographs of their houses under construction. A photograph of the

Farnsworth House shows the lonely figure of Mies with his back to the camera somberly appraising the empty frame. His enormous figure cuts a black silhouette into the frigid landscape. With his coat and hat on, he stands like one of Caspar David Friedrich's figures confronting the sublime. At about the same time but a world away, the Eameses put on their new outfits, climb into their frame, and smile at the camera. 187

33 "Furniture Showroom by Charles Eames," *Arts & Architecture*, October 1949, 26–29.

34 "California Bold Look," *Life*, June 1954, 90–97; "California Ideas: Spreading West to East," *Vogue*, April 15, 1954, 60–87.

Chapter 4
The Lawn at War

During World War II, the lawn became a battlefield. Maintaining the lawn was a form of war, a national duty performed for the morale of both those at home and those in the armed forces. Keeping the lawn amounted to no less than keeping the face of the nation. Advertisements in popular magazines presented a comprehensive and sustained polemic about the lawn's key role in simultaneously defining domestic architecture and national ideology. An advertisement for Vigoro plant food in *House Beautiful* says: "Probably you, too, have a loved one in the service . . . a boy whose too few leisure hours are spent in dreaming of home." Symptomatically, what the GIs are supposed to remember as "home" is not a house but a lawn: "Wherever he is, he dreams of velvety lawns, beautiful flowers . . . he wants to come home to them. Keep them growing their best awaiting that day! They will contribute immeasurably toward a winning home front."[1] The lawn is home for the American soldier.

Countless images of the lawn were sent to the front. Inserts in *Life* reminded readers to pass the magazines along to their relatives in the armed forces,[2] and articles addressed to the soldiers were dominated by lawn pictures. An issue of September 1944 shows a full-page image of a suburban street with front lawns: "This street could be almost anywhere in America, but it happens to be Fair Oaks Avenue in Oak Park, Illinois. The people who live on Fair Oaks Avenue mostly work in Chicago, ten miles east. In the evening, after supper, they sit in rocking chairs on their porches, water their lawns, or listen to the radio tell them what their sons and daughters are doing overseas."[3] Another full-page image in the same article shows the back lawn with a woman hanging laundry: "Home: It's the Same as Ever. Bill's mother still hangs the family wash in the yard below his bedroom window."[4] Eighteen out of the twenty-nine photographs in "An American Block: War Has Made Few Marks on Progress Avenue," a November 1943 article in *Life*, are of lawns: families posing on the front yards of their houses, the postman delivering mail on the lawn, a boy delivering the paper, a group of children reading comics on the lawn, a woman raking the leaves, a woman with children and a baby carriage on the sidewalk, women on the lawn doing the wash, a woman leaving the house for her war job. And finally, most arresting, is a photograph of children playing war in a backyard foxhole with machine guns made out of wood and aluminum mixing bowls as helmets.[5] **188**

The lawn is not just a makeshift battlefield, the site of a playful war game. Keeping the home front is keeping the lawn, which one article in *House Beautiful* describes as "a challenge for fighters in the home front."[6] Popular magazines continually give advice while acknowledging it is not an easy task: "Without any help it's quite a job, this keeping the home place up. What can you do to control shrubbery? The hedge? Do junipers beside the door have to be clipped? Would the lawn get full of weeds if you let it grow the rest of the summer?" writes *Better Homes and Gardens* in 1944.[7] The home front in fact is a lawn, a green facade, a horizontal facade, as if seen from the air—as in the endless aerial views of the suburbs that recall the aerial photography that played such a strategic role in military reconnaissance and bombings. **209**

The cover of the July 1942 issue of *Better Homes and Gardens* shows a bird's-eye view of an isolated house on a rectangular lawn with a victory garden in a corner. The lawn floats like a magic carpet on a blue background, while a huge American flag flies overhead. The caption reads, "Home is the strength of

---

1 Advertisement for Vigoro, *House Beautiful* and *Better Homes and Gardens*, April 1944.
2 "Pass along LIFE to others. . . . make sure this copy goes the rounds of your family and then to your friends or the men in the armed services," *Life*, April 13, 1942, 107. "Pass along this copy to a man in the armed forces," *Life*, January 25, 1943, 96.
3 *Life*, September 18, 1944, 83.
4 Ibid., 86–87.
5 *Life*, November 8, 1943, 95–103.
6 "Have Your Garden and Eat It Too!" *House Beautiful*, March 1942, 63.
7 Harvey Philips Dean, "Keep the Home Place Trim," *Better Homes and Gardens*, April 1944, 26–27.

the nation." **190** At about the same time, a similar, closer-up image appears on the cover of the rival magazine *House Beautiful*. The house now recedes into the background, visible only as fragment. The focus is on the lawn, pinned in the middle by another enormous American flag. The family and dog stand on the grass below, looking up proudly. Readers are urged: "Pledge Your Support: Buy War Savings Bonds and Stamps."[8] The lawn has become a national symbol as vital as the flag. The defense of the nation is the defense of the lawn.

During the war, the government encouraged people to stay at home and keep the lawn when they were not at work. As Virginia Scott Jenkins has noted, lawn care was a hobby that saved gasoline, automobile tires, and public transportation, all of which were critical for the war effort.[9] People were, moreover, encouraged to turn part of their lawn into a "victory garden." Growing vegetables for personal use relieved not only farm producers but also shippers and packers of their expanding war load. Popular magazines contributed extensively to the campaign: "Have Your Garden AND EAT IT TOO!" wrote *House Beautiful*. "You can—and should—grow Vegetables for Victory. Grow them side-by-side with flowers, as part of the whole decorative pattern."[10] Advertisers capitalized on the message: "Needed! 20,000,000 Victory Gardeners," read an ad for the Stum & Walter seed company.[11] While Stum & Walter would, obviously, benefit from the corresponding increase in sales, what the advertisement spelled out was the patriotic obligation to have a victory garden. The biggest-selling suntan lotion, Gaby, advertised itself with a woman in a bikini wearing sunglasses in the shape of two blazing suns: "With Our Armed Forces under blazing tropical skies . . . in Victory gardens—Gaby is performing miracles!"[12] Even Coca-Cola promoted itself as "Hospitality . . . in a Victory Garden." The ad features a large image of a vegetable patch on a lawn, while a smaller image above it shows two women, one in gardening clothes, near a set of chairs and a table with Coca-Cola bottles. Coca-Cola is for that moment of relaxation when the gardener entertains the neighbor who has come over to admire the garden: "They eat tomatoes right off the vine and munch carrots fresh from the earth.... They drink ice-cold Coca-Cola and enjoy perfect refreshment while contemplating the results of their work."[13]

Yet the greatest benefit of having a garden seems to have been psychological: "Check the WAR at your garden gate," writes *House Beautiful* in 1943. The garden, according to the article, is the antidote to war: "War glares at you from the morning newspapers on your doorstop. It crowds into the bus with you as you rush for the 8:16. It strikes at you from the grocer's shelves. But there's one place war *can't* touch you—your garden."[14] A 1942 article in *Life*, "Gardens for the U.S. at War," first recounts the economic benefits and patriotic obligation of having a lawn and then writes: "But over all these gains, are the simple joys of growing things— the primitive pleasure of feeling damp earth in the fingers in April, the wonder of watching corn sprout and tomatoes swell and ripen overnight, the fierce delight of annihilating enemy weeds and bugs, the pleasant pain of hot sun on back and hands.... These are things that bring satisfied peace to wartime worriers and transform mute men into poets."[15]

The lawn was war therapy. During the war, gardening was considered more effective than any other kind of therapy for healing hospitalized veterans in the South Pacific: "Somehow, in the garden, these tired, anxious men found new self

8 Cover of *House Beautiful*, July–August 1942.
9 Virginia Scott Jenkins, *The Lawn: A History of an American Obsession* (Washington, DC: Smithsonian Institution Press, 1994), 95.
10 "Have Your Garden and Eat it Too!" 63.
11 Advertisement in *House Beautiful*, May 1945, pt. 1.
12 Advertisement for Gaby, *Life*, July 17, 1944, 41.
13 Advertisement for Coca-Cola, *Better Homes and Gardens*, August 1943.
14 Stephen Gale, "Check the War at Your Garden Gate," *House Beautiful*, April 1943, pt. 1, 47.
15 "Gardens for the U.S. at War: Six Million Amateurs Work the Soil," *Life*, March 30, 1942, 81.

confidence and peace."[16] After the war, gardening established itself as the "leading healer" in army and navy hospitals everywhere. Women for the Garden Club of New Jersey developed a gardening camp, Camp Kilmer, one among many offering therapy for wounded soldiers. In an article in *Better Homes and Gardens* entitled "The Men Come Out of It in the Garden," the chair of Camp Kilmer describes her experience:

> There wasn't any glory to it—we didn't even have uniforms—we wore pants and just a jacket, but I'm very happy to be able to tell you that gardening therapy has done something for our boys. . . . Some of the boys are mental cases, and when you're a mental case soil does more than grow crops for you. It has a great healing property, far beyond the power many of us realize. Some of these mental cases are on the borderline. A little push means an awful lot—they come out of it.[17]

Mobilized at last, even if without a uniform, the grandmother figure becomes a soldier in the war of the lawn: "I've been told I was too old to be a gray lady, too old to go overseas and do my bit but I wasn't too old to stand out in the sun at 115 degrees that summer, and I thank God for that."[18] She had been mobilized as a psychotherapist of the garden variety. With veterans returning from the front psychologically destroyed, mental health was the number-one medical issue in postwar America. Psychiatric-hospital admissions doubled between 1940 and 1956.[19]

The therapy of the lawn was not without its own violence. "The fierce delight of annihilating enemy weeds and bugs" becomes an active call for violence in a 1944 *Better Homes and Gardens* article instructing women on the care of the lawn: "About moles—you can dig them out if you're patient. And if you are mad enough about what a mole has done to your lawn and flowers, you won't mind in the least giving him the knockout with the flat of your spade. Wait until you see the soil heaving and are sure which way he's headed. Then sock your spade down back of him and give a quick heave."[20] Women are encouraged by the (male) author to exercise direct, bodily violence. For the fainthearted, however, there are more advanced, almost military strategies: "Some people drown moles out, but with a badly mole-ridden lawn I don't know what your water bill would be. Gassing is probably easiest. Ask your seedman for his best brand of cartridges."[21] The most feared tactics of war had become household strategies, with the lawn itself the site of a form of war. **192** "Time Your Attack on Your Garden Pests," writes *House Beautiful* in 1944. "It's as important to know when the enemy will strike as to know what he looks like. Prepare your weapons and strategy early, and have a better garden all year long."[22] Bugs are represented as enemy soldiers and flying insects as Japanese air fighters. An advertisement for the insecticide Bug-a-boo, "with or without D.D.T.," presents bugs as retreating soldiers: "G'BYE BOYS, IT'S Bug-a-boo"[23]; another one, for the insect repellent Skat, presents flying insects with dots painted on their wings: "Ready to STRIKE but . . . SKAT will drive them away."[24] The motif of flying insects as Japanese air fighters is ubiquitous. Cartoons show GIs aiming their insecticide guns at incoming insects decorated with the insignia of warplanes.[25] **193**

---

16 Mrs. S. G. Van Hoesen, "The Men Come Out of It in the Garden," *Better Homes and Gardens*, June 1945, 24.

17 Ibid., 24–25.

18 Ibid., 24.

19 Margot A. Henriksen, *Dr. Strangelove's America: Society and Culture in the Atomic Age* (Berkeley and Los Angeles: University of California Press, 1997), 107. Statistics from William Leuchtenberg, *A Troubled Feast* (Boston: Little, Brown, 1973), 104.

20 Dean, "Keep the Home Place Trim," 27.

21 Ibid.

22 "Time Your Attack on Garden Pests," *House Beautiful*, February 1944, pt. 1, 48-49.

23 Advertisement for Bug-a-boo, *Life*, July–August 1946, 105.

24 Advertisement for Skat, *Life*, June 18, 1945, 106.

25 For example, in an advertisement for FLIT, a cartoon presents insects with dots in their wings attacking a soldier equipped with an spray bottle of insecticide as a gun: "Man the Flit Guns, here they come boys!" *Life*, July 19, 1943, 92.

The rhetoric of battle reaches its climax with the Japanese beetle, often referred to as the Jap beetle. The control of this garden pest becomes the occasion not only to echo the war in the Pacific but also to express outright racism and bigotry, as when a July 1944 article in *Life*, "Japanese Beetle: Voracious, Libidinous, Prolific," [191] writes:

> Japanese beetles, unlike the Japanese, are without guile. There are, however, many parallels between the two. Both are small but very numerous and prolific, as well as voracious, greedy and devouring. Both have single-track minds. Both are inscrutable, the beetles particularly. . . . The Japanese-Beetle invasion antedated Pearl Harbor by about 25 years. We were quite unprepared for it, but we have some excuse, because it was impossible to know that there was anything to be prepared against. . . . Long ago we declared war on them, and though we have little chance of total victory—which will mean exterminating every single beetle on our shores—we may hope to achieve a more limited success, with the insects so harassed and persecuted that their numbers would be kept within decency's limit, although their character would never be changed.[26]

The article proceeds to explain the extent of the problem and the tactics of the beetle's advance since its "illegal entry" into the US[27] and the countertactics in a battle in which complete victory has already been renounced:

> 29,000 square miles in Massachusetts, Connecticut, New York, New Jersey, Pennsylvania, Delaware, Maryland, and Virginia . . . [are] the territory firmly held by the enemy; in addition it has outposts at scattered points over a much larger area than this. . . . Sometimes the beetles spread by a frontal assault.

In 1933 they held the southern part of New Jersey, but had not yet obtained a firm foothold in Delaware, in that summer large quantities of them in flight were carried by the wind over Delaware Bay, and after falling into the water they drifted about until many of them were washed up on the other side. Eighty percent of them were dead by then, but the 20% still alive were quite enough to carry the beachhead. They also conquered Staten Island and Long Island in the same ruthless way.... These beetle advances are truly Japanese, with total disregard for expendables. As long as some get through, it does not matter how many perish.[28]

Not only were these beetles suicidal warriors, kamikazes; they also seemed to indulge in excessive pleasures. According to *Life*, they slept late and devoted their days to a continuous orgy of food and sex in which these two got confused: "It is quite easy to find 50 or 100 of them on one apple, which they will eat down to the core, while an apple a few inches away is untouched. In part, this habit is due to their active love life, which they indulge in while they are eating."[29]

The first line of defense in dealing with such a vicious creature was to quarantine or contain the enemy, as the government had advised people to do since 1919. Once contained, attacks would be launched against the Japanese beetle with an array of weapons, including spray guns, poisons, and traps. The Department of Agriculture enlisted scientists as advanced scouts in the battle: "Beginning in 1920, entomologists were sent out to the far East to study these friendly insects [ones that attack Japanese beetles].... Two of our entomologists were caught

---

26 Anthony Standen, "Japanese Beetle: Voracious, Libidinous, Prolific, He is Eating His Way Across the U.S., Destroying $7,000,000 Worth of Plant Life Every Year," *Life*, July 17, 1944, 39–46.

27 "The exact date and the port of arrival of its illegal entry are unknown; all that is known is that, in the summer of 1916, around Riverton, N.J., a few little beetles were found, which the entomologists called Popillia japonica." Ibid., 40.

28 Ibid., 39–46.

29 Ibid., 43.

in Japan at the outbreak of the war. . . . They had found and sent back no less than 26 species of useful insects."[30] The most useful were small Japanese wasps that ate beetles. But for the most part, imported insects did not adapt, and the department turned to more aggressive methods: "A more effective way of harassing the beetles is to spread disease epidemics among them. Every year more than half million of the grubs [are collected] for this purpose." The grubs were treated, one by one, by impaling them on a hypodermic needle to give them a shot of the disease. They were anesthetized before this is done, not for humanitarian reasons, but to make them easier to handle and to prevent them from biting one another.[31]

The war of the lawn, in this way, became a medical war, paralleling, once again, actual war: "Against one enemy Americans need have no scruples in waging bacterial warfare. This is the Japanese Beetle, scourge of many urban and suburban gardeners," states *Better Homes and Gardens* in 1944, as it promotes the use of a packaged bacteria called Japidemic.[32] In fact, the insecticide industry began as a spin-off of military research on chemical warfare during World War II. Some of the chemicals developed turned out to be lethal to insects, which is not surprising since insects were widely used as surrogates for men to test chemicals.[33] In this sense, when insects were portrayed as soldiers in advertisements for insecticides, it was not just a metaphor.

But there is another sense in which insecticides were weapons. During the war, they were used extensively to protect soldiers from foreign insects: "Our soldiers are sure glad to get FLIT—and all other super-slaying insecticides. They're real weapons of war on many insect infected battle-fronts," an advertisement

[30] Ibid., 44–46.
[31] Ibid., 46.
[32] Katherine M. Palmer, *Better Homes and Gardens*, April 1944, 26–27.
[33] Rachel Carson, *Silent Spring* (Cambridge, MA: Riverside Press, 1962), 16.

124 ↑194

for FLIT reads, while a cartoon shows a soldier writing a letter behind a barricade made out of boxes labeled FLIT that separates him from attacking insects with dotted wings: "Honest, Mom, if the FLIT hadn't come we would have been eaten alive!"[34] **193**

DDT, first synthesized in 1874, was discovered to be an insecticide in 1939 by Paul Müller of Switzerland, who received the Nobel Prize.[35] Used during the war, it was found to be so effective that all supplies were reserved for the military. Only in 1945 was the general population, many of whom were returning from war and already familiar with the product, given access to DDT.[36] The chemical arms that had been developed to protect soldiers and attack other humans were made available to all. DDT was hailed as "the atomic bomb of the insect world."[37]

Even military techniques of delivering the chemical were used. In 1948 an article in *Life* celebrates the covering of entire towns with DDT by helicopters equipped with "fogging machines." **194** Acclaimed as a much more efficient system than traditional sprays, the fogging machine was an adaptation of the navy's smoke generator: "The fog covers everything with a submicroscopic and stainless film of poison, lethal to insects but harmless to humans, animals and food. Mounted in a helicopter or a truck, the machine in one to two minutes bugproofs an acre of land."[38] The images show a small town being fogged by helicopter to kill black flies, children romping in the fog as the fog truck passes, cows in the fog ("unbitten cows give more milk"), and a woman in a bikini emerging from the fog with a hot dog in one hand and a soda bottle in the other ("unlike dust or spray the fog will not contaminate food"). **196** But the fallout from these weapons did increasingly begin to encroach on human as well as insect life. In the '50s, there were many forms of protest to these domestic attacks, but only years later would the extent of the damage on civilians be identified.[39]

Other insecticides made available in the postwar years were even more dangerous than DDT. As Rachel Carson pointed out in her 1962 book *Silent Spring*, esters of phosphoric acid, discovered as insecticides by chemist Gerhard Schrader in the late 1930s, were recognized by the German government as chemical weapons. Some became nerve gases, while others were developed into insecticides such as malathion and parathion, widely used in the United States.[40] The devastating effects of these toxins were more immediately obvious when hundreds of people died instantly after eating parathion-coated vegetables and fruit or by coming into contact with empty chemical containers. Nevertheless, parathion continued to be used widely in agriculture. Carson quoted a medical authority to the effect that in 1961 "the amount [of parathion] used in California farms alone could provide a lethal dose for 5 to 10 times the whole world's population."[41]

The confusion of insects with the enemy may explain the popularity of insects as a topic in popular magazines throughout the war years. At the end of the war, an article in *Life* entitled "Enemy Insects" compared the annual cost of insects to agriculture in the US, three billion dollars, with the cost of producing the atomic bomb, which was one billion dollars less. The damage that worms cause to a plant is depicted in terms of a time bomb. A series of photographs documents the total destruction of a bean leaf by an attack of "army worms" over a period of less than ten hours, with a clock indicating the time at every stage of the destruction.[42]

---

34 Advertisement in *Life*, August 16, 1943, 8.
35 Ibid., 20.
36 Jenkins, *The Lawn*, 153–54.
37 James Whorton, *Before Silent Spring: Pesticides and Public Health in Pre-DDT America* (Princeton: Princeton University Press, 1974), 248–49, quoted in Jenkins, *The Lawn*, 154.
38 "Fogging: New Process Makes Insect Control Safe, Stainless and 90% Cheaper," *Life*, July–August 1948, 49–51.
39 Carson writes about the 1956 and 1957 campaign to eradicate the gypsy moth. One million acres were aerially sprayed in the states of Pennsylvania, New Jersey, Michigan and New York in 1956 and three million in 1957. Milk and farm produce were contaminated, and beekeepers lost all their colonies. Several lawsuits ensued. See Carson, *Silent Spring*, 158–60.
40 Carson, *Silent Spring*, 28.
41 Ibid., 30.
42 "Insect Enemies: They Cost the U.S. 3 Billion Dollars Annually," *Life*, August 27, 1945, 59–64.

The fascination with war imagery and military rhetoric continued during the immediate postwar years, as is evident in magazine articles and in the styling and advertising of lawn equipment and pesticides. A "dust gun" called Bug Blaster looks like a bazooka, although it is handled like a broom.[43] Lawn mowers were advertised as weapons and carried remarkable names like Savage Superchief, one of three models produced by the Savage Arms Corporation and targeted for women as "effortless," "noiseless," "efficient," and "built by gun craftsmen": "Imagine *Me* Enjoying This!" exclaims the "Lady of the House" as she pushes one.[44]

Even sprinklers were advertised as weapons. In an ad for engineering products by B-W (Borg-Warner), sprinklers that "disappear when not in use" are presented together with the technology that allows a jet pilot to "hit planes that are never where he sees them."[45] "Speaking of Pictures," a 1946 *Life* photo-essay, presents the death of a mosquito by DDT in a series of detailed frames reminiscent of plane-crash footage. **198** The article acknowledges that DDT is not the panacea it was once believed to be, "when it cleared malarial mosquitoes from Pacific islands, wiped out a typhus plague in Naples and gave North African Arabs their first itchless night's sleep in centuries." Not only is it ineffective against many bugs, but it harms "useful insects" such as bees and "kills fish and animals that eat the poisoned bugs."[46]

The lawn is a medical hazard, and yet the lawn stands for health, mental and bodily. If the lawn was prescribed as a form of therapy, it was also used extensively as background in advertisements of medications, where it was presented as the antithesis of the prevailing illness, be it tetanus, poliomyelitis, epilepsy, heart disease, or cancer. The figure of the physician on the lawn making a house call is even used in advertisements for Camel: "More Doctors Smoke Camels Than Any Other Cigarettes."[47] Nothing bad can happen on the lawn. "Johnny Can Walk," an advertisement for Wyeth medical products, shows a boy recovering from poliomyelitis slowly moving with the help of a cane from the veranda of his house onto the lawn, where his friends wait—from the inside of the house, where illness harbors, to the outside, where health, represented by the lawn, reigns. An advertisement for Parke, Davis pharmaceuticals compares the chances of a boy punctured by a nail with those of a wounded soldier. The soldier, the ad implies, is better protected against tetanus because he was immunized against it when he entered the army. The hurt boy, meanwhile, is sitting by his house on the ground just outside the lawn—which represents the security that he would achieve with the vaccine. Another Parke, Davis advertisement shows also a double image: a man having a heart attack while mowing the lawn and another one having a heart attack in the office. The man on the lawn survives, while the one indoors dies suddenly. An advertisement for Shell celebrates the discovery of a new chemical recovery process by which the production of penicillin, badly needed for the hundreds of thousands of sick or wounded, could be substantially increased. Shell scientists, with their expertise in recovering lost elements from petroleum for use in explosives like TNT, have just achieved this feat. A man, his crutches on the floor, moves from the dark space of war and destruction into the green space of health and well-being.

The lawn is also present in advertisements for products concerned with hygiene: hand cream, toothpaste, shaving cream, toilet paper, and baby-care products. The care of the lawn was the care of a body, mostly of a male body, whose outgrowths had to be kept in check: it had to be trimmed, like a man's hair, beard, or mustache—groomed, clipped, and manicured; *Better Homes and Gardens*

43 Advertisement for Bug Blaster, *Life*, May–June 1947, 60.
44 Advertisement for Savage Arms Corporation, *House Beautiful*, July 1946, pt. 2, 112.
45 Advertisement for Borg-Warner, *Life*, July 22, 1957, 8–9.
46 "Speaking of Pictures," *Life*, January 21, 1946, 10–11.
47 Advertisement for Camel, *Life*, July–August 1946.

compared an unmowed lawn to an unshaven man.⁴⁸ After the war, the Motor Wheel Corporation introduced a power mower capable of delivering a "clipped, brushed, military trim" to the lawn, a close-to-the-surface cut that easily navigated obstacles, cut grass so fine that clippings disappeared, and made the lawn look neat without much handiwork: a military cut.⁴⁹

There are also references to women's and even infants' bodies, as when an article in *Life* juxtaposes images of young women's hair and lawns or when an article titled "Fall Hair—Do Your Lawn" in the *Christian Science Monitor* encourages women to take care of the lawn as they take care of their own hair.⁵⁰ During the 1930s, as Scott Jenkins has noted, lawn articles and advertisements appealed to women by addressing the lawn in terms of beauty problems: the new grasses "give you a landscape skin you love to touch, . . . massage is good for the complexion of your lawn. It keeps out blotches, black heads, and wild whiskers."⁵¹ The lawn was also associated with the soft, unmarked skin of babies and young children. An advertisement for Northern toilet paper shows a cartoon of a young boy lying in a lawn: "Mighty Soft . . . Northern Tissue."⁵² Numerous advertisements for child-care products, such as those by Johnson's, used the lawn as background.

Not only was the lawn considered hygienic, it also represented the safety women were supposed to provide to the family during the war, when all women became de facto nurses. With wartime shortages of hospital beds and doctors, civilians were encouraged to take care of themselves. Prevention was never so important.

Wartime toilet-paper advertisements are symptomatic. Starting in 1943 and for the duration of the war, Scott Paper ran a series of advertisements in *Life* magazine in which a woman wearing a mask made of ScotTissue takes care of a young baby. **199** The series began with three ads featuring the delivery of a newborn, with a woman in bed and a doctor wearing a clinical mask. A smaller image in the corner shows the mother herself, wearing a mask while feeding the baby. The text of each ad insisted on the new wartime responsibilities: "For the duration, you are going to have to be more self-reliant about your baby's precious welfare—almost from the moment your overworked, war-busy doctor places him in your arms." "Today your doctor brings your baby into the world—frequently in your own house—and turns him over to you for the duration. From Now on—it's up to *you* to see he doesn't need a doctor."

The woman has been made into a medic for her baby. A free booklet "Helpful Wartime Suggestions on Mother & Baby Care" was offered with the ad. But more than that, the woman seems to be joining the armed forces with the task of safeguarding the welfare of her baby, as becomes clear in subsequent advertisements in the series. The masked woman with baby has jumped into the main picture, while the secondary image is of two rolls of toilet paper, one wrapped, the other unfolding, resting in what appears to be a lawn or a thick, lawnlike carpet. The image and the admonition vary from one ad to the next: "How Safe Can You Make His War-Changed World?" "The Family Cold—Most Dread Menace to Your Baby's Safety." The toilet paper on the lawn/carpet remains. The common cold has to be kept from the baby, in the same way that soldiers are keeping the front at war. The mother has been mobilized, and her task is to man the war at the gate. She has been made into a warrior, a wartime Madonna, a masked woman, the Madonna of the toilet-paper mask.

The carpet and the lawn are thoroughly confused in war and postwar ads. Scott offered free bulletins on lawn care that "tell you how to make your lawn

48 "An unmowed lawn looks as bad as a man without a shave," *Better Homes and Gardens*, April 1944, 27.
49 Advertisement for Reo, *Life*, May 14, 1956.
50 Morris A. Hall, "Fall Hair—Do Your Lawn," *Christian Science Monitor*, September 7, 1946, 9, quoted in Jenkins, *The Lawn*, 123.
51 Elias J. Beach, "5 Steps to a Good Lawn for Next Year," *Better Homes and Gardens*, September 1935, 17, 16, quoted in Jenkins, *The Lawn*, 121.
52 *Life*, July 1945.

into a green carpet."[53] A "hormone-treated" lawn is referred to as an "Earth Carpet" in an ad for L. Teweles Seed.[54] And an ad for Eclipse lawn mowers takes the form of a cartoon in which a man pulls up some grass, turns over to a woman, and says to her, "It's not a green carpet, it IS grass. These people must use an Eclipse."[55] In fact, a well-tended lawn is often referred to as a carpet, a soft, velvety, surface offering protection to the house that rests on it, as if it were a security ring isolating it from neighboring homes, dust, and health hazards. The lawn is an antiseptic surface on which the family's activities can be extended into the open air. Some advertisements for General Electric lamps explicitly present the lawn as an open-air living room, even a classroom.[56]

If the lawn is a carpet, then the carpet is also a lawn. An advertisement for Belmont Radio and Television shows a boy in a baseball uniform watching a baseball game on television in a carpeted room. Inside the house, it is as if he were on a baseball field.[57] In another ad, this one for children's shoes, a girl dressed as a ballerina practices her steps in the green carpet of her house while her brother kicks a football on an open green field.[58] The gender split in these ads—the girl inside, on the carpet; the boy outside, on the grass—reproduces the separation of domestic tasks in the suburban house. The postwar lawn was the territory of men or grown boys (taking care of the lawn was considered a rite of passage), while women kept to the green Formica pastures of the interior. Green—judging by advertisements and magazine articles—was the most popular color for the inside of homes during and after the war years. Carpets were often green, as were the curtains, the upholstery, the walls, the towels, the dinnerware. . . . Green was everywhere.

Indeed, like homegrown vegetables, much of America's postwar consumable durables seemed to have grown out of the lawn. A 1944 advertisement for Revere

Copper and Brass shows new automobiles as produce of a "Victory Garden in Detroit." Two men in business suits kneel over a garden plot pinned with labels: Buick, Cadillac, Chevrolet, Chrysler, Ford, Dodge, Plymouth, Pontiac, Lincoln, Mercury, De Soto, all planted in the soil: 201

> A new car! To us Americans, the thrill of those words baffles description. There's a heavy fragrance like wine's in the very idea of driving once more across the bosom of the continent. . . . We *know* that the automobile brains which yearly created better and more beautiful cars, have been learning new magic while they were producing the world's finest guns and trucks and tanks and planes. We *know* that the seeds of this new knowledge are planted in a Victory Garden whose blooming, when the war is won, will seem like a miracle when we see it.[59]

A drawing in *Life* published after the war presents the General Motors corporation as a flower garden "with a rich soil of consumer dollars in which to grow, and rich nourishment in the form of legal, financial, research and engineering advice, and distribution and styling help" that has produced "opulent blooms" such as Chevrolet, Buick, GMC Truck and Coach, Frigidaire, Electromotive, Pontiac, Cadillac (soon to make tanks), Oldsmobile, Delco Appliance, and Allison aircraft engines.[60] 201

---

53 Advertisement for Scott and Son, *House Beautiful*, January 1945, 128.
54 Advertisement for L. Teweles Seed Co., *House Beautiful*, April 1949, 257.
55 *House Beautiful*, October 1949, 271.
56 An ad for General Electric in *House Beautiful*, 1944, pt. 2, presents a living room with the walls removed sitting on a lawn: "This is a picture of you in your postwar living room." In the June 1945 issue of *House Beautiful* and in *Life*, October 2, 1944, 15, General Electric presents a classroom on a lawn. The new GE lamps will bring, after the war, "amazing indoor light . . . that compares with sunshine . . . ultraviolet light that produces essential Vitamin D . . . short wave ultraviolet that kills germs in the air around you." At the end of the war, *Life* announced that "[a] universal American wish is to spend more time in the garden. The indoor-outdoor living room is a partial answer to that desire. It has a glass wall across the garden side." A view of the indoor-outdoor living room shows the lawn meeting the carpet in the glass wall. *Life*, May 28, 1945, 54–55.
57 Advertisement for Belmont Radio and Television, *Life*, May–June 1945.
58 Advertisement for Poll Parrot (children's shoes), *Life*, August 19, 1946, 95.
59 "Victory Garden in Detroit," advertisement for Revere Copper and Brass, *Life*, March 20, 1944, 51.
60 "How GM's Garden Grows," *Life*, May 14, 1956. See also *Life*, June 4, 1956, 54.

From victory garden in war to flower garden in peace, the products of postwar US industry are represented as those of a domestic garden, a productive lawn. Perhaps this explains why the lawn became the surface for the display of everything in postwar production: cars, strollers, bicycles, alcohol, candy, shoes, soap, soup, rubber tires, soft drinks, appliances, prefabricated houses, cameras, film, cigarettes, coffee, silverware, trailers, vitamins, medicines, fashion, hosiery, beauty products, telephone companies, and, of course, all tools related to lawn care, such as lawn mowers, pesticides, plant food, and sprinklers.

The lawn was an image of American affluence. Always on show, the lawn was used to display the consumer products that were the by-products of war or, as wartime advertisements announced, the American way of life that the soldiers were fighting for.[61] Postwar industry was the result of war: cars, lawn mowers, appliances, insecticides, medicines, even fast food—everything that made America in the '50s had been developed as part of the military effort. Cars were given names like Commander V-8, for a new Studebaker advertised on a lawn in 1951. Lawn mowers, fabricated by the same companies that had once made tanks, happily advertised their products as weapons, descendants of those that had won the war. But war doesn't go away. The same companies that made cars and appliances—General Motors, Chrysler, General Electric, Goodyear, and Westinghouse—were also the leading defense contractors in the postwar years,[62] dependent on the defense budget for the sophistication of their products.

Every company—selling everything from meat to golf balls—advertised itself during the war years as invested in the war effort and at the same time waiting for the day all the techniques developed could be applied to domestic use. "And We'll Live Happily Ever After," an advertisement for Kelvinator early in 1945, shows a woman inside her house looking adoringly through the window at a man in uniform and a boy who are sitting in the yard behind a white picket fence:

> "I know it will just be the way your letters describe it to me. . . a bright sunny house.. a garden where you can dig while sunshine warms you through and through . . . and a kitchen for me that's full of magical things. A wonderful new electric range (the kind they are planning now) that starts coffee perking and biscuits browning before we wake up . . . and cooks dinners while we're away. . . . A refrigerator . . . with glistening shelves. . . . A deep freezer. . . . Oh!, it's easy to see how happy we'll be . . ."

Here, at Kelvinator, we pledge you this. When our war job is done—all our strength, all our new skills born of war, will be turned to production for peace. This will be our part in the building of a greater, a happier nation. For we believe all of us owe to those who have fought to preserve it, a strong, vital and growing America—where all men and women will have the chance to make their dreams come true.[63]

Appliances topped the list of the most desirable objects in the postwar years. In 1946, a double-page spread in *Life* titled "Family Utopia" presents "the dream to which all Americans aspired" displayed on the lawn. **202** The magazine claims that it is an "honest representation of the dream of most U.S. families . . . based on statistics of consumer demands and manufacturers' unfilled orders."[64] Beginning with a suburban house and a lawn, what Americans wanted most was a convertible station wagon, an electric stove, a television-phonograph-radio, a washing machine, a vacuum cleaner, a dishwasher, a toaster, an iron, a lawn sweeper, a power mower,

---

61 Elaine Tyler May, *Homeward Bound: American Families in the Cold War Era* (New York: Basic Books, 1988), 168; John Morton Blum, *V Was for Victory: Politics and American Culture During World War II* (San Diego: Harcourt, Brace, 1976), 100–101.

62 Stephen J. Whitfield, *The Culture of the Cold War* (Baltimore: Johns Hopkins University Press, 1991), 74.

63 Advertisement for Kelvinator, *Life*, April 16, 1945, 57.

64 "Family Utopia," *Life*, November 25, 1946, 58–59.

aluminum porch furniture, an aluminum slide, a doll carriage . . . and a helicopter. The prototypical family stands on the lawn, surrounded by its gadgets.

The advertisement displayed the postwar dream on the lawn in the same way that ones for credit cards, first introduced in 1950,[65] still do today. An ad for American Express in 1996 presented today's objects of desire—fax machine, gardening tools, ski gear, baby jogger, Yard-Man riding mower, gourmet gas range, telescope, paper shredder, Maalox—displayed on the lawn with power couple James Carville and Mary Matalin, their baby, and two dogs. **205** The display of dream objects on the lawn is the display of the victory of American consumer culture.

The lawn is the surface for the display of victory—military victory, as when soldiers parade on the lawn,[66] but also medical victory. A 1949 photograph in *Life* shows, exhibited on the lawn, an impressive array of bottles, bandages, and intravenous needles; they are all the drugs and medical materials used to save the life of a badly burned young boy, also displayed on a bed on the lawn, with his mother and all the doctors, nurses, technicians, Red Cross workers, and skin donors who kept him alive. Even political victory requires the lawn in postwar years. Politicians were always photographed on the lawn, sometimes even in hilarious positions, as when *Life* photographed a "Virile Governor" in 1947 doing a headstand on the lawn of his mansion.[67] **206** In 1946 a California senatorial candidate practices his speech in a modern house where the lawn extends to the inside of the house.[68] In other *Life* photos, Senator Robert Taft plays golf on the lawn,[69] and statesman Bernard Baruch, waiting to address the United Nations Atomic Energy Commission with his plan to ban the atom bomb, sits on a bench on a lawn with the speech in his pocket.[70] Every president is photographed repeatedly on the lawn of the White House.

The lawn represents democracy, understood in postwar terms. Everybody can have a lawn. The lawn is a right and, as such, a sign of postwar patriotism. "Meet a solid American citizen," an advertisement for the American Trucking Industry in 1947, shows a man and a child watering flowerpots on a lawn while a woman in the background sits on a lounge chair and reads a book: "Right in your hometown—right up your block—may live the driver of one of the trucks you often pass on the streets and highways. A family man. A taxpayer. A man with standing in the community . . . the *typical* truck driver owns his own home and car . . . is raising a family." A "solid American citizen" stands on the lawn, or in suburban builder William Levitt's famous words, "No man who owns his own house and lot can be a communist. He has too much to do."[71] **209** Wartime propaganda also expressed these themes. One poster, from a 1942 series called "This Is America," shows a family on their suburban lawn, the mother holding a baby, the father and the boy working on the finishing touches of the yard: "This is America . . . a nation with more homes, more motor cars, more telephones—more comforts than any nation on earth. Where free workers and free enterprise are building a better world for all people. This is your America. . . . Keep it Free!"[72]

Affluence itself was a form of victory. The battle of the appliance continued during the cold war when the US established its superiority over Communist Russia on the basis of its gadgets, not its weapons. The suburban house was the

---

65 Credit cards were launched in 1950 with the Diners Club card. Whitfield, *The Culture of the Cold War*, 71.
66 Even women soldiers were represented on the lawn. An article on the Women's Army Auxiliary Corps (WAACS) at Fort des Moines, the first women soldiers to join the army, presents them parading, doing calisthenics, and playing softball on the lawn. *Life*, September 7, 1942, 74–81.
67 *Life*, November–December 1947, 44.
68 Will Rogers Jr. in *Life*, October 1946, 33.
69 *Life*, June 2, 1947, 33.
70 "The Baruch Plan for Banning the Atom Bomb," *Life*, June 1946, 34.
71 Whitfield, *The Culture of the Cold War*, 73. William Levitt's words were originally quoted in Eric Larrabee, "The Six Thousand Houses That Levitt Built," *Harper's*, September 1948, 79–88.
72 Poster in the Warshaw Collection of Business Americana, Archives Center, National Museum of American History, Smithsonian Institution, Washington, DC.

ideal represented in the 1959 American National Exhibition in Moscow, where the most symbolic exhibit of the American way of life, an appliance-filled six-room ranch house, became the forum for the famous Kitchen Debates between Nikita Khrushchev and Richard Nixon.[73] 94 362 Circarama, Disney's 360-degree film presentation of the rituals of life in the USA, also an exhibit in Moscow, included a barbecue scene on the lawn. The suburban house had become a weapon.

The militarization of the domestic lawn after World War II was also evident in bomb shelters constructed during the cold war. Often on the lawn or under it, the bomb shelter was, as Elaine Taylor May has argued, a surrogate home, an image of the American home in the nuclear age.[74] 98 210 It was as isolated, self-sufficient, and stocked up with supplies as the suburban house that sat on the lawn.

Postwar America was split. The smiling face of abundance and gadgets barely hid the dark side of depression, tranquilizers, and mental illness. Veterans were plagued with psychological problems, exacerbated by the isolation of the suburbs, and psychologists discovered a new kind of disorder: housewife blues.[75] The lawn represented this divided psyche. Underneath its contented surface was the threat of nuclear annihilation, a major cause of psychological troubles. On the outside, the lawn displayed the goods, the American dream, all the gadgets for which the war had been fought; below it lay the possibility of its absolute destruction. Tranquilizers were recommended among the necessary supplies of a shelter.[76] One hundred pills—a civil defense film argued—would be a suitable supply for a family of four.[77]

Perhaps nowhere was this schizophrenia more acutely represented than in an article in *Life* about a couple in Florida who spent their fourteen-day honeymoon in their fallout shelter. "Their Sheltered Honeymoon" portrays them sitting in the lawn—before going under—with their provisions spread out around them on the grass like "wedding gifts."[78] 96 97

The fallout-shelter craze reached its climax in 1961 when, with the deepening of the crisis over Berlin, President John F. Kennedy delivered a televised address on civil defense. In what is considered "one of the most alarming speeches by an American President in the whole, nerve wracking course of the Cold War,"[79] Kennedy handed over responsibility to individual homeowners: "In the coming months I hope to let every citizen know what steps he can take to protect his family in case of attack."[80] **211** A thirty-two-page Department of Defense pamphlet, *The Family Fallout Shelter*, became a national best seller. According to *Time* magazine, until August 1961 monthly request of the free booklet had averaged 260,000 copies. In August, 2,400,000 copies were distributed, and in the first half of September, even *that* rate doubled.[81] A Wide World photograph captioned "War Games, 1961" shows a woman with two small children running happily across the lawn toward their home shelter as they practice evacuation. **207**

But it was not all so sweet. Only a few weeks after the speech and before their shelters were finished, people across the United States were already announcing how they were going to defend their shelters from the neighbors' assault. An article in *Time* entitled "Gun Thy Neighbor?" quoted a suburban Chicago man:

> When I get my shelter finished, I am going to mount a machine gun at the hatch to keep the neighbors out if the bomb falls. I'm deadly serious about it.

---

73 About the Kitchen Debates and the 1959 American National Exhibition in Moscow see May, *Homeward Bound*, 16–18; Karal Ann Marling, *As Seen on TV: The Visual Culture of Everyday Life in the 1950s* (Cambridge, MA: Harvard University Press, 1994), 243–83; and Eric J. Sandeen, *Picturing an Exhibition: The Family of Man and 1950s America* (Albuquerque: University of New Mexico Press, 1995).
74 May, *Homeward Bound*, 3.
75 Henriksen, *Dr. Strangelove's America*, 81–111.
76 "Shelters—How Soon—How Big—How Safe," *Time*, October 20, 1961, 21–25.
77 Film on civil defense included in the film *The Atomic Cafe*, dir. and prod. Kevin Rafferty, Jayne Loader, and Pierce Rafferty (New York: Archives Project, 1982).
78 "Their Sheltered Honeymoon," *Life*, August 10, 1959, 51–52.
79 International analyst Michael Mandelbaum quoted in Allan M. Winkler, *Life under a Cloud: American Anxiety about the Atom* (New York: Oxford University Press, 1993), 126. See Henriksen, *Dr. Strangelove's America*, 200–201.
80 Kennedy's July 25, 1961, speech on civil defense in *Time*, October 2, 1961, 21. See also Walter Karp, "When Bunkers Last in the Backyard Bloom'd," *American Heritage*, February–March 1980, 85–93.
81 "The Cold War," *Time*, September 29, 1961, 13.

> If the stupid American public will not do what they have to save themselves, I'm not going to run the risk of not being able to use the shelter I've taken the trouble to provide to save my family.[82]

A hardware dealer in Austin, Texas, had also constructed a well-armed shelter with four rifles and a .357 magnum pistol. But in case his neighbors reached the shelter before he did, he kept a tear-gas gun at home: "If I fire six or seven tear-gas bullets into the shelter, they'll either come out or the gas will get them."[83] Even religious leaders sanctioned the deadly use of force against neighbors trying to "invade" shelters. A huge national debate on nuclear ethics ensued.[84] Once again, the lawn became a battlefield, this time in an imaginary battle over shelters that were not yet built—Americans for the most part ignored the call to build them.

If World War II defended the national lawns, after the war, each private lawn became the site of a war waged with weapons derived from military technology and paranoia—insecticides, lawn mowers, shelters, appliances—but this militarization remained more or less hidden from view. Such hiding was at the very heart of the cold war. It is as if the ideal American postwar suburb were a network of buried surrogate houses, bunkers beneath the lawn acting as the counterpart to the fragile pavilions above, row upon row of hidden concrete fortifications topped by transparent boxes.

---

[82] "Gun Thy Neighbor?" *Time*, August 18, 1961, 58, quoted in Henriksen, *Dr. Strangelove's America*, 204.

[83] Ibid.

[84] Walter Karp, "When Bunkers," 85–93.

141

FAMILY UTOPIA

The posed scene above is an honest representation of the dream of most U.S. families. Fanciful as it looks, it is based on the hard statistics of consumer demand and manufacturers' unfilled orders. Beginning with the trim Colonial house and its generous plot which affo portunity for gardening, what Americans want are (from left background, working to foreground) ible station wagon, $2,890; blankets and towels

50; aluminum ladder, $22; set of stainless-steel pans, $33; automatic washing machine, $241; on-phonograph-radio, $1,795; vacuum cleaner gets, $107, being unloaded from truck with plastic hose, $15; electric stove, $266, with (to right) dishwashing unit, $299. Behind the bemused couple is a freezing unit, $200. On aluminum porch furniture, $115, sit percolator, $47, toaster, $19, and iron, $10. Behind is a lawn sweeper, $37. Farther to right is power mower, $200; aluminum slide, $37; doll carriage, $35, and a portable radio, $60. Hovering over them all, the dream's supreme moment just before waking, is helicopter, $48,500.

CONTINUED ON NEXT PAGE 59

Chapter 5
X-Ray Architecture

1.

In *Highlights and Shadows*, a 1937 Kodak Research Laboratories film analyzed by Lisa Cartwright in *Screening the Body*,[1] a woman wearing a swimsuit is shown strapped to a laboratory table while her body is subjected to x-rays. 212 213 Screening a whole population with x-rays, as it became common in the United States at midcentury, put the private space of the body under public scrutiny. The film associated this exposure of the body with the exposure of the domestic space of a glass house. As the photographic image of the woman gives way to the image of her x-rayed body, the male narrator announces, "This young lady, to whom henceforth a glass house should hold no terrors, will after an examination of her radiographs, be reassured that she is *indeed* physically fit."[2] What is remarkable about this is not that the woman will be reassured that she is healthy after finding out that her x-ray is clean; the real surprise lies in the claim that this will make her unafraid of being in a glass house. The glass house acted as a symbol not only of the new form of surveillance and health but also of terror.

The development of the x-ray and that of the modern house coincide. Just as the x-ray exposes the inside of the body to the public eye, the modern house exposes its interior. 214 Likewise, screening the body for TB meant penetrating with the gaze areas of the body previously invisible. The technology of x-rays had been available in sanatoriums since the beginning of the century. By the 1920s, it was a routine part of the examination for those with visible symptoms. 215 Diagnosis of tuberculosis continued to be difficult, with physicians confusing it with a variety of other illnesses, including bronchitis, chronic indigestion, malaria, neurasthenia, and typhoid fever. Doctors wanted to see inside the body to evaluate the damage already done. Only in the 1930s did mass x-raying of citizens on a regular basis start. With this development, the now-visible interior of the body became not just a tool for diagnosis but also the site of a new form of public surveillance. Policing the population by scrutinizing their insides, public institutions such as schools and the military took over the management of the most private spaces of the body.

Highlights and Shadows was part of this national campaign. Prepared by a filmmaker-radiographer, it appeared precisely around the time the antituberculosis campaign was being stepped up to a new level. The National Tuberculosis Association reported that the "rebirth of interest in the control of tuberculosis has marked the fourth decade of the twentieth century." More than six times as many articles regarding TB were published in the *Journal of the American Medical Association* in 1939 as had been in 1933.[3] By the 1940s, most areas of the country had experienced a major resurgence of efforts to detect and treat the disease. The war accelerated the campaign even more.[4] Screening soldiers led to a new awareness of the degree of undetected TB in the general population. The US Public Service established an Office of Tuberculosis Control in 1943. Among the programs was the chest x-ray examination of workers in war industries.

Military metaphors that had long accompanied TB work in the earlier twentieth century became even more popular. Fighting one's disease was seen as a patriotic obligation: "Our immediate danger is the insidious forces in our bodies, the conquering of which, in the long run, leads to victory for the USA within the larger arena of war." The TB germ was seen as an invader of the body that had to be militarily defeated. During the 1950s, public-health films such as *Target TB* (a 1950 film sponsored by General Electric) represented the TB bacteria as Japanese

---

1 Lisa Cartwright, *Screening the Body: Tracing Medicine's Visual Culture* (Minneapolis: University of Minnesota Press, 1995), 154–55.
2 James Sibley Watson Jr., *Highlights and Shadows* (Kodak, 1937), quoted in Cartwright, *Screening the Body*, 155.
3 Barron H. Lerner, *Contagion and Confinement: Controlling Tuberculosis along the Skid Road* (Baltimore: Johns Hopkins University Press, 1998), 34–35.
4 Ibid., 40.

soldiers penetrating the lungs and causing cavities. What the x-ray reveals is understood as war damage.[5]

The postwar mobilization against TB included programs for the mass x-ray surveying of the entire population using mobile x-ray machines in places such as department stores, industries, schools, suburban streets, and public markets. The campaign was supported by a barrage of newspaper articles, radio broadcasts, films, and even buttons bearing such slogans as "O.K. Let's X-Ray" and "I've Had My Chest X-Ray." Over a period of a half century, an experimental medical tool had been transformed into a mechanism of surveillance for the whole population.

Still today, the x-ray is a mechanism of policing. Our baggage is x-rayed in airports, embassies, consulates, and other targets of terrorism, something that, incidentally, started immediately after the war, with the Inspectoscope used to detect contraband. A few years ago, the *New York Times* showed us an x-ray image of a truck that revealed it was full of people trying to smuggle themselves into England. They were from Kosovo and had been caught by the machine at the Calais checkpoint.

These images have had a major effect on architects, but more important, they have transformed our sense of what architecture is. It would not be an exaggeration to say that twentieth-century architecture is all about surveillance: from the polemical windows of Loos and Le Corbusier to the glass architecture of midcentury, to recent experiments with video and computer surveillance.

2.

The surveillance technologies of the x-ray and modern architecture evolved in parallel. While one could argue about when modern architecture began, historians like Nikolaus Pevsner and Sigfried Giedion point to the all-glass corner of the Gropius 1911 Fagus Work building, and others point to earlier uses of glass walls. Either way, we are talking about an x-ray effect. Look again at the famous images of the Fagus Work, for example: magically, we see through the corner, and the inner structure is revealed, even painted white, like bones—an effect that can be seen in image after image. **220** Books on modern architecture look like collections of chest x-rays. Our slide libraries in schools of architecture all over the world are filled with images of translucent glass skins revealing inner bones and organs. Think, for example, about Le Corbusier's project for the Glass Skyscraper (1925), Walter Gropius's Bauhaus (1925–26), Brinkman & Van der Vlugt's van Nelle factory in Rotterdam (1925–31), Eric Mendelshon's Schocken department store in Stuttgart (1926–28), George Keck's Crystal House at the 1933–34 World's Fair in Chicago, Paul Nelson's Suspended House (1935), Frits Peutz's Schunck Glass Palace in Heerlen, The Netherlands (1935), and countless other examples. **221 222 223 224 225 226**

If experiments with glass were numerous in the early years of the century, they still tended to be isolated esoteric projects by avant-garde architects. Only by midcentury did the see-through house become a mass phenomena just as the x-ray itself was becoming a mass phenomena as well. And it was not just the house: it would seem that everything in the house had to be see-through, from the Pyrex cookware to Saran Wrap to windows in ovens and washing machines and so on. Likewise, the x-rays are not just to see inside the body for medical reasons. Everything is subject to x-rays. Even cars, as in a 1946 image of a Jeep in *Life* ("World's Biggest X-Ray"), to the house itself, which, even if too big to be x-rayed, was imagined that way in advertisements and films. **227**

---

5 And when the cartoon shows the microscopic view of the bacilli they appear as a dot, resembling the Japanese flag. Cartwright, *Screening the Body*, 152–53.

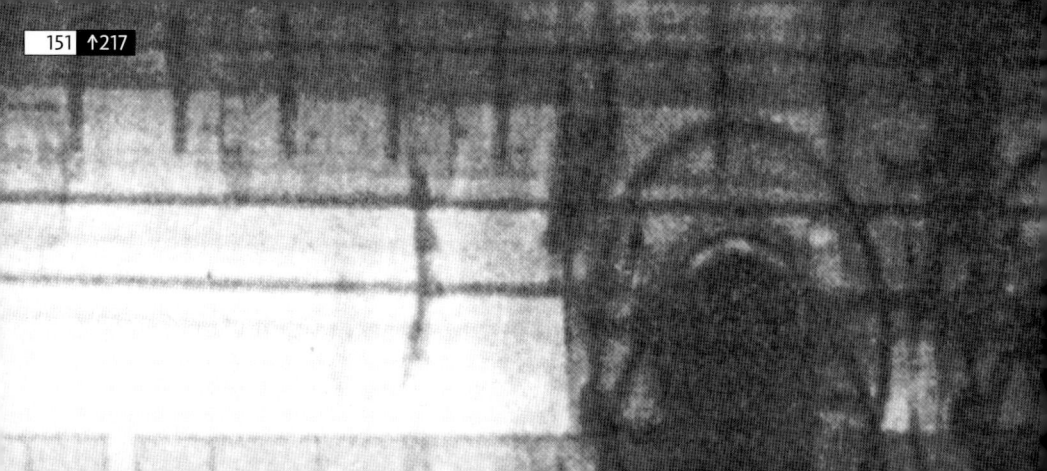

Glass walls, like x-rays, are instruments of control. From the outside, the glass exposes the house to the public, as if guaranteeing conformity to the community. The glass also enables an internal policing of the suburban house. It permits the surveying eye of the mother, already mobile through the open plan, to extend itself into the yard to monitor the movements of children playing outside and of approaching visitors and deliverymen. **228**

If architectural ideas and medical ideas have always been entangled, it should come as no surprise that twentieth-century architecture is shaped by the dominant medical obsession with tuberculosis. Exactly the same set of associations as in the Kodak film can be seen in the discourse around canonical works of the architectural avant-garde, for example the Farnsworth House of 1949. **229** In the course of an interview in *House Beautiful*, Edith Farnsworth, a successful doctor in Chicago, compares her weekend house, designed by Mies van der Rohe, to an x-ray:

> I don't keep a garbage can under my sink. Do you know why? Because you can see the whole "kitchen" from the road on the way in here and the can would spoil the appearance of the whole house. So I hide it in the closet further down from the sink. Mies talks about "free space": but his space is very fixed. I can't even put a clothes hanger in my house without considering how it affects everything from the outside. Any arrangement of furniture becomes a major problem, because the house is transparent, like an X-ray.[6]

The metaphor of the x-ray was not accidental. Already in the early 1920s, in the context of the publication of his Office Building project, Mies had written about his work as "skin and bone" architecture and referred to the structure of his Glass Skyscraper of 1922 as "the skeleton," rendering the building as if seen

---

[6] Edith Farnsworth quoted in Joseph A. Barry, "Report on the American Battle between Good and Bad Modern," *House Beautiful*, May 1953, 270.

under x-rays. 230 231 This is more than an aesthetic. It is a symptom of a deep-seated philosophy of design deriving from medical discourse and inseparable from it. Not by chance does Farnsworth go on to say of her house: "There is already the local rumor that it's a tuberculosis sanatorium."[7]

Modern architecture cannot be understood outside tuberculosis. Indeed, it would seem as if modern architects and their promoters were advocating life in a sanatorium. Take, for example, Sigfried Giedion's little 1929 book *Befreites Wohnen* (Liberated Dwelling), which is subtitled *Licht, Luft, Öffnung* (Light, Air, Opening), almost like the slogan of a sanatorium. 232 Under the cover of a book on the modern house, we find more than half of the illustrations dedicated to hospitals and to sports: Richard Döcker's sanatorium in Waiblingen (1926–28), Byvoet and Duiker's Zonnestraal in Hilversum (1927), a 1907 sanatorium in Davos (the famous site of Thomas Mann's novel *The Magic Mountain*), athletic stadiums, images of gymnastics, sunbathing, and tennis. 234 237 238 239 And when we finally get to the houses, they seemed to have turned themselves into sanatoriums, with convalescents resting on long chairs on terraces, as in a picture of a Max Häfeli house in Zurich of 1928, or into gyms, as in the Marcel Breuer's bedroom for Piscator in Berlin (1927–28), with its gymnastic equipment, or André Lurcat's gym on the roof of the Guggenbühl House in Paris (1926–27). 233

And it is not just Giedion. Another influential book of that time, Richard Döcker's *Terrassentyp* of 1927, follows the development of the terrace in modern architecture from the sanatorium to the home, starting with Döcker's own sanatorium in Waiblingen and proceeding to Zonnestraal, Davos, and so on, delineating a seamless transition from the terraces of sanatoriums to those of modern houses. 236 237 Diagrams show the penetration of the sun rays in modern sanatoriums and in modern terrace houses, and the book concludes with a series of photographs of domestic terraces furnished with exercise equipment, as in Döcker's apartment in the Weissenhof in Stuttgart or Le Corbusier's terraces or the swimming pool of Mallet-Steven's Villa Noailles in Hyeres. 235

Not only did modern architects emphasize health and exercise in opposition to the dangers of disease, but their architecture was understood that way. 240 The buildings became unconsciously identified with the healthy body. For example, Mies van der Rohe's Tugendhat House in Brno of 1929–30, which had been abandoned during the German occupation of Czechoslovakia, was turned into a gymnasium for young children by communist bureaucrats who presumably were unaware that the house had been photographed in its early days in exactly that spirit. Early-1930s photographs of naked Tugendhat children playing in the sun on the terrace are uncannily echoed in the 1960s images of children exercising in the living room–gym. 241 242 Modern architecture was unproblematically understood as a kind of medical equipment, a mechanism for protecting and enhancing the body.

Even entire cities were thought in those terms. Tony Garnier's proposal for an Industrial City (1904), for instance, featured the heliotherapy building of the hospital complex occupying the highest point of the plan, dominating the city from the hillside, and a sports center right in the middle of town, as if replacing the cathedral of medieval times. Health had become a new form of religion. Giedion describes the project in his 1928 book *Building in France, Building in Iron, Building in Ferro-concrete*, "Elevators carry the convalescent in his bed to the generous terraces to which the roofs have been converted. . . . The eye, through the interplay of the various horizontal surfaces, has an impression of the air always separating and hovering."[8]

---

[7] Edith Farnsworth, "Memoirs" (unpublished manuscript), quoted in Alice T. Friedman, *Women and the Making of the Modern House: A Social and Architectural History* (New York: Abrams, 1998), 143.

[8] Sigfried Giedion, *Building in France, Building in Iron, Building in Ferro-concrete* (1928), 163.

Giedion's emphasis on the horizontality of both the convalescent and of modern architecture suggests perhaps a completely different explanation for the horizontal framing of the modern house than those that I myself have supported by linking the horizontal window with cinema. Could the relentless horizontal framing of modern architecture be related to the horizontality of the occupant—the TB convalescent lying on the chaise, the paradigmatic client of modern architecture? 244

The architecture of the early twentieth century cannot be understood outside of tuberculosis. Indeed, the principles of modern architecture seem to have been taken straight out of a medical text on the disease. A year before the German microbiologist Robert Koch discovered the tubercle bacillus in 1882, a standard medical book stated that among the causes of the disease were "unfavorable climate, sedentary indoor life, defective ventilation and deficiency of light."[9] It took a long time for these notions to lose credibility, as Susan Sontag writes: "The TB patient was thought to be helped, even cured, by a change in environment. There was a notion that TB was a wet disease, a disease of humid and dank cities. The inside of the body became damp ('moisture in the lungs' was a favored locution) and had to be dried out."[10]

Modern architects offered health by providing exactly such a change of environment. Nineteenth-century architecture was demonized as unhealthy, and sun, light, ventilation, exercise, roof terraces, hygiene, and whiteness were offered as means to prevent, if not cure, tuberculosis. The publicity campaign of modern architecture was organized around contemporary beliefs about tuberculosis and fears of the disease.

In his book *The Radiant City* of 1935, Le Corbusier dismisses the "natural ground" as "dispenser of rheumatism and tuberculosis" and declares it to be "the enemy of man." He insists on detaching the house, with the help of pilotis (thin columns), from the "wet, humid, ground, where disease breeds," and on using the roof as a garden for sunbathing and exercise. **247** To reinforce the point, he uses pictures taken from medical texts as architectural illustrations, showing the lungs and their inner workings, while giving architectural illustrations medical labels, as when a photograph of an old part of the city becomes "Historic Paris, tubercular Paris." **245** **246** Le Corbusier develops in this book a concept of "exact respiration" whereby the indoor air is continually circulated and cleaned, made "dust free, disinfected, . . . and ready to be consumed by the lung." Opening windows are eliminated, and the facades become walls of glass. One by one, the characteristic features of modern architecture, such as pilotis, roof garden, glass walls, and clean air, turn out to have been presented as medical devices. Even the walls are white to reveal any contamination. As Le Corbusier had put it in *L'art decoratif d'aujourd'hui* ten years earlier, in 1925:

> If the house is all white, the outline of things stands out from it without any possibility of mistake . . . everything stands out from it and is recorded absolutely, black on white; it is honest and dependable. Put on it anything dishonest or in bad taste—it hits you in the eye. It is rather like an X-ray of beauty. It is a court of assize in permanent session. It is the eye of truth.[11]

The historical European architectural avant-garde could therefore be reconsidered from the point of view of the associations between modern architecture and tuberculosis, focusing on the new paradigm of the x-ray.

9 August Flint and William H. Welch, *The Principles and Practice of Medicine*, 5th ed. (1881), cited in René and Jean Dubos, *The White Plague* (1952), 69, and in Susan Sontag, *Illness as Metaphor* (New York: Vintage Books, 1979), 53.

10 Sontag, *Illness as Metaphor*, 14–15.
11 Le Corbusier, *L'art decoratif d'aujourd'hui* (Paris, 1925), 190.

3.

A parallel analysis needs to explore the situation in the United States. While there may be, again, disagreement on when and how modern architecture developed in the US, the discourse around tuberculosis was undoubtedly modernizing architecture from the beginning of the century. As in Europe, the germ theory of tuberculosis turned the house into a battlefield. Doctors, popular magazines, and advertisements for cleaning products and devices were calling for war in the home.

The treatment of TB is never finished. If sanatoriums could, as they used to say, "arrest" in some cases the progress of the disease, they could never completely cure it. The bacilli remained in the cavities of the lungs, waiting for a lowering of the defenses to renew its attack.[12] The battle against TB had to be continuously fought in the house. Medical authorities such as William Osler characterized the home not as a private space but as a public theater for the staging of contagion. In 1903 he wrote:

> In its most important aspects the problem of tuberculosis is a home problem. In an immense proportion of all cases the scene of the drama is the home; on its stage the acts are played. . . . The battlefield of tuberculosis is not in the hospitals or in the sanitaria but in the homes, where practically the disease is born and bred.[13]

Visiting nurses recommended removing wallpaper and draperies from the sick person's room, whitewashing the walls, scrubbing the floors, opening the windows, replacing old furniture with just a clean bed and a simple chair, and so on. In other words, they were recommending that patients modernize their interior.

If the house was a battlefield, the woman became a combination of military commander, scientist, and doctor. Since the beginning of the century, the house had been her laboratory, kept scrupulously clean of dirt, dust, and, above all, germs. As Gwendolyn Wright has written, women were even advised "to leave out petri dishes, as did scientists who grew germ cultures, to see if they had successfully eliminated the bacteria in their living rooms."[14]

Unlike the European sanatoriums, which tended to be centralized institutional buildings, many American sanatoriums grew out of tent colonies under the auspices of physicians who often had moved to the area to treat their own health problems. **248** **249** Even in Saranac, the Magic Mountain of the USA, the treatment of tuberculosis patients by Edward Livingston Trudeau first started in tents. Over time, so-called cure cottages were built, and people from the village turned their houses into boardinghouses for consumptives by adding "sleeping" porches, "sitting-out" porches, and glass-enclosed verandas to the fresh-air treatment of tuberculosis. The architectural features of the cure cottage would soon spread to the private house: sleeping porches, for instance, became common in California, where many TB-afflicted people had gone to seek treatment.

The private house took on other characteristics of the public sanatorium as well, including large windows, clean surfaces, clean lines—meaning the absence of ornament, of draperies, of carpeting, of encumbering objects. White walls not only were considered sanitary but were believed to have a positive impact on the mental health of the inhabitants, their effect the equivalent of a rest cure. In other words, the full ideology of high modern architecture was present in the USA before the official representatives of the European avant-garde arrived.

12 This is one of the reasons TB again became a problem in the 1980s: it was a serious threat to AIDS patients. The *New York Times* writes often about the continuous problem of TB, which today is still the leading infectious killer in the world, with many antibiotic resistant strains of the disease emerging.

13 Barbara Bates, *Bargaining for Life: A Social History of Tuberculosis, 1976–1938* (Phladelphia: University of Pennsylvania Press, 1992), 234.
14 Gwendolyn Wright, *Building the Dream: A Social History of Housing in America* (New York: Pantheon Books, 1981), 159.

As the European avant-garde started to emigrate to the USA, this tradition combined with that of high modernism in projects such as the Schindler-Chase House of 1921–22, Schindler's Lovell Beach house of 1925, and Richard Neutra's Lovell "Health" House of 1928–29, all of which included sleeping porches and sleeping lofts. **251** Still in the late 1930s and 1940s Neutra included sleeping porches outside every bedroom in projects such as the 1939 Residence for Dr. Scioberetti in Berkeley. **252**

Neutra writes about the architect being a kind of physician and about the special role of the house in what he calls the "development of an architecture attuned to biology": **253**

> The client of a domestic project sits with his wife . . . very visibly and audibly before us. We can learn in practice how to conduct a revealing clinical interrogation.
>
> Designing a setting for human beings is an important branch of preventive medicine, an intuitive art with a scientific footing, like "Medical Art." . . . There is a difference, though, between a doctor and an architect: The first is visited by "depressives" worried about a threat to their vitals. . . . The architect is telephoned by "maniacs," by a man who is engaged to get married . . . expecting a rise in salary next quarter. . . . Is a manic or a depressive easier to handle, to treat, to advise? What is the architect's contribution toward psychosomatic medicine?

After the war, Neutra, like many other architects, shifted his preoccupations with physical health of the late '20s and '30s to preoccupations with mental and psychological factors, as Sylvia Lavin's research has analyzed.[15] It is as if the horizontality of the TB patient had been replaced by the horizontality of the psychoanalytic patient, on the couch.

The shift reflects a more general shift in the country. In the first half of the century, popular magazine writers and architects had stressed the role of the house in the prevention of illness and the promotion of health and physical fitness. Cleanliness, open interior spaces, sleeping porches, and sanitary kitchens and bathrooms were all seen as promoting a new healthy lifestyle and a new body. There was an emphasis of outdoor activities and sports. The languid body of the TB patient, so romanticized in nineteenth-century literature, was suddenly out of fashion, and new bodies had to be designed—at times literally: some patients had multiple ribs surgically removed as part of the treatment of TB.

Midcentury books such as Royal Barry Wills's *Houses for Good Living* of 1940 described the function of house design as "to preserve the vital health and happiness" of the family group[16] and portrayed the professional architect as a doctor: "If you picked a druggist in place of a physician to medicate your great-aunt and she happened to get well, you would never know whether it was by virtue of the medicine or her indomitable will to live. It would be a chance you took needlessly, where much was at stake."[17] But in the two decades following World War II, the ideal home was expanded to include an emphasis on psychological well-being. The house was now understood as the "bulwark of the family's psychological health."[18]

McCall's Book of Modern Houses, a collection of homes that had first appeared in *McCall's* and some of which had been commissioned by the magazine, offers a "Primer for Modern Houses":

---

15 Sylvia Lavin, "The Avant-Garde Is Not at Home: Richard Neutra and the American Psychologizing of Modernity," in *Autonomy and Ideology: Positioning an Avant-garde in America*, ed. R. E. Somol (New York: Monacelli Press, 1997).
16 Royal Barry Wills, *Houses for Good Living* (New York: Architectural Book Publishing Co., 1946), 6.
17 Ibid., 16.
18 Clifford Edward Clark Jr., *The American Family Home 1800–1960* (Chapel Hill: University of North Carolina Press, 1986), 240.

It is important to answer three questions:
Who am I?
What do I/we want out of life?
What do I/we want for the family?

But the book argues that "since psychological factors to a certain extent supersede purely physical factors in today's house, where do we start? . . . What methods can we use to discover and develop our taste, to see clearly our ambitions and circumstances? How can we be our own psychoanalyst?" And then it provides a questionnaire "to help you get acquainted with yourself and your family": that is, *McCall's* offers guidelines to psychoanalyze yourself.[19]

As tuberculosis started to be controlled in the 1950s, mental illnesses took over as a national obsession. One-third of all prescriptions in the postwar years were for tranquilizers. In the middle of the decade, then–vice president Richard Nixon declared National Mental Health Week.[20] And all of a sudden, the house was seen in a new light. Even the kitchen was now a mental rather than a sanitary problem. **254** The much-publicized health-inducing properties of the modern house began to be extended into the psychological realm. But the modern house itself produced psychological problems. As the Kodak film of 1937 had already intimated, the glass house could be a source of terrors.

4.

The glass house produced fear for the same reason x-rays did. Loss of control, of privacy. **256** This fear was explicit in 1950s literature. Bernard Rudofsky, in *Behind the Picture Window*, writes that in the modern house, only the precious little time spent in the bathroom could be considered really private and is for that reason a source of creative inspiration.[21] When women were asked by a women's magazine how their suburban houses could be improved, the report observed that those who had a space for themselves, no matter how small, where they could escape not just from everybody else but also from TV and radio noise were less likely "to need the services of a mental health professional" and also less likely to divorce. Whether madness and divorce were related remains unclear, but of course the postwar years saw also a skyrocketing divorce rate.

Not only did the open plan eliminate individual private spaces inside the house, but the picture window and the glass wall exposed everything to the ruthless public gaze. Once again, Edith Farnsworth is a perceptive witness. The house invades her privacy, makes her anxious. As Alice Friedman has written, Farnsworth complained repeatedly about feeling vulnerable to the prying eyes of others both inside and outside the house. "Do I feel implacable calm?" she repeated in her interview in *House Beautiful*. "The truth is that in this house with its four walls of glass I feel like a prowling animal, always on the alert. I am always restless. Even in the evening. I feel like a sentinel on guard day and night. I can rarely stretch out and relax."[22] **257** Moreover, the house made her self-conscious about her body. She wrote: "I am six feet tall and I wanted to be able to change my clothes without my head looking like it was wandering over the top of the partitions without a body."[23] She could not even hide behind the five-foot-high partitions.

The x-ray house challenges the body it exposes; the healthy occupant becomes distressed. The Kodak film of 1937 tried to reassure us that, for the woman who has had her insides exposed by the x-ray, "a glass house should hold no terrors."

---

19 Mary David Gillies, *McCall's Book of Modern Houses* (New York: Simon and Schuster, 1951), 162.
20 Margot A. Henriksen, *Dr. Strangelove's America: Society and Culture in the Atomic Age* (Berkeley and Los Angeles: University of California Press, 1997), 81–111.
21 Bernard Rudofsky, *Behind the Picture Window* (New York: Oxford University Press, 1955), 193.
22 Farnsworth quoted in Barry, "Report on the American Battle," 270.
23 "Glass House Stones," *Newsweek*, June 8, 1953, 90, quoted in Friedman, *Modern House*, p. 142.

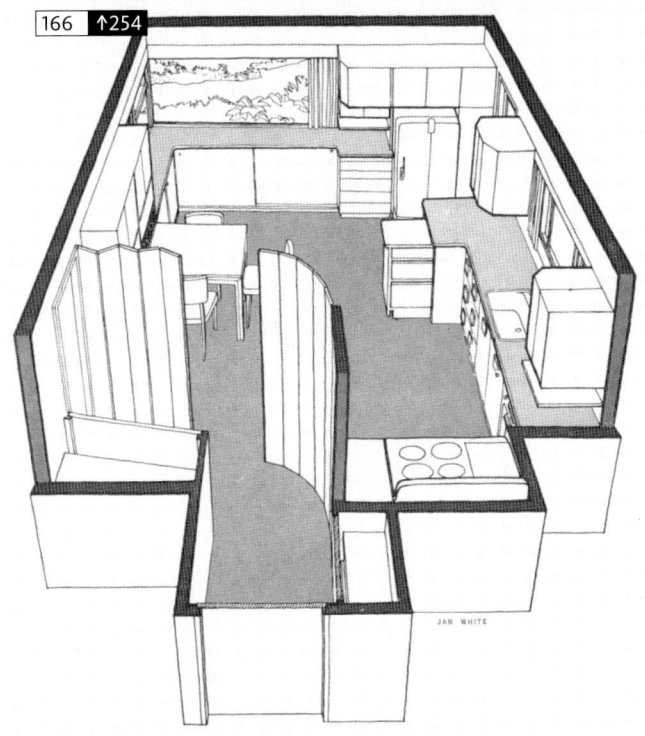

Sketch of remodeled kitchen shows what good planning and detailed thinking can accomplish. Every inch of possible storage space has been used to the best advantage. Counter space is available anywhere in the room. Cabinet manufacturers might well give serious study to these workable innovations in kitchen storage. With common sense, serious study and a good carpenter, Mrs. Zundel achieved a better kitchen than most experts could have planned. Only she could know her own wants and needs.

It wasn't a psychiatrist Mother wanted— it was a new kitchen

By LOYE Y. ZUNDEL

Mother is out of danger, now that she has her new kitchen. It is part of her five-year plan to remodel our Pacific Northwest home, vintage 1930 or thereabouts.

Our old kitchen proved a constant frustration to the four members of our family. Storage space was poorly organized and utensils difficult to find. Lights glared and clutter was everywhere. It would be insufficient to call it inefficient.

The poor arrangements caused Mother to take twice the steps necessary in preparing daily meals. No wonder she had to spend extra hours in the kitchen when there were so many things to do. And after she finally had dinner on the table, she was often too tired to eat.

"This kitchen was built for someone who died 100 years ago," Mother would say. "They had so many servants they weren't concerned with saving time or energy."

Mother always frankly admitted that she didn't like to cook. It was too time consuming. (*Please turn the page*)

Having your inner structure revealed by the machine was supposed to acclimatize you to a house that exposed all your movements. But, of course, it did not.

Furthermore, the x-ray effect of the glass wall works two ways. Not only does it expose the inside of the building and the inhabitants. It is also a traumatic exposure of the exterior. The picture window, an integral element of the postwar American house, turns the building into a showcase of domesticity. It is not, as is commonly assumed, that the house exposes its interiority. There *is* no interior. What the huge window exposes is not a private space but a public representation of conventional domesticity. The picture window is like a shopwindow selling the middle-class American dream or like a billboard in which the passerby's eyes will not stop for too long, will not scrutinize the scene but will glance quickly and then move on, as if not wanting to know too much, to detect something out of the ordinary. A furtive look. It is not that the spectator is trying to be polite. It is her own identity that is at stake.

It is the passerby who is really exposed in the suburbs, subjected to all these eyes behind every window, every venetian blind, every curtain—inquisitive, implacable eyes. There is no restraint here. Every pedestrian is suspect, an intruder.

The pedestrian is scrutinized by all these eyes that cannot be seen and that, as Lacan wrote, referring to Jean-Paul Sartre's *Being and Nothingness*, do not need to be there to be felt:

> I can feel myself under the gaze of someone whose eyes I do not even see, not even discern. All that is necessary is for something to signify to me that there may be others there. The window if it gets a bit dark and if I have reasons for thinking that there is someone behind it, is straightway a gaze. From the moment this gaze exists, I am already something other, in that I feel myself becoming an object for the gaze of others. But in this position, which is a reciprocal one, others also know that I am an object who knows himself to be seen.[24]

This is a kind of reverse exposure, an x-ray of the people outside the building. If the modern house is an x-ray machine, the medical equipment actually works in two directions, and there is an unwritten history of the way we are examined by our buildings.

5.

In Dan Graham's work *Alteration to a Suburban House* (1978), the entire facade of a typical suburban house has been removed and replaced by a full sheet of transparent glass. **258** Midway between this glass wall and the back of the house is a huge mirror that runs the full length of the house, cutting it in half. The result is that the front section is completely exposed to the public, while the rear is hidden. Since the mirror faces the glass facade and the street, it reflects not only the house's interior but also the street and the environment outside the house. In fact, viewers will see the facades of the houses on the opposite side of the street.

Alteration makes visible the optical structure of postwar suburban life. Passersby are exposed, swallowed up by the house, incorporated into the interior as part of the decoration, as a kind of wallpaper. Visitors and passersby will see themselves inside the house, moving around in the virtual living room with the landscape of the suburb, the street, the sidewalk, the lawn, and neighboring houses behind them. They see themselves in an interior but also in an exterior that has now been made part of the interior. On the other side of the glass wall, inhabitants of *Alteration* will see themselves outside, in the street reflected in the mirror. Their domestic setup is displayed in the mirror as an open-air room surrounded by clouds, lawns,

---

24 Jacques Lacan, *The Seminar of Jacques Lacan: Book I, Freud's Papers on Technique 1953–1954*, ed. Jacques-Alain Miller, trans. John Forrester (New York: W. W. Norton, 1988), 215.

and the facades of houses. Passersby and inhabitants share the same convoluted space in the mirror.

The effect recalls that of Mies van der Rohe's Barcelona Pavilion of 1929, **260** where visitors saw themselves reflected in the dark glass, with the clouds, the sky, and the trees appearing behind them. They saw themselves within an interior that they stood outside of. Very few people seem to have noticed this effect. What has come to be understood in the architectural world as the most influential building of the twentieth century was apparently seen by "nobody": virtual architecture. Despite its prominent location in the layout of the International Exhibition in Barcelona, journalists sent by professional architectural magazines passed it over entirely, unable to detect its significance. Naive visitors and local journalists provided the only testimony to its existence. They commented on its "mysterious" effect, "because a person standing in front of one of these glass walls sees himself reflected as if by a mirror, but if he moves behind them, he then sees the exterior perfectly. Not all the visitors notice this curious particularity whose cause remains ignored."[25] It was only in the 1950s, in the aftermath of the 1947 Mies exhibition curated by Philip Johnson at the Museum of Modern Art, that the pavilion burst into every architectural publication.[26] **178** As glass architecture became dominant, the pavilion was hailed as the most beautiful building of the century, exemplifying the cult of transparency. A building that was known only through magazine images (it was dismantled at the closing of the exhibition in Barcelona and its fragments misplaced during its return trip to Germany) became the most significant monument of modern architecture.

Glass architecture also made it to the suburbs in the 1950s through magazine images. The picture window, which had its origins in high-art architecture, became a feature of suburban tract houses. But, as Thomas Hine has noted, the largest windows in the houses of Frank Lloyd Wright, Mies van der Rohe, and Richard Neutra framed the most spectacular views of the landscape, while picture windows in developers' houses would "look out on whatever happened to be outside."[27] 261 As each tract house faced the identical one across the street, the picture window became another screen of identification, a form of a mirror. People in the suburbs took cues for their behavior and consumer habits from their neighbors, in similar ways that they took them from advertisements and television programs.

Alteration was the culmination of an ongoing reflection on the postwar suburban house in the work of Dan Graham beginning with his "Homes for America," published in *Arts Magazine* in November 1965 and considered by some critics to be his first artwork. 262 In *Video Projection Outside Home* of 1978, a large video screen is placed on the front lawn of the house, facing the street. 264 It shows an image of the TV set being watched by the family inside the house. If television in the '50s brought the public realm into the private, here the private—the family's choice of TV program—is publicized. Graham argues that video, from the Latin "I see," "in architecture will function . . . as window and as mirror simultaneously, but subvert the effects and functions of both."[28] But in *Alteration* of the same year, Graham removes all the video equipment. There is not even a TV in sight. Is it that the whole facade is a TV screen? And which way is it facing? Who is watching what?

Unlike such high-art works as Johnson's Glass House (1949) and Mies's Farnsworth House (1949–52), which expose the four sides of the structure to

---

25 Local journalist from Barcelona reviewing the pavilion, quoted in Jose Quetglas, "Fear of Glass: The Barcelona Pavilion," *Revisions* 2, ed. Beatriz Colomina (New York: Princeton Architectural Press, 1988), 130.
26 Juan Pablo Bonta, *Architecture and Its Interpretation: A Study of Expressive Systems in Architecture* (New York: Rizzoli International, 1979), 131–74.
27 Thomas Hine, *Populuxe: From Tailfins and TV Dinners to Barbie Dolls and Fallout Shelters* (New York: MJF Books, 1999), 49.
28 Dan Graham, *Video-Architecture-Television: Writings on Video and Video Works 1970–1978*, ed. Benjamin H. D. Buchloh (Halifax, NS: Press of the Nova Scotia College of Art & Design; New York: New York University Press, 1979), 64.

the landscape of the private estates in which they are placed, Graham's *Alteration* remains frontal to the viewer, like a film screen or a TV set. **258** The postwar house, the house that had to make space for the TV, rearranging its living room to provide everybody with a view, itself operated as a television set, airing representations of family life to passersby.

In the age of TV, there is no privacy. In the early 1970s, at the same time that Graham started to work on the suburban house, the everyday domestic life of a real American family, the Louds of Santa Barbara, was presented on TV. In the course of the program, the couple split. It was not the stress of being on view. As Graham recalls it, the couple's marriage was already in crisis, with a philandering husband. The wife thought being on TV would solve their problems, serve as a form of therapy—that they could expose themselves to get a hold of themselves. The public reaction was initially very negative. But then everybody became a star. The wife appeared on *The Tonight Show* with Johnny Carson, and the audience identified with her. One son worked with Andy Warhol.[29] With each passing year, this exposure of the private has become more extreme. Not by chance, the current television program *Big Brother* originated in the Netherlands, where the inside of houses has traditionally been fully on display through sheer glass. **265**

Nothing could seem to be farther from the high-art world of Mies. And yet his former students and associates Edward Duckett and Joseph Fujikawa said of him, "He liked boxing, or at least he enjoyed watching it on television. . . . He had the largest television screen of anybody I knew. I think Herb Greenwald picked it out for him."[30] Indeed, the popular televisual logic of the picture window can be seen in Mies's high-art experiments with transparency.

Greenwald was a rabbinical scholar turned real-estate developer whom Mies met in 1946.[31] **266** Among other projects, the two built the 860–880 Lake Shore

Drive apartments in Chicago, twin twenty-five-story glass-and-steel structures on the shores of Lake Michigan containing 275 glass apartments each. **267** The project represented, according to one reporter, the fulfillment of Mies's thirty-year dream of a "skin and bone construction. . . . [Mies] wanted to give city apartment dwellers the feeling of living close to the out of doors, as people in suburbs do who have floor-to-ceiling picture windows in their houses."[32] Lake Shore Drive brings the suburbs to the city, as if stacking suburban houses on top of one another. The apartments are glass houses suspended in the air, their walls allowing "breathtaking" views of the lake from every apartment and at the same time turning each apartment into a display. At night, the towers become multiplex theaters providing an audience for each other. **268** Each looks on its identical twin as in a mirror image. Inhabitants seemed to feel perfectly at ease. As one of the first tenants put it: "I feel quite tucked in, and not nearly as exposed as I thought I'd feel, now the furniture is in place."[33]

Twinning is a common suburban condition explored by Graham in *Alteration* and in many other works. As he puts it, "I often think in doubles."[34] He traces the genesis of *Alteration* to *Two Audiences/Public Space*, his contribution to the 1976 Venice Biennale exhibition Arte Ambiente, organized by Germano Celant, where a room in the shape of a golden mirror rectangle was divided into two square rooms by an acoustic pane. **270** One of the far walls was a mirror, and the other far wall was painted white. Graham says that the Venice Biennale and other international art

---

29 Beatriz Colomina, interview with Dan Graham, February 2000.
30 William S. Shell, *Impressions of Mies: An Interview on Mies van der Rohe, His Early Chicago Years 1938–1958, with Former Students and Associates Edward A. Duckett and Joseph Y. Fujikawa*, pamphlet (Knoxville: University of Tennessee, 1988), 30.
31 Franz Schulze, *Mies van der Rohe: A Critical Biography* (Chicago: University of Chicago Press, 1985), 239.

32 Grace Miller, "People Who Live in Glass Apartments Throw Verbal Stones at Scoffers: Chicago Tenants Praise Lake Shore Drive Cooperatives," clipping from an unidentified newspaper, n.d., Mies van der Rohe Archive, Museum of Modern Art, New York.
33 Ibid.
34 Graham, interview.

Two Entrance Doorways, 'Two Home Homes', Jersey City, N.J.

two-story house is usually called 'colonial.' If it consists of contiguous boxes with one slightly higher elevation it is a 'split level.' Such stylistic differentiation is advantageous to the basic structure (with the possible exception of the split level whose plan simplifies construction on discontinuous ground levels).

There is a recent trend toward 'two home homes' which are two boxes split by adjoining walls and having separate entrances. The left and right hand units are mirror reproductions of each other. Often sold as private units are strings of apartment-like, quasi-discrete cells formed by subdividing laterally an extended rectangular parallelopiped into as many as ten or twelve separate dwellings.

Developers usually build large groups of individual homes sharing similar floor plans and whose overall grouping possesses a discrete flow plan. Regional shopping centers and industrial parks are sometimes integrated as well into the general scheme. Each development is sectioned into blocked-out areas containing a series of identical or sequentially related types of houses all of which have uniform or staggered set-backs and land plots.

Housing Development, rear view, Bayonne, New Jersey

Housing Development, front view, Bayonne, New Jersey

Center Court, Entrances, Development, Jersey City

In addition, there is a choice of eight exterior colors:
1 White
2 Moonstone Grey
3 Nickle

LAWN GREEN

4 Seafoam Green
5 Lawn Green
6 Bamboo
7 Coral Pink
8 Colonial Red

As the color series usually varies independently of the model series, a block of eight houses utilizing four models and four colors might have forty-eight times forty-eight or 2,304 possible arrangements.

CCDDAABB	CDABCDAB
CCDDBBAA	CDBACDBA
	DACBDACB
	DABCDABC
DDBBAACC	DBACDBAC
DDBBCCAA	DBCADBCA
DDCCAABB	DCABDCAB
DDCCBBAA	DCBADCBA

Lawn Green	Patio White
Colonial Red	Fawn
Patio White	Colonial Red
Moonstone Grey	Moonstone Grey
Fawn	Yellow Chiffon
Yellow Chiffon	Lawn Green
Nickle	Skyway Blue
Skyway Blue	Nickle

side of its immediate 'here and now' context it is useless, designed to be thrown away. Both architecture and craftsmanship as values are subverted by the dependence on simplified and easily duplicated techniques of fabrication and standardized modular plans. Contingencies such as mass production technology and hand use economics make the final decisions, denying the architect his former 'unique' role. Developments stand in an altered relationship to their environment. Designed to fill in 'dead' land areas, the houses needn't adapt to or attempt to withstand Nature. There is no organic unity connecting the land site and the home. Both are without roots — separate parts in a larger, predetermined, synthetic order.

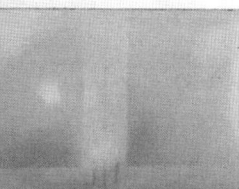

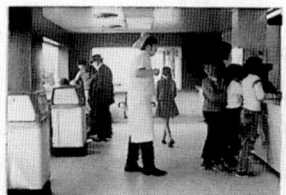

Car Hop, Jersey City, N.J.

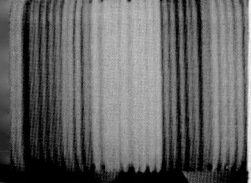

A given development might use, perhaps, four of these possibilities as an arbitrary scheme for different sectors; then select four from another scheme which utilizes the remaining four unused models and colors; then select four from another scheme which utilizes all eight models and eight colors; then four from another scheme which utilizes a single model and all eight colors (or four or two colors); and finally utilize that single scheme for one model and one color. This serial logic might follow consistently until, at the edges, it is abruptly terminated by pre-existent highways, bowling alleys, shopping plazas, car hops, discount houses, lumber yards or factories.

Kitchen Trays, Different Houses, New Jersey

ARTS MAGAZINE/December 1966-January 1967

fairs are like World's Fairs, where each country is represented by a pavilion and art is the commodity. In Venice he attempted to upset the system by making the audience the exhibit; visitors to the pavilion would see themselves seeing themselves as the commodity.

Mies and Graham are linked by the idea of the pavilion. **271** When commissioned to build the German pavilion for the International Exhibition of Barcelona in 1929, Mies asked the Ministry of Foreign Affairs what was to be exhibited. "Nothing will be exhibited," he was told. "The pavilion itself will be the exhibit."[35] In the absence of a traditional program, the pavilion became an exhibit about exhibition, presenting only a new way of looking. As with Dan Graham, the work was simply a space in which people encountered themselves, a space of reflection. What Graham took from Mies was not simply the look of Mies, in the sense of a reproducible visual style, but Mies's way of exposing the very act of looking, the new ways we look at ourselves and the world. Graham inherited Mies's sense of architecture as a vision machine.

Perhaps that's what attracted architects to the x-ray from the beginning. More than simply an image of the body, it is an image of the body being imaged. The x-ray is not about just showing the inside. The exterior volume is still visible as a kind of shadow or blur, and you feel yourself looking through it. **213** To look at an x-ray is to feel one's eye penetrating the surface of the body, moving through space. The very act of looking is exposed. With Mies, the glass is never completely transparent. Even at night, one feels the outer limit of the building and the eye passing through that limit. One feels the exposure.

Modern architecture exposes itself, but not by revealing everything. Rather, it stages the act of exposure, calling the eye in. These buildings are not simply acting like pieces of medical technology, scanning themselves and their occupants. They also scan those who look at the work from the outside. The glass box became a crucial piece of defense equipment in the cold war, continuously monitoring the exterior, a fragile surveillance device acting as the counterpoint to buried concrete shelters.

6.

Two persistent dreams of the twentieth century, that of the all-glass house and that of television, were finally realized at around the same time and in the same place, the suburbs of America. If experiments with glass and glass fantasies had played a dominant role in science fiction and in modern architecture since the mid-nineteenth century, only by the mid-twentieth century was the dream inhabited, in Mies van der Rohe's Farnsworth House in Plano, Illinois, and Philip Johnson's Glass House in New Canaan, Connecticut. 272 273 274 Two spacecrafts had landed: the Farnsworth, floating just above the ground like a craft coming in to land, and the Glass House, finally resting on the ground, down on its solid pad, anchored in place and yet somewhat a "raft," in Johnson's words, or, one could even say, a flying carpet. What had been experimented with in drawings, models, writings, and pavilions in fairs had become useful. As Louis Kahn put it in a television program with Philip Johnson: "The Glass House is a marvelous building because it stated very elegantly what was in the secret recesses of everybody's mind at the time of its conception. It brought out the picture of what modern architecture wanted to be."[36] The house as an image, then, a photograph of what everybody had in mind, a dream in physical form. The dream of transparency finally inhabited. 276

The Glass House represented the realization of the century-old dream of a transparent house that extended from the science fiction–like quality of Paul

---

35 Julius Posener, "Los primeros años: De Schinkel a De Stijl," *Mies van der Rohe, A&V: Monografías de Arquitectura y Vivienda* 6 (1986): 33.

36 Louis Kahn, "The Architect (Philip Johnson and Louis Kahn)," *Accent*, CBS, May, 14, 1961.

178 ↑268

179 ↑269

Scheerbart's images of glass buildings in an ideal future in his novels and in his 1914 collection of aphorisms, *Glasarchitektur*, dedicated to Bruno Taut, to Taut's own Glashaus (the pavilion for the glass industry in the Werkbund Exhibition of Cologne of 1914); to Mies van der Rohe and Lilly Reich's Glass Room in Stuttgart (1927), German Pavilion at the International Exhibition of Barcelona of 1929, and project for a Glass House on a Hillside (1934); to George Fred Keck's House of Tomorrow and the Crystal House (photographed with Fuller's Dymaxion car parked in the garage), both built at the 1933–34 Century of Progress International Exhibition in Chicago, and so on. 168 223 278

By 1949 this dream of a house defined only by glass walls—or, we could even say, the absence of walls—was fully realized in Mies's and Johnson's houses. But the absence of traditional walls does mean that the inhabitants of glass houses are exposed. As a Danish reporter seeing American houses with big picture windows put it: "A glass house bespeaks more security than a stone house because the owner can afford to dispense with the safety of the stone."[37] Or as Johnson said of his house in the 1965 CBS program *This Is Philip Johnson*, it was "an opportunity to live in the woods."[38] He insisted that "a wall is only an idea on your mind. If you have a sense of enclosure you are in a room." And to the repeated question of whether his house was a fishbowl that exposed his body to the eyes of others, he answered that in the sixteen years that he had lived in the house, nobody had come up to glue their face on the glass: "I think it is because people are afraid that you are looking at them."[39] The glass house operates both ways, as artists like Dan Graham have been exploiting since the 1970s. 258 Johnson didn't even experience the glass as transparent but as wallpaper. In another TV program, he says the Glass House "works very well for the simple reason that the wall paper is so handsome. It is perhaps a very expensive wall paper but you have wall paper that changes every five minutes throughout the day and surrounds you with the beautiful nature that sometimes—not this year—Connecticut gives us."[40] [278] The glass provides enclosure, containment, rather than openness:

> I built this Glass house shortly after Mies van der Rohe gave us all the model with his famous glass house near Chicago. This one came first, so people think I'm the original. I'm not. I knew the plans of the Farnsworth House very well. . . . But of course, there are differences. . . . I wanted to live on the ground. I wanted to be contained. I don't believe in indoor-outdoor architecture. What you want is a contained house to cuddle you, to hold you, to hold you near the hearth. You want to get your back up to a fireplace—any Anglo-Saxon does. Maybe the Italians don't care about that, but we do. . . . So this house is contained. I must admit the containment is a rather small feature—a black band that runs around the house—but it keeps the landscape away. It turns the landscape into a kind of wallpaper—expensive wallpaper to be sure—but wall paper, where the sun and the moon and the stars make different patterns.[41] [280] [281]

It is this sense of complete envelopment that makes the minimalist statement architecture: "If you are in a good piece of architecture you have the feeling that you are surrounded."[42] Rather than dematerialize architecture, the glass reinforces its traditional role. "Architecture is how you enclose space. That's why I hate photographs, TV and motion pictures," Johnson says during the same interview.[43]

37 Quoted in "Glass House Permits Its Owner to Live in a Room in Nature," *Architectural Forum*, November 1949.
38 *This Is Philip Johnson*, documentary, directed by Merrill Brockway, 1965.
39 Ibid.
40 Philip Johnson, *Accent*.
41 Philip Johnson, three-part interview by Rosamond Bernier, *Camera 3*, CBS, 1976, partially transcribed in Rosamond Bernier, "Fons et Origo: The Glass House and What Came of It," working draft, 13–15. A shorter version was later made for the Museum of Television and Radio seminar series The Artist at Work: Philip Johnson, September 26, 1991.
42 Ibid.
43 Ibid.

Television, too, arrived in the USA at midcentury. **283** Long part of science-fiction fantasies of the future, television was featured at its first public demonstration in 1927, prompting Buckminster Fuller to state that his Dymaxion House, designed the same year, was organized around a TV communication center. The Dymaxion House was equipped with the latest media technology (telephone, radio, television, phonograph, dictaphone, loudspeakers, microphone, and so on), but some of these technologies barely existed in 1927. Only in the late 1940s and 1950s was TV widely introduced to the American public. DuMont and RCA offered their first sets to the public in 1946, and between 1948 and 1955 nearly two-thirds of American families purchased a television set.[44] In 1950 the most famous of mass-produced suburbs, Levittown in Long Island, offered a television set built into the wall of its prefabricated Cape Cod house. Television had become part of the architecture of the American house. **282**

Johnson's Glass House, built at the time when most Americans owned a television, avoided all media technology. **284** There was not a TV set in sight in any of Johnson's houses, including the Hodgson House of 1951, whose client was a CBS executive. In one TV interview, Johnson insisted that the Glass House has "no television, no telephone, no gramophone, ... no noise of any kind."[45] No media in a house designed for the media.

And yet the Glass House itself was operating as a TV set, but not in the obvious sense of the views that the house makes possible. If the postwar suburban house operated as a television set, broadcasting family life through the picture window, the Johnson's Glass House closed itself to the outside, much more radically than a stone house could, to become a TV broadcasting studio.

The model was picked up later by authorities on the American house like Martha Stewart, who not only uses her own houses as a broadcast studio but owns a country estate in Westport, Connecticut, with a series of model houses, in the same way that Johnson had his estate with a series of model structures built over the years, each of which became an opportunity for broadcast. Each time the Glass House seemed to run out of steam, Johnson built a new pavilion, one that renewed the discussion of both the earlier house and of himself. "I keep building around the place because I get itchy," he said. "Nobody asks me to build funny things, so I do them myself as sort of tests. Clients always want something definite with toilets and other unnecessary gadgets but I can always build what I like for myself. So about every five or six years I build another funny thing."[46]

The Glass House was built first, in 1949; the brick guesthouse, also of 1949, was remodeled in 1953, the pavilion in the lake added in 1962, and "the swimming pool, which is an essential part of the composition, wasn't built until 1963. 285 286 287 In 1965, I had some pictures I wanted to hang, so I thought, 'good opportunity, we'll try something funny for a gallery.' Since I didn't want to build it too close to the Glass House, I put it in a bunker. People think it is an underground gallery, but it's not underground at all. . . . 1970 was the sculpture gallery. I had nothing to build for a long time, and about 1978 I was itchy again, the land next door came up for sale, so I kept expanding."[47] The studio was built in 1980, the Lincoln Kirstein Tower and the Ghost House in 1985, and a visitor's pavilion, Da Monsta, in 1995.

The official story, passed on in architectural scholarship, is that the Glass House is Johnson's laboratory. As Johnson himself put it: "I consider my own house not so much as a home (though it is that to me) as a clearing house of ideas which can filter down later, through my own work or that of others."[48] What he doesn't

44 Lynn Spigel, *Make Room for TV: Television and the Family Ideal in Postwar America* (Chicago: University of Chicago Press, 1992).
45 In fact, there was a telephone in the Glass House and a television set in the guesthouse, many people recalled.
46 Bernier, "Fons et Origo," 23.
47 Ibid., 24, 41–42.
48 "Philip Johnson (I)" and "Philip Johnson (II)," in Selden Rodamn, *Conversations with Artists* (New York: Devin-Adair, 1957), 52–56, 60–70, quoted in Peter Eisenman, introduction to *Philip Johnson Writings* (New York: Oxford University Press, 1979), 21.

tell you is that the house is a platform for him on the media—and not only the professional media of the architectural journals, but also the popular media of *Life*, *Look*, *House Beautiful*, *Ladies Home Journal*, the *New York Times Magazine*, *Newsweek*, *Business Week*, *House & Garden*, *Show Magazine*, and so on. **276** Johnson also appeared with astonishing regularity on TV programs, from the 1951 *Car Style Show* for CBS to his last interview, with Charlie Rose for PBS. The house is almost always at the center of these programs, every new construction an opportunity for reviving the fire.

So what is this house?

The best descriptions are still those of Johnson. He likens his house to a "celestial elevator in which when it snows, you seem to be going up because everything is coming down."[49] It is akin to the common experience of sitting on a train stopped at a station and feeling that it is moving only to realize that it is only the train across the platform that moves, the same feeling in the stomach, the same sense of displacement, except that in the house the movement is vertical rather than horizontal as in a train or in a Mies or Le Corbusier house, where the framing is relentlessly horizontal. And this is precisely the point at which the Glass House, described by Michael Graves as more Miesian than Mies, departs from that lineage.

What is curious about the idea of an elevator is that Johnson also repeatedly noted how much he disliked elevators, how elevators represented the end of architecture, the end of the experience of space in movement. Of the Seagram Building, for example, he wrote: "Unfortunately, the entire experience of Seagram's leads but to the elevator. . . . That claustrophobic box brings visual, processional beauty to a complete dead stop. The visitor can only be restored, if at all, by looking out of a high window. Elevators are here to stay, but one is not forced to love them."[50]

But then in *This Is Philip Johnson*, he theatrically and proudly crosses the lobby of the Seagram Building and goes where? Into the elevator, where he repeatedly presses the button frenetically while the camera follows him all the way up to his office.

It seems as if the claustrophobia of the elevator goes away when there is only the elevator in the landscape. A free box. A glass elevator with four doors? Stay clear. The containing gesture is now exactly what allows the box to move. Even the black band going around the glass makes sense now, as if it is something to hold on to when the box moves. 290 291

Already in 1947, in his book on Mies accompanying the exhibition at MoMA, Johnson had described the Farnsworth House as a "floating self contained cage."[51] And Henry-Russell Hitchcock described it as "beached yacht" with no provisions for outer living beyond the very confined space of the fly-screened "deck" and the small travertine "dock" below it.[52] The idea of floating can already be found in early articles in the popular press, as when *House & Garden* calls the house "a glass shelf that 'floats' in the air."[53] 289 Johnson happily picked up the same metaphor for his house, describing it as floating on the sea, even if he disliked the sea as much as he disliked elevators: "That's why I don't like the seaside. There's nothing there, unless it's a boat. If there's a boat, it's O.K. In the East River wonderful barges go by. But God keep me from the Atlantic Ocean. There are a lot of glass houses that face the ocean, and people like them. But I say there's nothing there."[54]

49 Quoted in Kenneth Frampton, "The Glass House Revisited," *Catalogue* 9 (September/October 1978), reprinted in David Whitney and Jeffrey Kipnis, eds., *Philip Johnson: The Glass House* (New York: Pantheon Books, 1993), 99.

50 Philip Johnson, "Whence and Whither: The Processional Element in Architecture," *Perspecta* 9/10 (1965).

51 Philip Johnson, *Mies van der Rohe* (New York: Museum of Modern Art, 1947).

52 Henry-Russell Hitchcock, "The Current Work of Philip Johnson," *Zodiac* 8 (1961): 66.

53 "A Glass Shell That 'Floats' In the Air," *House & Garden*, February 1952.

54 Rosamond Bernier, "Improving His View," *House & Garden*, June 1986, reprinted in Whitney and Kipnis, *Philip Johnson*, 149.

If Mies's house is a beached yacht, Johnson would rather have his own house be at sea. The Glass House, Johnson says, was designed like a "Chinese box":

> You have a box, then you take the lid off and there's another one, there's another one, there's another one. So what we do, we start with a room—but it's a rather large room. It is the landscape from the forest on the road to the forest in the forest. And from the north to the south it's the same way. That's the room. Within that room we create a raft of space—the green lawn around you. On the green lawn we make another raft, which is the house, separate entirely form the green lawn. On this brown lawn, as it where, of the brick floor, we make another lawn: the white rug . . . . So the living room is just this raft in the brown sea, or the brown lawn (lets mix metaphors) of the paving. That again is on a green lawn, which again is on a forest lawn around. So here we have the microcosm, and that's the macrocosm.[55]

To experience the house is to move from floating raft to floating raft, each one providing a sense of containment. Space is defined by the outer lines of these rafts, the lawn, the pavement, the rug . . . The glass house is not a glass box but a horizontal surface, a raft, drifting among other rafts and having rafts drifting within it.

Is this horizontal movement contradictory to the idea of the vertical elevator or to Johnson's distaste for glass houses by the seaside? Not at all. Johnson accumulates metaphors and repeats them in different combinations. The raft lacks direction; it is floating in the sea, not looking at it from an anchored position as does the modern house. If the raft is an enclosure, if it provides shelter from the sea, which it does, it is in the vertical volume defined by the perimeter of the raft:

The intimacy of the raft is as great as the intimacy of a closed room. That's what's hard for older architects, who didn't have glass, to understand. On the ocean, on a raft, boy, you are enclosed. You can't step out. Well, you can't step off this white carpet either. And it brings you emotionally together so you can have a conversation.[56]

This evocative idea of the house as a raft had already been launched by Arthur Drexler within a month of the house's completion. In an article in *Interiors*, he describes the site of the house as itself a room with carpets laid out within it, the brick platform with the herringbone pattern, and within the platform the "sand-colored carpet, like a raft in the ocean, provides safe passage for a low couch."[57] Was Drexler listening to Johnson, or was Johnson listening to Drexler? Did Johnson do the same thing with his words as he did with the design of the house, picking up ideas from all his critics? Probably. He was a sponge, soaking up things and refining them, simplifying them, like a TV personality, a journalist reporting on his own life in an easily understood language. There is no difference between the reporter and the thing being reported on. Johnson was simply a TV program, a reality-TV show that ran longer than anybody could have imagined.

The x-ray house not only exposed itself along with anyone inside it, and the world outside along with whoever comes near it, but also broadcast images out into the world. The glass pavilion simultaneously absorbed images from the outside and threw images into the outside. It was a delicate but efficient media machine attached to a bunker, Johnson's fortified guesthouse, an early warning sign of the cold war's buried partner to the suburbs' ubiquitous picture windows.

55 "Philip Johnson Interviewed by Rosamond Bernier," 16–17.
56 Ibid.
57 Arthur Drexler, "Architecture Opaque and Transparent: Philip Johnson's Glass and Brick Houses in Connecticut," *Interiors*, October 1949.

Chapter 6
Unbreathed Air

Mies could take quietness for granted in the first half of the century. He could be sure of the individual rights of the undisturbed, inhabited place situated away from industry until almost at the end of his life, when the new state highway was built directly opposite his last pavilion, the Farnsworth house. A mobile home camp grew on the other side of the river; the tree screen had to be left so dense one is barely conscious of the river when in the house or on the property. . . . Starting to work in the 1950s we never could make the innocent assumptions available to the Heroic Period of Modern Architecture. *In the American magazines of the 1940s and 1950s we could foresee the consumer-oriented society that would, through advertisements, change all our lives. . . . World War II had acted as the great divide between ourselves and our grandparent architects, who built for the few tall cars and for the genteel who shopped for rarely replaced objects.*
—Alison Smithson[1]

Outside it was a wooden rectangular box of almost blank walls. The words "House of the Future" flashed on and off, projected onto one of the longer walls. 292 293 A small opening to one end of the wall acted as an entrance. Inside was another blank box. Visitors would circle around it, peeping in at ground level through a few openings that had been cut in the walls for that purpose before ascending to an upper level, where a viewing platform circled the inner box again, allowing a bird's-eye view into its interior, before leaving the outer box through another discreet opening on one of the short sides and finally descending to the ground of the vast Olympia exhibition hall in London. 294 295 The mysterious structure had been commissioned by the *Daily Mail* for their Jubilee Ideal Home Exhibition and displayed there for twenty-five days in March 1956. Afterward, it was carefully dismantled, stored, and transported to Edinburgh for the *Scottish Daily Mail* Ideal Home Exhibition in July of 1956. Its subsequent fate is unknown.[2]

How are we to understand the Smithsons' House of the Future? How can we discuss today a 1956 project that tried to imagine the house of 1981, that is, a house halfway between then and now? How can we look back at a forward-looking house? For years it was considered, or ignored, as an anomaly in their career, the project that didn't fit with anything else—despite the architects' repeated attempts to locate it within their multiple chronologies of their own work.[3] Much discussed at the time, in both the professional and popular media, the House of the Future (H.O.F., in the Smithsons' private notes) faded away from everybody's memory, almost disappearing, until the last few years when it has regained some currency. After almost half a century, the house seems almost impossible to ignore. Is it because its sinuous curves resonate with a renewed interest in biomorphism and the growing sense that new moldable materials are a driving force in architecture? **296** Or is it the contemporary fascination with the 1950s and British Pop in particular? Or the inevitable reassessment that occurs when a generation of architects reach the end of their careers? Or the rise of architectural archives that reveal new angles on familiar things? Or is there perhaps something about the house itself that, as it were, forces itself back on us? To echo the title of Richard Hamilton's famous collage from the same year: Just what is it that makes this house of the future so different, so appealing?

---

1 Alison Smithson, "Patio and Pavilion, 1956, Reconstructed U.S.A. 1990," *Places: A Quarterly Journal of Environmental Design* 7, no. 3 (1991): 11.
2 The technical specifications of the contractor established that construction would start "at 8am on 15th of February 1956 . . . to be completed as soon as possible . . . and no later than 10 am on 1st March,1956. Dismantling and clearing away is to commence at midnight on 31st March, 1956, and is to be completed by midnight on 7th April, 1956." Trevor Smith (exhibition architect), "Technical Specifications," November 11, 1955, manuscript, A&P Smithson Archives, London. The words "House of the Future," in lettering designed by Edward Wright, were in the end attached to the outer box rather than projected as originally intended. See "Ideal Homes. House of the Future. Suggestions for Outer Case and Viewing Platforms," manuscript, n.d., A&P Smithson Archives, London.
3 The Smithsons repeatedly insisted that Patio and Pavilion, in the exhibition This Is Tomorrow later the same year, was essentially a continuation of the same research idea of the H.O.F., that the H.O.F. was part of their larger investigations on the Appliance House, the Put Away House, and the Sky House. They also saw continuity between the H.O.F. and their work in Team 10, and in the meeting in Dubrovnik, also in 1956, they demonstrated the "grouping characteristics" built into its design, how it could come together in a dense "mat-cluster" of similar dwellings. In 2001 Peter was still insisting on the connection between these projects. See "1956 . . . The DS: The H.O.F. (AND DUBROVNIK!)," manuscript, September 28, 2001, A&P Smithson Archives, London.

Plastic

If there is one word that comes to mind when thinking about the House of the Future, it is *plastic*. The building was all plastic and filled with plastic objects.[4] The chairs, designed especially by the Smithsons for this house and fabricated by Thermoplastics Ltd., were all experiments in the new material: the folding "Pogo" chairs—seen by the Smithsons as "relics of the previous constructed technology"—were in steel and transparent Perspex, while the "Egg" chairs (one honey colored and the other citrus yellow), the "Petal" (in pimento red and honey color), and the white "Saddle" were molded in reinforced polyester resins and seem to share the character of the doubly curved modeling of the house itself. **297** **299** **321** The kitchen sink, like the sunken bath, all the hand basins, and the cubicle for the shower and drier, were a Bakelite polyester/fiberglass molding in pimento red made by Fibromold. **300** **345** The mattress and headrests for the bed were made of latex foam by Dunlopillo and covered with nylon. The bedclothes consisted of a single red nylon fitted sheet. **301** **328** The cushion in the living room was covered in royal blue nylon fur. The curtains that screened the bathroom from the entrance hall were made of orange-colored fiberglass. A never-realized suspended cloud was envisioned in pale blue nylon stretched over a light metal structure. **298** The working surfaces and cupboard doors in the kitchen were in Pitch Pine Warerite. Even the food had been packed in airtight plastic containers. **302** *House Beautiful* described the house as a "Wellsian fantasy in plastic," with "herrings wrapped in polythene"[5] and eggs without shells individually packed in little plastic sachets, the whites separated from the yolks.[6]

The H.O.F. was a veritable showcase of plastic, and the showcase itself took its logic from plastic, with journalists and critics insisting, probably after the Smithsons, that "plastic materials are used not as substitutes for conventional materials . . .

but in a way that seeks to utilise the inherent characteristics of plastics."[7] The exhibition catalog describes the structure of the house as "moulded in plastic-impregnated plaster, a kind of skin structure built up in units comprising floor, walls and ceiling as a continuous surface."[8] The exterior wall was sprayed with a protective plastic skin, and throughout the interior of the house the partly translucent, honey-colored rounded walls, floors, and ceilings were to be plastic, with brown "gasket" joints. Even the curved glass wall to the garden was to be molded in metal-reinforced plastic.

So is that all the H.O.F. was, a plastic house with curves? A skin structure, the smooth, rounded look of mid- to late-1950s architecture and design, of the Monsanto House of the Future of 1956, of Lionel Schein's *maison plastique* and cabine hoteliers, both of 1956, of Eames and Saarinen fiberglass chairs, of Tupperware bowls, and so on? **304** **305** A house, that is, that looked like a plastic consumer product? A house that was meant to be mass produced, easily transported on the back of a truck, and arrayed in a "dense mat of similar dwellings"—a "mat-cluster," as Alison put it?[9] **307** A plastic version of the 1920s dream of the industrialized house, then? But the dream was no longer of a series of standard elements that could be combined in different ways to produce different houses. Rather, it was of a series of unique molded shapes that could fit together in only one form. Prefabrication in

---

[4] Plastics seem to be also what struck contemporaries. Many newspapers and magazines referred to the plastics in the house. An article under the pseudonym "Polly Ester," for example, relentlessly listed every use of plastic in the house. "Polly Ester," "Rubber and Plastics: House of the Future," April 1956, clipping, A&P Smithson Archives, London.
[5] "House of the Future," *House Beautiful*, May 1956, clipping, A&P Smithson Archives, London.
[6] "House of the Future," *The Scottish Daily Mail Ideal Home Exhibition*, Waverley Market, June 29–July 14, 1956, 6, manuscript, A&P Smithson Archives, London.
[7] Polly Ester, "Rubber and Plastics," 247.

[8] Alison and Peter Smithson, "The House of the Future," *Daily Mail Ideal Home Exhibition, Olympia, 1956*, exhibition catalog, 97.
[9] Alison Smithson described the H.O.F. as "The House within the Community: the house of twenty-five years hence will be different not only in itself but also in the way in which it is arranged within the framework of the community. This particular house has been thought of as a town house, it is not set in its own garden but contains a garden within it. Such houses can be grouped together to form a compact community [a mat-cluster]." "The House of the Future, Ideal Home Exhibition, Olympia, end August 1955 to March 1956," manuscript, n.d., A&P Smithson Archives, London.

the H.O.F. represented not infinite flexibility but a singular, self-supporting shape that would, like any other consumer product, be abandoned as soon as a new model came out.

The H.O.F. learned from plastic. It had the aura of plastic, the dream material of the time. That is why it was talked about so intensely when it was constructed and perhaps why it is being celebrated again now. Popular magazines had been heralding the arrival of the new material in the house for some years. A 1952 article in *Life* magazine entitled "House Full of Plastics," for example, cataloged the endless plastic contents of an American ranch-style house. **204** A house, any house, could be turned into a dream house simply by filling it with dream material. Four years later, experimental architects were turning the container, the house itself, into plastic.

But in fact this plastic house was not made of plastic. It was a simulation, a full-scale mock-up in plywood, plaster, and emulsion paint, traditional materials collaborating to produce the effect of a continuous molded-plastic surface. **306** As Peter put it:

> It wasn't real. It was made of plywood. It was like an early airplane, where you make a series of forms, then you run the skin over them. The house was made in ten days. The exhibition contractor was fantastically fast. It was not a prototype. It was like the design for a masque, like theatre. Which is extraordinary.[10]

It was "make-believe." The most important thing, according to the specifications of the contractor, was that "the completed work gives the effect of continuous molded surfaces of the same material throughout." Even the transparent plastic wall to the garden of the house was fake. Thin chromium wires tensioned between the floor and the ceiling created for the viewer the illusion of the curved transparent wall molded in metal-reinforced plastic described in the brochure of the house when in fact the opening was left unglazed.[11] 322 The Smithsons saw the tradition of such temporary theatrical structures as a centuries-old tradition in architecture that played a crucial role in stimulating the evolution of ideas and tastes:

> The architects of the Renaissance established ways of going about things which perhaps we unconsciously follow: for example, between the idea sketchily stated and the commission for the permanent building came the stage-architecture of the court masque; the architectural settings and decorations for the birthday of the prince, for the wedding of a ducal daughter, for the entry of a Pope into a city state; these events were used as opportunities for the realisation of the new style; the new sort of space; the new weight of decoration; made real perhaps for a single day . . . the transient enjoyably consumed, creating the taste for the permanent.[12]

Like in the Renaissance, the H.O.F. was staged architecture, a shimmering masque, which made the proposal not less provocative but perhaps more: "Like all exhibitions, they live a life of say a week or four weeks in reality, then they go on and on forever. Like the Barcelona pavilion before it was reconstructed."[13] The temporary turned out to be permanent.

Image

The most extreme and influential proposals in the history of modern architecture were made in the context of temporary exhibitions. The Smithsons saw the H.O.F.

[10] Beatriz Colomina, "Friends of the Future: A Conversation with Peter Smithson," *October* 94 (Fall 2000): 24.

[11] Trevor Smith, "Technical specifications."

[12] Alison and Peter Smithson, "Staging the Possible," in *Alison + Peter Smithson, Italian Thoughts* (Sweden: A&P Smithson, 1993), 16. See also the earlier version of the same argument in "The Masque and the Exhibition: Stages Toward the Real," *ILA&UD Year Book*, July 1982.

[13] Colomina, "Friends of the Future," 24.

as following this tradition: Le Corbusier and Pierre Jeanneret's L'Esprit Nouveau Pavilion (1925) and Nestlé Pavilion (1929), Kostantin Melnikov's Market in Moscow (1924) and his USSR Pavilion in Paris (1925), Mies and Lilly Reich's Velvet and Silk Café at the exhibition Die Mode der Dame, Berlin (1927), Gropius's Werkbund Exhibition in Paris (1930).[14] As always, the Smithsons positioned their work in a genealogy of "three generations," each building on and transforming the vision of the previous one. In particular, they saw the H.O.F. as the inheritor of a twentieth-century tradition, a third-generation work extending the strategies of Le Corbusier's pavilion of 1925 (from the first generation) and the exhibition design of the Eameses (from the second generation):

> The House of the Future . . . "staged" as an exhibition house, confronted the changes that domestic machines, the emergent consumerism, the anticipated technology of the nineteen eighties; as two generations earlier the *Pavilion de L'Esprit Nouveau* had confronted the use of the products and the technology which it assumed would soon be generally available.[15]

The Smithsons' house echoes the way Le Corbusier constructed a model apartment and filled it with everyday objects to present his vision of modern living—with the difference that the Smithsons would display and draw from the "transient materials" of an ever-changing market. Found objects, perfected types like the Thonet chair or the generic wineglass, gave way to imagined disposable objects and food packaging. More important, it could be argued that they moved from displaying the object as such to displaying the image of the object, as exemplified in the glossy ads they collected, the shining fantasy world of consumer goods. The H.O.F. was itself just a seductive advertisement. As Reyner Banham put it at the time, the H.O.F. was successful in producing a "powerful and memorable visual image."[16]

From the Eameses, the Smithsons had learned how to transform the images on display into the architecture: "the exhibition material becoming itself the means of spatial organisation."[17] This was already evident in their 1953 exhibition with Nigel Henderson and Eduardo Paolozzi, Parallel of Life and Art, where an architecture of images was inserted into a traditional room, creating a room inside a room. `308` And it would continue when the same team assembled Patio and Pavilion in 1956, essentially another room within a room except that now the inside walls of the outer room (the patio) were lined in aluminum, making the visitor, endlessly reflected on the walls, part of the exhibit. `309` The space was filled with found archaic objects treated as images, laid out like a large painting to be walked through in the patio with the visitors incorporated into the image, or looked at from behind the wires that replaced the missing wall of the pavilion to keep visitors out, or looked up through the translucent corrugated plastic roof of the pavilion that had the effect of an almost photographic vision. The H.O.F., on the other hand, was a display case that, like the objects it displayed, was pure image. Both the house and the objects inside were treated as images, and they combined to produce one single smooth, glossy ad that could be placed alongside any other ad, participating in the flow of popular imagery, intense images that dominated for a moment only to be quickly replaced.

The house itself was as expendable as the objects within it. Looking at the H.O.F. was like looking at a futuristic prototype of a car, which, while it has not arrived yet, will no doubt leave soon after it does. The H.O.F. was not a vision

---

14 Alison and Peter Smithson, "Staging the Possible," 16.
15 Ibid., 20. The publication reads "although staged," but in the copy in the A&P Smithson Archives, "although" is thoroughly crossed out, as if an annoying typo or a copy-editorial mistake.
16 Reyner Banham, "Things to Come: Architecture and Industry Look into the Future," *Design*, July 1956, 28.

17 Alison and Peter Smithson, "Staging the Possible," 18.
18 The Smithsons understood the H.O.F. not as a universal housing solution but as a model to be added to the existing stock of houses.

of how we would all live in the foreseeable future. It was not *the* house of 1981 but *a* "house of 1981," a vision of a type of house that might for a short while be added to the accumulated stock of already existing houses.[18]

Car

The Smithsons explicitly thought of the H.O.F. as a car, both in its concentrated attempt to provide a particular level of performance ("The House of the Future was designed—like a car—as one thing, for a limited role"[19]) and in its construction (the flexible gasket joints between the panels are like those in a refrigerator or a car). In this, they were obviously continuing another twentieth-century tradition, except that here the car is standing not only for a particular shape or a construction technique but also for mobility itself: "Mobility has become the characteristic of our period. Social and Physical mobility, the feeling of a certain kind of freedom. . . . And the symbol of that freedom is the individually owned motor car."[20] Unlike the luxury sports cars that Le Corbusier placed in front of his villas to emphasize their modernity or the minimal Citroën car that acted as his reference for the 1921 "mass-production house" Maison Citrohan,[21] the model of the Smithsons' house seems closer to the freedom offered by a caravan, a continual fascination of theirs. **310 311** As Alison wrote:

> Caravans are the nearest to an expendable architecture that the market has to offer. . . . For against the standard solution of the permanent dwelling, the caravan is neat, like a big piece of equipment; has a place for everything, like a well-run office; has miniature appliances in scale with the space, like a toy home; is as comfortable as this year's space-heated car, and like the car, the caravan represents a new freedom.[22]

One car in particular fascinated the Smithsons, the Citroën DS 19, designed the same year as the H.O.F. They would eventually acquire a DS—in fact, several models in succession: first the less expensive ID, then the DS 19, and finally the DS Safari station wagon. Echoing Le Corbusier, they photographed the car in front of their country house in Fonthill. **312** **313** Alison would write an entire book dedicated to the DS, *AS in DS*, a book that even took the shape of the car.[23] **314** The DS became (although perhaps only in retrospect) an explicit reference for the H.O.F. In a short typed manuscript entitled "1956 . . . The DS: The H.O.F. (AND DUBROVNIK!)," dated September 28, 2001, a very late entry to the H.O.F. file in A&P Smithson Archives, Peter wrote:

> My memory tells me that in 1956 Citroën launched its first post-war car, the Citroën D.S. It was a miraculous wholly new idea of a car. Its body-panels were visually and actually separated . . . water passed between them and was collected in a gutter-pressing behind; flowing out by air-pressure and gravity at low level. It was an aesthetic of explicit joints.
> DS = DÉESSE = GODDESS
> ID = IDÉE = IDEA
> The house of the future played a similar game of doubly-curved body panels and explicit joints. Joints whose placing quietly made the curvature apparent (like the seaming of jeans—which also made their first appearance outside of true North American work-clothes in the fifties).[24]

19 Alison and Peter Smithson, "The Appliance House," *Design*, May 1958, 47. Reprinted in Alison and Peter Smithson, *Changing the Art of Inhabitation* (London: Artemis, 1994), 115.

20 Alison and Peter Smithson, "Mobility," in *Architectural Design*, October 1958, 385–86, reprinted in Alison and Peter Smithson, *Ordinariness and Light: Urban Theories 1952–60, and Their Application in a Building Project* (Cambridge, MA: MIT Press, 1970), 144–53.

21 "'Citrohan' (not to say Citroën). That is to say, a house like a motor-car, conceived and carried out like an omnibus or a ship's cabin. The actual needs of the dwelling can be formulated and demand their solution." Le Corbusier, *Towards a New Architecture*, trans. F. Etchels (London: John Rodker 1931), 240.

22 Alison and Peter Smithson, *Changing*, 119. Originally published in a slightly different version in Alison Smithson, "Caravan, Embryo, Appliance House," *Architectural Design*, September 1959, 348.

23 Alison Smithson, *AS in DS: An Eye on the Road* (Delft: Delft University Press, 1983).

24 Peter Smithson, "1956 . . . The DS."

Peter's text alludes to Roland Barthes's famous ode to the DS, "The New Citroën," in *Mythologies* (1957), where he calls the DS the *Déesse* (the Goddess) and equates the cars of the time with "the great Gothic cathedrals," much as Le Corbusier had once famously associated the Delage and Voisin sports cars of his time with the Parthenon: "I mean," wrote Barthes, "the supreme creation of an era, conceived with passion by unknown artists, and consumed in image if not in usage by a whole population which appropriates them as a purely magical object."[25] The H.O.F., likewise, aspires to the magical status of a mass consumers' image.

In another sense the DS was for Barthes already architecture, more "homely" than a car: "The dashboard looks more like the working surface of a modern kitchen than the control room of a factory." Likewise for the Smithsons, it would seem that the DS was a combination of sports car, family car, and caravan (particularly in the station-wagon model, the DS Safari, that they later owned). In the 1950s, the house wanted to be more like a car and the car more like a house.

In *AS in DS*, which is constructed as a diary of life in the DS, mostly on the road from London to their country house in Fonthill and back, Alison writes about a car that has become a moving living room in a time of "car inhabitation," with children in the backseat drawing or playing invented board games to do with the car and architects sketching and photographing the landscape as seen through the windshield.[26] Snapshots of the car itself, photographed in the affectionate way usually reserved for family members, appear throughout the book with captions reminiscent of those portraying the life of a child: first photograph of DS, DS first trip north, DS in the grass after washing, DS in front of house at Fonthill, DS at a picnic, DS covered in snow, DS parked in Priory Walk (their home in London at the time) and last photograph of DS, in the snow.[27]

Like houses, cars could even have an effect on relationships. In 1982 Peter wrote:

> I remember thinking you were so close together in the Volks and so far apart in the DS your relationship as a married couple was bound to subtly change. Now you could stand off the situation of each other. Then it was love in a box. After it a big car was a kind of physical divorce.[28]

Perhaps the real influence in the H.O.F. was not the Citroën DS but the Volkswagen Beetle owned by the Smithsons at the time they were working on the project. **316** The working drawings for the H.O.F. were completed in October 1955, more or less at the same time the DS 19, which had been developed in great secrecy, was introduced at the Paris Motor Show.[29] The compact efficiency of the Beetle was closer to the logic of the house, a single shape with everything built into it. It is not by chance that Banham had used a beetle (the insect) as one of the illustrations accompanying his more substantial article on the H.O.F.[30] **317** The Smithsons' reference to the DS was an afterthought. In 1958, much closer to the time of the H.O.F., they wrote: "A house designed like a car is at some disadvantage, for the appliances would be so closely integrated into the structure, that to change the refrigerator would be like getting a larger glove compartment in a 'Volkswagen' dashboard—it would be simpler to get a new car."[31] The house

---

25 Roland Barthes, "The New Citroën," in *Mythologies* (1957), trans. Annette Lavers (New York: Hill and Wang, 1972), 88.

26 "Usually, a notebook has been carried in the Citroëns. In some period of car inhabitation we carried drawing books on the back floor, with the back ashtray full of pencil stubs and still in the early seventies used to find an occasional passenger had put ash among pencils." Alison Smithson, *AS in DS*, 15.

27 "Citroën ID 93 DLT at Upper Lawn, Fonthill, 1962"; "Citroën ID 93 DLT: picnic at Garesdale Head, spring 1965"; "Citroën DS 9 FGK at Upper Lawn, Fonthill, February 1966"; "Citroën DS 9 FGK in grass, after washing, Upper Lawn, Fonthill, September 1966"; "Citroën DS Safari's first trip north, autumn 1973"; "Citroën DS Safari: last photograph; in snow, in yard, Gilston Road, November 1981"; "Citroën CX Reflex: first photograph; in snow, in Priory Walk; November 1981." All in Alison Smithson, *AS in DS*, 157–63.

28 Peter Smithson in Alison Smithson, *AS in DS*, 13.

29 The DS was introduced on October 5, 1955, at the Paris Motor Show. The drawings of the house were also completed and submitted to the *Daily Mail* in October 1955.

30 Reyner Banham, "Things to Come," 27. Banham saw the structure of the house "on analogy with jointed, molded natural structures like a beetle's wing cases."

31 Alison and Peter Smithson, "The Appliance House," *Design*, May 1958, 47. Reprinted in Alison and Peter Smithson, *Changing*, 116.

had become expendable, a throwaway object. The H.O.F. not only looked like a car (has the shape of motion) and was conceived in terms of the prefabrication of cars but presumed in its program the mobility of its occupants. The house was designed for a "young couple without children": that is, sooner or later they would have to move.

Even the very idea of the house of the future was transient. By the end of 1956, the Smithsons had already moved on, leaving it to the following generation to pick up the thread. Banham expressed disappointment in his friends for having so abruptly abandoned the Pop and technological sensibility in their next project, Patio and Pavilion. When Archigram, obsessed with the ready-made architecture provided by the car, picked up and transformed the House of the Future, a fourth generation was born. As Peter Cook, a student of the Smithsons, put it:

> For those of us in the next generation, the puzzlement remained as to why the Smithsons chose not to continue on the line of exploration started by the House of the Future: and in the projects by my friends David Greene and Warren Chalk (the Pod and the Capsule respectively), homage is offered quite openly to them. Indeed one could, by the outset of the 1960s, select out one's own myopic segment of the Smithsons' work. . . . I could dream of a mechanised Cluster City invaded by stacked-up Houses of the Future.[32]

Clothing

Not by chance did the Smithsons think of cars also in terms of clothing. Indeed, they spoke of the Volkswagen as something that was worn rather than simply occupied, a close-fitting but comfortable garment rather than a room: "As for the Beatle [*sic*] generation—the mini got them. But for the middle-aged there is no forgetting your Volkswagen. It was not only love of animals or machines or sound (it was like a speed boat). You wore the Volks."[33]

Clothing was architecture for the Smithsons, one of their multiple media of operation. [318] [319] As Peter Cook has pointed out, they always wore the most remarkable clothes: "Certainly by the time that I came to London in the late '50s, they would stand out in a crowd by skilful wardrobeship in day-glo, loud checks, plastic, rubber, flags."[34] Alison was a talented dress designer and maker and perhaps this explains the built-in sewing machine in the H.O.F.—a rather incongruous piece of equipment for a future that anticipated the disappearance of housework, a future that envisioned every labor-saving device. [320] The H.O.F. catalog even points out that the laundry area had "enough space to cut out a dress" and a "work table at which one sits to sew and iron."[35] The future did not include prêt-a-porter! The design of the clothes of the future was carefully established. As a journalist described it: "FOR HIM.—A Superman space outfit of nylon sweats and tights with foam rubber fitted soles. FOR HER.—The Pixie look—a sort of nylon skirt with scalloped edge, and tights with high-heeled fitted soles."[36] [322] [324] [325] [343]

The clothes of the actors daily enacting the inhabitation of the house for the visitors of the exhibition were designed by Teddy Tinling, a prominent designer of sportswear who had designed tennis outfits for Wimbledon. "Therefore," Peter recalls, "the language he was speaking was of movement."[37]

Tinling first sought the opinion of a famous costume historian, James Laver.[38]

---

32 Peter Cook, "Regarding the Smithsons," *Architectural Review*, July 1982, 40.
33 Peter Smithson, *AS in DS*, 13.
34 Cook, "Regarding the Smithsons," 38.
35 "The Ideal Home Exhibition 'House of the Future,' 1956. General Statement," manuscript, n.d., 3, A&P Smithson Archives, London. The original 1956 text was edited by Peter Smithson, March 2000. See also Alison and Peter Smithson, "House of the Future," 99.
36 Arthur Butler, "Housewife's Dream—It May Be 1984," *News Chronicle*, March 6, 1956, clipping, A&P Smithson Archives, London.
37 Colomina, "Friends of the Future," 23.
38 Alison and Peter Smithson, "The House of the Future," 100.

To forecast the clothes of the future, the designer consulted a man whose business was to study the past—looking back to look forward:

> I am sure that the trend, already beginning, for more colour in men's clothing, will develop. Especially in the house, men will revert to the bright colours which they wore before the Industrial Revolution. . . . Through history women have emphasised their femininity by décolleté necklines, and our woman of the future will be no exception.[39]

The Smithsons specified not only what they were expecting from the designer but how the clothes were to be displayed, and they claimed the right over the ultimate control of the design.[40] Clothing, they requested from the *Daily Mail*, should recognize the "atmosphere" of the house, by which they meant not only the controlled temperature in the house but the intended feeling of "glamour":

> Clothes for the woman for other occasions should be in evidence. Nightdress (maybe laid out), clothes for outdoor cover, etc. (will be on view when demonstrator slided [sic] back the folding doors on a section of 'her' wardrobe). . . . The garments should not excite laughter, nor detract from the house or the equipment the people are trying to demonstrate. . . . The overall impression given the public should be one of glamour.[41]

Nevertheless, *Model Housekeeping* reported that the clothes of the H.O.F.'s occupants "raised the most laughs": "male mannequin modelling gent's underwear," with "hacked-off hair do," and wife on the "dressy side" with "lacquered hair and heavy bangles." On the other hand, Peter Smithson, looking back in 2000 to the future they had envisioned for 1981, saw the clothes of the visitors as the most absurd: "Recently, I printed my own pictures, taken during the constructions, which show the actors and ordinary people together and I thought that the ordinary people looked absolutely ridiculous."[42]

But perhaps more interesting than the clothing in the house was the way that the house itself was understood by the architects as a form of clothing, a kind of blue-jeans house whose "explicit" seams, like those of the DS, emphasized the curvature of the body: "Joints whose placing quietly made the curvature apparent (like the seaming of jeans—which also made their first appearance outside of true North American work-clothes in the fifties)."[43] Like jeans, the H.O.F. was to be a mass-produced generic product assembled from a single prosaic, utilitarian material stitched together with a pattern of visible seams—functional, comfortable, and stylish. You wore your H.O.F.

Spaceship

The allusion to clothes resonates again with Barthes, who had already read the DS in terms of clothes, but not just any clothes—not the workers' jeans—but the immaculate, smooth clothes of Christ: "The 'smoothness' of the DS," he wrote, was an "attribute of [its] perfection," like the "seamless[ness]" of "Christ's robe" and of "the airships of science-fiction." In other words, the DS was otherworldly, visiting us from another place, like a spaceship or a science-fiction craft. Barthes saw the new Citroën as a vehicle that in 1956 must "have fallen from the sky" or risen up from the depths like Jules Verne's submarine: "The *D.S.*—'the Goddess'—has all the features . . . of one of those objects from another universe which have supplied fuel for the neomania of the eighteenth century and that of our own

---

39 Ibid.
40 "The architects would like to see the ideas of the dress designer to check this before they are too far committed." "Life in The House of the Future," manuscript, November 6, 1955, A&P Smithson Archives, London.
41 Ibid.
42 Colomina, "Friends of the Future," 23.
43 Smithson, "1956 . . . The DS."

science-fiction: the *Deessé* is *first and foremost* a new *Nautilus*."⁴⁴ The H.O.F. was likewise a science-fiction vehicle. Even what was playing on TV reinforced the sense of a moving space cut out from the terrestrial world. The Smithsons requested from the *Daily Mail* that a color film such as "Captain Cousteau's under water-film" be shown on the back projection TV "to run longer than it would take a person to complete a circuit of the house." **297** The H.O.F. became a submarine moving underwater with the TV built into the wall as a porthole and with the gasket joints running across every surface, preventing any leaks. The entrance to the house even looked like a submarine door, punched through a thick bulkhead, or even an air lock—as if to enter the house was to go on a long voyage. **326**

The H.O.F. was a "Space House," both in the sense of Kiesler's project Space House of 1933, where the curved skin already acted as the structure, and in the look and logic of the recently launched space program—a spaceship. **327** A significant part of the *Daily Mail* exhibition of 1956 was dedicated to the space program and filled with imaginary rockets and spaceships. It was the jubilee year, and the newspaper celebrated with a special display that looked back sixty years and tried to imagine sixty years ahead. The H.O.F. was commissioned to tie in with this display. It was the first time since the 1930s that the *Daily Mail* Ideal Home Exhibition had included a House of the Future.⁴⁵ But the Smithsons argued that you could accurately predict only twenty-five years ahead and chose this time frame for their H.O.F.:

> Why 25 years?: Because we found that consensus of opinion among the experts we consulted was that this period is likely to produce as many revolutionary

---

44 Barthes, "The New Citroën."
45 The first house of the future at the *Daily Mail* Ideal Home Exhibition was designed by architects S. Rowland Pierce and R. A. Duncan in 1928. It was a modernist house and anticipated many of the themes of the 1956 H.O.F., including the prediction that the house would be replaceable like a car. It also forecast color TV, automated household tasks and atomic energy. Deborah S. Ryan, *Daily Mail–Ideal Home Exhibition: The Ideal Home through the 20th Century* (London: Hazar Publishing, 1997), 113.

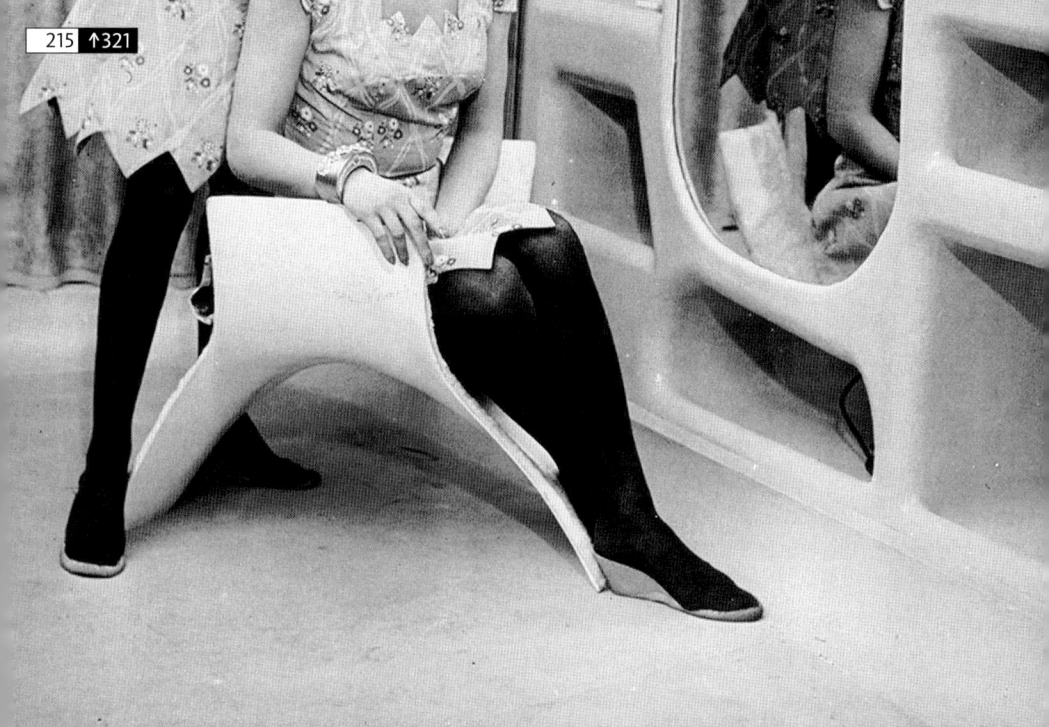

changes as the past one hundred years; changes not only in our way of life, but also in the design and techniques of building the homes in which we shall live.[46]

These radical changes included the conquest of space. Allusions to space fantasies were numerous in the H.O.F., starting with the architects' request to the organizers of the *Daily Mail* exhibition that among the list of objects to be included in the house should be a book, to lie open "at a space man plate" on one of the chairs, and a "snap of someone on MARS" to be placed in a silver frame in a compartment of the dressing room.[47] Correspondence between the Smithsons and Kenneth Corney, assistant organizer of the Ideal Home Exhibition, speaks of his efforts to find such an image: "I have covered such films as 'Rocket Ship', 'This Island Earth', 'It Came from Outer Space', and 'Thresholds of Space'. The most promising title was, of course, 'Destination Moon' this film was shown in 1950 but unfortunately the makers of it cannot now be traced in this country. They appear to have shipped themselves abroad to Turkey."[48]

The food in the house was radiated and packaged in airtight containers for long-term storage as if occupants had to survive an extended period of time in isolation. **302** Even the clothes designer forecasted the future of dressing in terms of the space program, attempting to translate the radical look of the space suit to everyday life: "The clothes worn by the man are plain and unembellished. This is in keeping with the times, a kind of Superman trend to fit in with the Space Age." Women, on the other hand, "will wear ultra-feminine clothes in the home. Out-of-doors their clothes will have to be almost as severe as men's. A woman's space suit, for instance, will be much the same as a man's. As a reaction to this, I feel sure she will want light, pretty clothes to wear in her well-heated home."[49] The popular press echoed these references with headlines such as "All Dressed for the Future"[50] or "When the Future Was Skin-Tight"[51] and using Tinling's words to describe the clothes: "Superman trend to fit with the space age," and so on.

Peep Show

The H.O.F. was both a house on exhibit and an exhibitionist house, a peep show. With its windowless facade and forbidden access, viewing the house meant peeping through openings made in the walls specially for that purpose, to see a couple, sometimes two couples, at home enacting the domestic life of the future—women wearing sexy miniskirts (ten years before British designers introduced them) and the men in tights, supermen of the future, as Tingling suggested, or men in underwear, as the popular press read it. The H.O.F. assumed, as the Smithsons put it, a "leisure time" with both husband and wife at home. Newsreels covering the 1956 *Daily Mail* exhibition show footage of the H.O.F. with the woman picking up a black lace semitransparent nightgown off the bed and holding it against her body for the man sitting on the bed. A photograph, among those circulated in the press, shows two almost identical couples in the bedroom, the black nightgown spread out on the bed, which makes one wonder what exactly is going on there, in this highly sexualized interior, with all those curved walls. **322** The bed, the bathtub, and all the basins are red; the curtains are orange; and the partly translucent honey-colored walls give a voyeuristic sense of x-ray vision. The bed is in the middle of the space, a theatrical stage with electronic controls. **328** The extreme visibility of the bathtub from the courtyard, through the transparent walls, "assumes," as Peter said in a late interview, "that the occupants are young people, when the body is still beautiful"[52]—the private house as an erotic space for both those inside it and those looking in. **300**

---

46 Alison and Peter Smithson, "House of the Future," 97.
47 "List of objects not covered by contract drawings or architect," manuscript, November 3, 1955, A&P Smithson Archives, London.
48 Kenneth Corney to Mr. Smithson, February 13, 1956, A&P Smithson Archives, London.
49 Alison and Peter Smithson, "House of the Future," 100.
50 Butler, "Housewife's Dream."
51 Dan O'Brien, "When the Future Was Skin-Tight," April 23, 1956, clipping, A&P Smithson Archives, London.
52 Colomina, "Friends of the Future," 22.

But is it the house itself or the occupants who are sexy? Despite the suggestive setup, the feeling of the enactment of life in the H.O.F. is rather aseptic. The separate headrests of the bed, for example, suggest those of car seats, as if the inhabitants were about to take off. The house itself, on the other hand, is highly sexualized. A series of organic shapes, a body of honey-colored translucent skin, and pimento red orifices, organized around a central, folded, furry opening: a sexual organ pushed into the face of the viewer like Marcel Duchamp's *Etant donnés*. **329**

Nineteen fifty-six was, after all, also the year of the first *Playboy* house. The *Playboy* Penthouse was published in the September and October issues of the magazine as a stage set for *Playboy*'s sexually liberated lifestyle.[53] **330** **331** The H.O.F. was related, on the one hand, to the American dream house of the 1950s as depicted in the advertisements the Smithsons collected—with the happy housewife surrounded by her new gadgets—and, on the other hand, to the *Playboy* house with swinging couples endlessly playing with their toys. Like those houses, the H.O.F. used the latest technologies and made housework disappear, transformed into a push-button game, a form of play.

The H.O.F. included all the latest electronic technologies available or imagined. **332** The telephone had loudspeakers to broadcast the conversation to the entire house and an earpiece to allow for privacy. In anticipation of the answering machine, the phone was connected to a tape recorder so it could take messages when the inhabitants where away or busy. Panels on the walls controlled the temperature and light, opened the front door, and made the dining-room table go up or down to coffee-table level or disappear completely. The TV/radio had a short-wave transmitter (proto–remote control) in the shape of a big die, which also controlled the table. **324** There were no children in this house, because the adults themselves had become children, playing with their toys, with their new electric gadgets, the peekaboo table and bed, the electrically operated doors, and so on. The most important symbols of domestic space, the table and the bed, were those that could be made to disappear without a trace, sinking into the floor as if the floor, like the walls, were a storage system and the house a flexible space that could hide its actual function. **333** A house in camouflage? A disappearing house? Or a theatrical stage set where fantasies of the future were scrutinized by an ever-curious, constantly watching audience?

Despite the fact that the presumed time of the H.O.F. was 1981 (twenty-five years from 1956),[54] reporters kept calling it the house of 1984 and referring to George Orwell's famous 1949 novel. "The loudspeaker telephone, the aluminium foil walls that form 'a discontinuous membrane between all houses,' the omnipresent eye of the colour television sets—these suggest 1984 more than 1981,"[55] read a review in a local newspaper, while another saw the house as "a cross between a Roman villa, a South American patio, and George Orwell's *1984* without the nightmare element."[56] An article in yet another newspaper was headlined "Housewife's Dream—It May Be 1984" and went on to say, "The year is 1984. If Big Brother is watching he will see that TIGHTS are definitely The Thing to wear."[57] **334**

Surveillance turned into voyeurism, which makes sense since the H.O.F. turned all viewers into voyeurs, even voyeurs of voyeurs. When walking along the avenue of the Ideal Home Exhibition, casual passersby could not look through the windows of the house in the same way they could with the other, more traditional

---

[53] Beatriz Preciado, "Pornotopia," in *Cold War/Hot Houses: From Cockpit to Playboy*, ed. Beatriz Colomina, Annmarie Brennan, and Jeannie Kim (New York: Princeton Architectural Press, 2004).

[54] "Why 25 years?: Because we found that consensus of opinion among the experts we consulted was that this period is likely to produce as many revolutionary changes as the past one hundred years; changes not only in our way of life, but also in the design and techniques of building the homes in which we shall live." Alison and Peter Smithson, "House of the Future," 97.

[55] "'Homes Past, Present and Future: The Ideal with a Touch of Fantasy' from our London Staff," clipping, A&P Smithson Archives, London.

[56] "A Look at Acacia-avenue, 1980, By 'Star' reporter," clipping, A&P Smithson Archives, London.

[57] Butler, "Housewife's Dream."

houses in the exhibition. The H.O.F. was isolated from the rest of the exhibition, at the end of a double row of conventional houses, closing that avenue. 294 295 It was encased in a box of blank walls, except for a horizontal slit at eye level running through the long facades that allowed peeking inside only when one was very close to the wall. 335 Thus the curious passerby became a voyeur looking at the other voyeurs, those inside the outer case who were looking at the actors playing out the life of the future. The outsiders look at the insiders looking at the inhabitants who look at one another. At a certain point, the eye might be able to pass through all the layers and see all the way through to the other side of the exhibition hall. But only by entering the case could the outsider see what the insider saw. And neither could see what the inhabitants saw.

Actual visitors to the house, unable to enter it, would peek inside through the viewing holes in the walls from the corridors surrounding the house at ground level or from the viewing platforms in the upper level where much of the roof had been removed to expose the interior, like in a doll's house. 293 296 336 The visitors occupying the gap between the two containers were carefully isolated from the rest of the *Daily Mail* exhibition—inside a case but unable to walk into the house. They looked inside it in complete absorption, as if watching a film or a TV program (in those early TV years, when spans of attention were longer) or a peep show.

The viewing mechanism resembled that of Adolf Loos's project for a House for Josephine Baker, another box inside a box with the visitors occupying the space between the walls, looking in through windows at a sexualized void, the swimming pool where the naked body of Josephine Baker moved.[58] The seductively fluid H.O.F. that viewers were seeing from behind walls was all Alison. In an interview in the summer of 2000, Peter said to me in passing that "the house of the future was entirely Alison's design."[59] While Alison was alive they had always referred to the H.O.F. as common work. But the original working drawings of the house, completed in late October 1955, were signed by A.M.S. (Alison Margaret Smithson), and the drawings of the "outer case" are by P.S. In that way, they reproduced in their work the traditional gender division. Alison's design was all interior, while Peter dealt with the "outside." But it is not so easy to separate the house from the case, Alison from Peter. Correspondence in the archives shows both of them deeply involved in the fabrication of the house, the furniture, the choice of objects, the contract, the press, and so on. Even if the house was carefully detailed in a different way and the case never touched the house,[60] they nevertheless combined to become one house. Indeed, the H.O.F. was produced as much by the exhibition as for it. The house was not simply put into the exhibition and framed by the case; its shoebox shape actually seemed to be coming from its allotted site in the exhibition hall. First sketches for the project saw it as a square with a round hole in the middle, and the architects spoke of using such exhibitions to go beyond their own aesthetic, beyond themselves: "Since our opportunities to build come so rarely, we always seize exhibition opportunities to project our ideas beyond our aesthetic—as if our ideas had already leavened the situation."[61]

The openings that had to be cut into the walls of the house to make its interior visible act like movie or TV screens temporarily set up for viewing the house. **296** Their detailing is clumsy, as if to make clear that they are not part of the design of the house itself. The big ones looking into the living room and bedroom could be mistaken for picture windows, but they are crudely detailed and at odds with the smooth, curved, precise look of the house. A series of small openings punched

58 For a reading of Josephine Baker's house see Beatriz Colomina, *Privacy and Publicity: Modern Architecture as Mass Media* (Cambridge, MA: MIT Press, 1994), 255–64, 280–81.
59 Colomina, "Friends of the Future," 17.
60 This was deliberate. In the manuscript "Suggestions for Outer Case and Viewing Platforms" they wrote, "The House and the surrounding structure should be absolutely separate." A&P Smithson Archives, London.
61 Alison and Peter Smithson, "Thirty Years of Thoughts on the House and Housing," in Denys Lasdun, *Architecture in the Age of Scepticism* (New York: Oxford University Press, 1984), 178.

an all-in-... colour TV
...switch
pressing buttons on a short-
wave transmitter which looks
like a giant dice. Good idea.
Two people called Anne and
Peter were showing us around
the house. They live there.
Their clothes are quite unusual,
but they say they are very comfortable. And they don't have
to iron anything because it's
all nylon.

... bed in the house has bright-
... nylon sheets, and you don't
... any blankets because the
temperature of the house is
... just right all the time.

... a lovely springy bed and
a funny shaped pillow was
... per, although lying on it made
... feel as if we were waiting to
... our heads chopped off,
... in the story-book.

... didn't want to leave the
... then. Almost everything
... to be electric.

... were no boiling rings, and
... just plug in all the frying-
... and saucepans and you
... all the dirty dishes in a
... and push them straight
into a dish-washer in the wall
which washes and dries them
and gobbles up all the scraps.

No answer

You can speak to anybody at
the front door by moving a
switch in the kitchen. We
showed it and said to the milk-
man: "Ten pints of milk
please." Then someone asked
us who we thought was going to
drink it. We didn't answer.

The house is built around a garden. Topsy-turvy, isn't it? But
just like any other house it had
a rainwater butt. This one was
built high so that nobody could
fall in.

Well, just about now we felt
hungry. Luckily we had some
sandwiches in our knapsacks.

Then we sat down to try to
remember all the things which
we had seen and forgotten to
make notes about.

No dust

And we remembered that the
roof was covered with
aluminium foil to reflect the
rays of the sun.

And that the walls were sound-
proof and fireproof;

And that the walls, floor and
ceiling were honey-coloured
with brown joints;

And that there was air conditioning which took away all
smells, such as cooking;

And that no dust at all could
get in the house;

And that in the living room was
an Italian standard lamp called
a relic of the past which was
made in 1955;

And that all the food like meat,
milk, butter, and fish had been
bombarded with gamma rays to
kill germs;

And that ... but just about now
we felt hungry again and we'd
eaten all our sandwiches, so we
asked if it was tea-time and
someone said tea-time had come

THE LIVING ROOM...with the gadgets which will one day be everyday

THE KITCHEN...with Hugh finding out

225 ↑347

into the outside wall corresponding to the dressing room are particularly confusing because their irregular shape and organic size resemble many of the interior details, bringing the openings closer to the spirit of the house. Perhaps for this reason, the Smithsons will have to insist their entire life that the openings in the H.O.F. were not windows,[62] eventually redrawing the plans and the axonometric so as to remove the viewing holes in the walls and roof and show how the house was meant to be understood.[63] But the image of the perforated walls has become indelible. The house is understood to have a hyperexposed interior, a space that is meant to be looked into and to reveal its seductive secrets.

In fact, the simulated occupants were not simply caught in the act of their private lives. They often looked back out at the visitors, as if looking directly at the camera, addressing the viewers on the other side of the walls. A photograph shows Ann in the kitchen, holding a microphone and explaining the "features and processes" of the house to the viewers on the walkways above. ▮336 The house was a three-dimensional television set even before it was broadcast on BBC and made part of newsreels. Like the *Big Brother* houses of today, the H.O.F. was closed to the outside by walls but wired to the world through the media. The house circulated not only through magazines and newspapers but also on TV and newsreels. Most remarkable, the H.O.F. itself was a media machine. More than including all the latest developments available or imagined, it actually broadcast itself. Throughout the day, the two "residents, dressed in the probable clothes of the period," explained the "modern intricacies" of the house over a loudspeaker system.[64] Submarines, spaceships, *Playboy* houses, and *Big Brother* houses are all intensely interiorized worlds that broadcast their intimacy through a multiplicity of media.

The H.O.F. was intensely privatized, closed to the outside, an architecture of paranoia, and yet relentlessly on exhibit, broadcasting its secrets: radical withdrawal combined with radical exposure. The image of playful domestic life that it transmitted cannot be separated from a fear of the outside. The H.O.F. cannot be separated from the thought of war. It was an escape both from the threats of the present and from the fresh memories of World War II. Like the *Playboy* house, the H.O.F. was itself a mechanism of escape, an all-interior space the overly happy inhabitants would never need to leave. A bunker.

Bunker

The H.O.F. is a kind of bomb shelter. There is no outside. The house is only an inside. The inside of an inside of an inside. A box (the H.O.F.) inside another box (the outer case) inside an exhibition hall (Olympia). Like a submarine or a spaceship, the walls of the craft are pierced at only one key point where entry is infrequent and carefully controlled. **326** The house is entirely closed to the outside except for the electrically operated steel door (controlled from the hall or the kitchen) that suggests hermetic closure by coming down between two very thick sets of walls to seal the house from the outside. Visitors can announce their business by ringing and be answered without entry. Postman and deliveryman leave their packages in either of two hatches by the door that can be accessed from the inside. The few visitors allowed entry find themselves "in the hallway facing the first of the fibreglass curtains that can be drawn to veil the rest of the house."[65] The structure smoothly seals itself off from the dangerous outside with a series of prophylactic layers.

---

[62] "The holes in the outside walls and the roof shown on this drawing are for the purposes of the exhibition . . . to allow visitors to see the inside without gaining access." Label of an axonometric drawing of the H.O.F., drawing HF5602, by A.S., 1956, A&P Smithson Archives, London.
[63] "In 1992 therefore to correct this, a new set of drawings was made of the volumes as they would be—that is without the holes." It was in connection with these new drawings that Peter acknowledged in a manuscript Alison's sole authorship of the H.O.F.: "This new set of drawings made in 1997, with exactly the same format as the originals, fills-in, as it were, the openings in the walls and roof to show the interior spaces as they were conceived by Alison Smithson in the years 1955–1956." Peter Smithson, "Drawings of Explanations from the House of the Future," manuscript, September 19, 1997, A&P Smithson Archives, London.
[64] "Latest Household Gadgets on Show," *Evening Dispatch* (Edinburgh), June 29, 1956.
[65] "Ideal Home Exhibition 'House of the Future,'" 2.

Food is stored and preserved for a long stay, and rainwater is collected from the roof, allowing inhabitants to eventually cut themselves off: **338** "Raw meat, milk, butter and even fresh fish are stored in quantities in a cupboard . . . packed in air tight plastics containers. . . . All the food is bombarded with gamma rays—an atomic byproduct to kill all bacteria. . . ."[66] Even this language of bombardment and atomic rays is the language of war: "You don't grill a steak here. You bombard it with gamma rays," said the *Daily Mail*.[67]

Bomb shelters, submarines, and spaceships defend themselves against the ultimate hostile environment outside. The latest technologies are used to establish a sense of security. Yet the Smithsons claim their inspiration for the H.O.F. had been an archaic form of architecture, the Caves Les Baux de Provence, near Remy, in the south of France, which they had visited in 1953. **339** They speak of the space of the H.O.F. as rooms of different sizes, shapes, and heights that flow into one another like the compartments of a cave. And as in a cave, "the skewed passage that joins one compartment to another effectively maintains privacy."[68] **340** Cave dwelling, like bomb shelters, submarines, and spaceships, corresponds to a time of extreme danger outside. Caves are all interiorized spaces, the first bunkers.

The elaborate plans, in the end unrealized, for an artificial sun (built as a light, open metalwork sphere, seven feet in diameter, with orange tungsten lamps projected radially over the whole surface and suspended from the Exhibition Hall roof) and a floating cloud (made of pale blue nylon stretched over a metal frame suspended from the roof and spot lit from above),[69] prefigured the bunker houses of the postwar years, in particular the "Underground House" presented at the New York World's Fair of 1964, where visitors descended into a kind of cave, an underground walled artificial garden, a safe space containing a freestanding suburban house.⁷⁰ 293 298 414 415 416 417 The walls of the house were protected by a second set of walls, producing a box inside a box.

Like the H.O.F., Patio and Pavilion of later the same year was a building of disaster, a tranquil garden erected in the face of an imagined horror. As Peter wrote: "Patio and Pavilion presented a sense of completeness—territory, pavilion, objects of occupation—complete in the sense of walking into a house abandoned by the owners during the course of the evening meal, or into a ruined mine shut down by impending disaster and never re-opened."⁷¹ This sense of disaster had already been picked up by early critics such as Banham, who responded to those who had described the exhibit as "the garden-shed aesthetic" by adding, "one could not help feeling that this particular garden shed, with its rusted bicycle wheels, a battered trumpet and other homely junk, had been excavated after the atomic holocaust."⁷² Later critics such as Kenneth Frampton also spoke of Patio and Pavilion as embodying the aesthetics of the day after, the landscape of waste, and war.

Despite Banham's criticism of their apparent turn from an idealized object for a perfect future to an archaic ruin in a destroyed landscape—or perhaps in response to it—the Smithsons repeatedly insisted on the continuity between the two projects: "Many of the ideas in Patio and Pavilion . . . had already been explored in the Spring of that same year in the House of the Future. . . . Patio and Pavilion was a pavilion in a patio. The House of the Future was a patio encapsuled by its pavilion."⁷³ Both patios were embattled. The absurdly happy, shiny world

---

66 Alison and Peter Smithson, "House of the Future," 99.
67 *Daily Mail*, March 6, 1956, late ed., partial clipping, A&P Smithson Archives, London.
68 Alison and Peter Smithson, "House of the Future," 97.
69 "Ideal Homes. House of the Future. Suggestions for Outer Case and Viewing Platforms." See also drawing 5526.

70 On the Underground House at the New York Fair of 1964, see chapter 8.
71 Alison Smithson, "Patio and Pavilion, 1956," 11.
72 Reyner Banham, *The New Brutalism: Ethic or Aesthetic?* (Stuttgart: Reinhold Publishing, 1966), 65.
73 Alison Smithson, "Patio and Pavilion, 1956," 10.

of American advertising for the perfect domestic life, embraced so fully by the H.O.F., was in fact a landscape of fear, a deceptive symptom of cultural paranoia. The H.O.F. was full of defenses. Almost every detail of the house can be explained as a defensive system against pollution, noise, dust, cold, views, germs, and visitors. It was precisely by actively countering each one of those threats that the H.O.F. was able to produce an image of idealized perfection, to construct the sense of "absolute tranquillity" in the face of the danger outside that Jules Verne describes for his science-fiction submarine:

> On the NAUTILUS men's hearts never fail them, No defects to be afraid of, for the double shell is as firm as iron, no rigging to attend to; no sails for the wind to carry away; no boilers to burst; no fire to fear, for the vessel is made of iron, not of wood; no coal to run short, for electricity is the only power; no collision to fear, for it alone swims in deep water; no tempest to brave, for when it dives below the water, it reaches absolute tranquillity. That is the perfection of vessels.[74]

Air

In the H.O.F., this tranquillity is to be found in the small garden at its center. **348** But while the double skin of the Nautilus allows its occupants to inhabit the ship without fear, the occupants of the H.O.F. live inside the double skin that surrounds the tranquil center. The house is basically a series of rooms wrapped en suite in a single loop around a green space. **340** Or, rather, the house is produced by wrapping a string of spaces around a garden, a fragment of the idealized outside that now appears at the heart of the inside. In this garden the Smithsons try to "recreate a piece of the country": a small patch of grass, deliberately kept "wild, rather than lawn turf—perhaps even with a moss base and scattered with spring flowers.

... A small tree ... in the centre of the widest part of the garden. A rock or boulder ... placed somewhere."[75] The garden, which the drawings insist on calling a "patio," is a peaceful site surrounded and preserved by the defensive mechanisms of the house. Daily life involves constantly removing any traces of the outside, as if in preparation for finally entering the garden.

The house's stubborn defense against the outside continues inside in a battle against all forms of contamination. Those few who enter the house by passing into the air lock in its hull are immediately subjected to a decontamination procedure that keeps the outside air out: "To admit the visitor the occupant operates the shutter control and automatically the anti-draught blast of warm air from the grille under the door comes into operation."[76] **326** From the front door, the visitor then passes through a curtain of warm air to remove dust. The house is air-conditioned throughout, and all smells are mechanically extracted. At the time, the United States was introducing the concept of air conditioners for widespread domestic use. Advertisements for window units used x-rays of lungs. Air conditioning stood for health as much as for comfort. Not by chance does the H.O.F. depicted in perspective resemble a lung inside a box, becoming, in its community form, a mat cluster of boxed lungs. The city of the future is a city of artificial lungs. **341** **342**

Not only is the air systematically controlled and purified, but every surface is obsessively cleansed of any trace of dirt, dust, or germs. The house's continuous surface with round corners, the architects insist, is easily maintained with a damp cloth. The sunken bathtub fills from the bottom and has an automatic rinsing system that swills down the bath with a foamless detergent. **343** The WC is "a room in

[74] Jules Verne, *Twenty Thousand Leagues under the Sea*, 1869.
[75] Alison and Peter Smithson, "General Statement," manuscript, n.d.,
A&P Smithson Archives, London.
[76] Ibid., 2.

its own right . . . and its continuously spinning self-digesting unit needs no flushing mechanism and makes no noise." The "glass" wall to the garden is "self-washing externally."[77] A "portable electro-static dust collector works on its own replacing the traditional vacuum cleaner to remove the little dust that may creep in."[78]

Towels are considered a health hazard. The shower in the bathroom is also a drier, with nozzles for water and warm air. **345** Disposable paper-towel dispensers are installed near all water sources. **344** A sun lamp is built into the lavatory wall. The bed has only one fitted nylon sheet because the controlled temperature of the house eliminates the need for bedclothes.[79] And so on and on. Even posture was carefully attended to in the H.O.F. as another form of hygiene.[80]

In the search for a completely controlled environment, the obsession with dust, hygiene, and cleanliness, the H.O.F. echoed Buckminster Fuller's Dymaxion House of 1927–29, which was also entirely air-conditioned, made free of dust, germs, and domestic drudgery. **346** Even the single fitted sheet on the bed recalls the Dymaxion House. In a famous photograph of Fuller with the model of the house, a naked doll has been laid on top of the bed to emphasize that the house was warm. (Or should one say hot? A less well-known photograph of the same model removes any doubt by showing the figure of a man in a business suit arriving home to find three naked dolls lounging around looking up at him.) Fuller's curvy Dymaxion bathroom was another obvious reference, as Banham had already pointed out: a seamless, molded, self-supporting, self-cleaning, lightweight, mass-produced unit that did with metal in the mid-1930s what the Smithsons did with plastic in the mid-1950s.

Yet Fuller's defenses against the outside also included defenses against surrounding buildings. His houses were disconnected from any fixed infrastructural links to the city. They were always ready to move, mobile even when seemingly fixed.

Likewise, all of the H.O.F.'s mechanisms echoed the way the disconnected moving private car kept the outside at bay by creating a supercontrolled environment, an enclave protected from the violent world outside:

> For the majority of people, the most interesting, carefree companionable times are spent in their cars; "Sealed in a glass box on wheels," we—again used in the collective sense—do not sense the air outside, smell something only after it has passed through the ventilation system, we read the weather through the glass of the windscreen or the side windows, feel the sun through this glass, are wonderfully protected from the most violent of storms in the wildest landscapes. This is a normality.[81]

This extremely controlled environment involved a new concept of privacy. Fuller had detached his domestic spaces from the surrounding local environment in order to make connection with the macro-environment, the planetary system. As his research on geodesic domes evolved, his houses increasingly asked the occupant to look up at the sky—a departure from the Dymaxion and Wichita houses, which framed a horizontal, all-around view of the world immediately outside. But from the first plastic "Garden of Eden" dome constructed at Black Mountain College in 1948 to the "sky-break" houses of the early 1950s, the primary purpose of the building was simply to create a controlled environment, an idyllic garden in which the occupants could claim the sky above as their own territory, "your private sky," as Fuller put it.[82]

77 Ibid., 2–3.
78 "How We May Live 25 Years From Now," *Evening Dispatch* (Edinburgh), June 29, 1956.
79 Fitted sheets were then unknown in England, and the clothes designer had to mock them up.
80 In the kitchen all fittings are above waist level, even the storage cupboard. This was often pointed out by the popular press. For some years after World War I, the Ideal Home Exhibition was replaced by the Efficiency Exhibition, which focused on the disabled (war veterans). Labor-saving devices in the workplace proposed in the Efficiency Exhibition have much in common with those proposed for the domestic sphere in the Ideal Home Exhibition. Ryan, *Daily Mail–Ideal Home*, 40.
81 Alison Smithson, *AS in DS*, 17.
82 See Joachim Krausse and Claude Lichtenstein, eds., *Your Private Sky: R. Buckminster Fuller, the Art of Design Science* (Baden: Lars Müller, 1999).

For the Smithsons, Patio and Pavilion was linked to the H.O.F. because "both speak to a portion of the sky, for this was also the period in which we had created our 'Private Sky' diagram that would allow dwellings their right to address a portion of the sky with its, as yet unbreathed air."[83] **347** Patio and Pavilion, which does not look like a house, was a "symbolic habitat" precisely because it responded to basic human needs such as "a view of the sky." In the H.O.F., the only view outside is up, with the house framing the sky as in a photograph. In fact, "there was preliminary discussion as to the feasibility of a mock-up of a winterseason-closure—as a camera's shutter—over the patio."[84] If Le Corbusier's house was a camera pointing horizontally to the landscape outside it, the H.O.F. ignored the horizontal landscape to face the vertical landscape. It was a camera pointing up, to the sky, to outer space—a kind of telescope looking beyond the contemporary world. In 1956, with Sputnik about to be launched, the spatial order was about to change. Site was no longer global, as it had become with the previous generation of modern architects, but planetary. The house itself was in orbit. Superman was everyman in the space age.

A change from the "venerable pavilions" of the Modern Movement, L'Esprit Nouveau, Barcelona, and so on, is that "we try to protect the occupants,"[85] wrote Alison. But protect them from what? What did this image of a secure "private sky" mean to a generation that had grown up during the war, watching the sky for bombers, a sky that could at any moment become the source of the most extreme threat? Alison, who lived on the Tyne during a period of aerial bombardments, wrote eloquently about her childhood experience, "sky-watching" with her father's makeshift telescope. As Peter later told me: "Children of that age were able to identify planes like butterflies."[86] The garden of her house, which had high walls, had to be turned first into an "air raid shelter built of re-creosoted railway sleepers; then, as the war settled in, had built a concrete skin to make the back scullery a dry shelter: all in a period of eighteen months . . . while I was evacuated."[87] This scene of a walled garden with a protective box inside it would literally return in Patio and Pavilion. The garden at the center of the H.O.F. is therefore best understood as a safe space in an imaginary world after or before fear. Indeed, its precise purpose seems to be to use the latest technology, real or imagined, to reconstruct the garden that preceded all technologies, all fear: the Garden of Eden.

It was in fact a fifteenth-century German panel painting, *The Garden of Paradise* (ca. 1410–20), by the Master of Middle-Rhine, that was one of the "conscious cribs" of the H.O.F., according to Peter—the other one being the caves of Les Baux.[88] **349** It is not just that the coloration for the house had been taken this painting, as he said, but that the entire scene is reproduced in the house. The Smithsons requested from the *Daily Mail* exhibition organizers that the garden include a tree, some spring flowers, water, a bird (for which they provided a molded drinking bowl on the counter), a musical instrument "appropriate for the future," and so on. Even the design of the one-legged, hexagonal plastic dining table comes directly from the painting, as does the big cushion for sitting in the living room.

The garden in the H.O.F. is all about Edenic innocence and purity. The primary role of the house is to filter out the world and produce a quasi-theological encounter with an empty sky, a sky made private by the house. In a certain sense, the house allows the sky to come down to touch the inhabitant. The air of the house

---

83 Alison Smithson, "Patio and Pavilion, 1956," 10.
84 Peter Smithson, "The House of the Future, Ideal Home Exhibition, Olympia, end August 1955 to March 1956."
85 Alison Smithson, "Patio and Pavilion, 1956," 10.
86 Colomina, "Friends of the Future," 10.

87 Alison Smithson, "Outbreak of War, 1939, February 7, 1989," manuscript, A&P Smithson Archives, London, reprinted in Colomina, "Friends of the Future," 12.
88 Colomina, "Friends of the Future," 24.

is cleansed to make way for a pure "as yet unbreathed air" to descend into the void and then into the body of the inhabitants—uncannily anticipating the current obsession with unbreathed air in airplanes, restaurants, and public buildings. Unbreathed air as the ultimate measure of privacy in an ever more congested world.

Air, then, rather than plastic, is the real material of the house. Unbreathed air with a glass wall wrapped around it, which in turn is wrapped by a blank wall, which in turn is wrapped by another wall, and then by an exhibition hall, and then by a city. The Smithsons built a hole. They took an empty space, and all the rest of the design was just a means of fixing that emptiness. Is it any wonder that this house will always elude our grasp?

Chapter 7
Enclosed by Images

1.

We are surrounded today, everywhere, all the time, by arrays of multiple, simultaneous images—in the streets, airports, shopping centers, and gyms but also on our computers and television sets. **350** **351** **352** The idea of a single image commanding our attention has faded away. It seems as if we need to be distracted in order to concentrate, as if we—all of us living in this new kind of space, the space of information—could be diagnosed en masse with attention deficit disorder. The state of distraction in the metropolis, described so eloquently by Walter Benjamin early in the twentieth century, seems to have been replaced by a new form of distraction, which is to say, a new form of attention. Rather than wander cinematically through the city, we now look in one direction and see many juxtaposed moving images, more than we can possibly synthesize or reduce to a single impression. We sit in front of our computers on our ergonomically perfected chairs, staring with a fixed gaze at many simultaneously "open" windows through which different kinds of information stream toward us. We hardly even notice it. It seems natural, as if we were simply breathing in the information.

How would one go about writing a history of this form of perception? Should one go back to the organization of the television studio, with its wall of monitors from which the director chooses the camera angle that will be presented to the viewer or should one look at the control rooms of Electronic Data Systems or traffic networks; or should one go to Cape Canaveral and look at its mission-control room; or should one even go back to World War II, when so-called situation rooms were envisioned with multiple projections bringing information from all over the world and presenting it side by side for instant analysis by political leaders and military commanders? **353** **354** **356** **357** **358**

But it is not simply the military or war technology that has defined this new form of perception. Designers, architects, and artists were involved from the beginning, playing a crucial role in the evolution of the multiscreen and multimedia techniques of information presentation. While artists' use of these techniques tends to be associated with the Happenings and expanded cinema of the 1960s, architects were involved much earlier and in very different contexts, such as military operations and governmental propaganda campaigns.

Take the 1959 American National Exhibition in Moscow, where the government enlisted some of the country's most sophisticated designers. **361** **359** Site of the famous Kitchen Debate between Richard Nixon and Nikita Khrushchev, the exhibition was a cold-war operation in which the Eameses' multiscreen technique turned out to be a powerful weapon.

To reconstruct a little bit of the atmosphere: The USA and USSR had agreed in 1958 to exchange national exhibits on "science, technology and culture." The Soviet exhibition opened in the New York Coliseum at Columbus Circle in New York City in June 1959, and the American exhibition opened in Sokolniki Park in Moscow in July of the same year. Vice President Nixon, in Moscow to open the exhibition, engaged in a heated debate with Khrushchev over the virtues of the American way of life. **360** The exchange became known as the Kitchen Debate because it took place—in an event that appeared impromptu but was actually staged by the Americans—in the kitchen of a suburban house split in half to allow easy viewing. **362** The Russians called the house the "Splitnik," a pun on "Sputnik," the name of the satellite the Soviets had put into orbit two years before. **364**

What was remarkable about this debate was the focus. As historian Elaine Tyler May has noted, instead of discussing "missiles, bombs, or even modes of

government . . . [the two leaders] argued over the relative merits of American and Soviet washing machines, televisions, and electric ranges."[1] For Nixon, American superiority rested on the ideal of the suburban home, complete with modern appliances and distinct gender roles. He proclaimed that this "model" suburban home represented nothing less than American freedom:

> To us, diversity, the right to choose, is the most important thing. . . . We don't have one decision made at the top by one government official. . . . We have many different manufacturers and many different kinds of washing machines so that the housewife has a choice.[2]

The exhibition captivated the national and international media. Newspapers, illustrated magazines, and television networks reported on the event. Symptomatically, *Life* magazine put the wives instead of the politicians on its cover. **365** Pat Nixon appears as the prototype of the American woman depicted in advertisements of the 1950s: slim, well groomed, fashionable, happy. In contrast, the Soviet ladies appear stocky and dowdy, and while two of them, Mrs. Khrushchev and Mrs. Mikoyan, look proudly toward the camera, the third one, Mrs. Kozlov, in what Roland Barthes may have seen as the *punctum* of this photograph, cannot keep her eyes off Pat Nixon's dress.[3]

Envy: that is what the American exhibition seems to have been designed to produce (despite vigorous denials by Nixon in his debate with Khrushchev: "We do not claim to astonish the Soviet people"[4])—yet not envy of scientific, military, or industrial achievements but envy of washing machines, dishwashers, color televisions, suburban houses, lawn mowers, supermarkets stocked full of groceries, Cadillac convertibles, makeup colors, lipstick, spike-heeled shoes, hi-fi sets, cake mixes, TV dinners, Pepsi-Cola, and so on. **366 367 370 371** "What is this," the newspaper *Izvestia* asked itself in its news report, "a national exhibit of a great country or a branch department store? Where is American science, American industry, and particularly their factory techniques?"[5] And a Russian teacher is quoted by the *Wall Street Journal*: "You have lots of dolls, furniture, dishes, but where are your technical exhibits?"[6] Even American newspapers described the main pavilion of the exhibition as a "lush bargain basement" but one that, owing to the dust from a concrete floor that had crumbled forty-eight hours after the opening, already looked as if it "had barely survived a fire sale."[7]

It was for this context that the Eameses produced their film *Glimpses of the USA*, projecting it onto seven twenty-by-thirty-foot screens suspended within a vast (250 feet in diameter) golden geodesic dome designed by Buckminster Fuller. **368 372 374 382 384** More than 2,200 still and moving images (some from Billy Wilder's *Some Like It Hot*) presented "a typical work day" in the life of the United States in nine minutes and "a typical weekend day" in three minutes.[8] Pulled from many different sources, including photo archives (such as Magnum Photos, Photo Researchers, and the magazines *Fortune*, *Holiday*, *Life*, *Look*, the *Saturday Evening Post*, *Sports Illustrated*, *Sunset*, and *Time*), individual photographers (such as Ferenc Berko, Julius Shulman, Ezra Stoller, Ernst Braun, George Zimbel, and Charles

1 Elaine Tyler May, *Homeward Bound: American Families in the Cold War Era* (New York: Basic Books, 1988), 16. See also Karal Ann Marling, *As Seen on TV: The Visual Culture of Everyday Life in the 1950s* (Cambridge, MA: Harvard University Press, 1994).
2 Quoted by May, *Homeward Bound*, 17. For transcripts of the debate see "The Two Worlds: A Day-Long Debate," *New York Times*, July 15, 1959, 1–3; "When Nixon Took on Khrushchev," a report of the meeting, and the text of Nixon's address at the opening of the American National Exhibition in Moscow on July 24, 1959, in "Setting Russia Straight On Facts about U.S.," *U.S. News and World Report*, August 3, 1959, 36–39, 70–72; "Encounter," *Newsweek*, August 3, 1959, 15–19; and "Better to See Once," *Time*, August 3, 1959, 12–14.
3 *Life*, August 10, 1959.
4 Khrushchev: "You Americans expect that the Soviet people will be amazed. It is not so. We have all these things in our new apartments." Nixon: "We do not claim to astonish the Soviet people." "Setting Russia Straight," 36–37.
5 Quoted in Alan L. Otten, "Russians Eagerly Tour U.S. Exhibit Despite Cool Official Attitude," *Wall Street Journal*, July 28, 1959, 16.
6 Ibid.
7 Max Frankel, "Dust from Floor Plagues U.S. Fair," *New York Times*, July 28, 1959, 12.
8 John Neuhart, Marilyn Neuhart, and Ray Eames, *Eames Design: The Work of the Office of Charles and Ray Eames* (New York: Harry N. Abrams, 1989), 238–41. See also Hélène Lipstadt, "Natural Overlap: Charles and Ray Eames and the Federal Government," in Donald Albrecht, ed., *The Work of Charles and Ray Eames: A Legacy of Invention* (New York: Abrams, 1997), 160–66.

Eames himself), and friends and associates of the Eameses (including Eliot Noyes, George Nelson, Alexander Girard, Eero Saarinen, Billy Wilder, Don Albinson, and Robert Staples),[9] the images were combined into seven separate film reels and projected simultaneously through seven interlocked projectors.

The Eameses did not simply install their film in Fuller's space: they were involved in the organization of the entire exhibition from the beginning. Jack Masey of the United Stated Information Agency (USIA) and George Nelson, who had been commissioned by the USIA to design the exhibition, brought them onto the team. According to Nelson, it was in an evening meeting in the Eames House in Los Angeles, culminating three days of discussions, where "all the basic decisions for the fair were made. Present were Nelson, Ray and Charles (the latter occasionally swooping past on a swing hung from the ceiling), the movie director Billy Wilder, and Masey."[10] According to Nelson, by the end of the evening a basic scheme had emerged:

> 1 A dome (by Bucky Fuller).
> 2 A glass pavilion (by Welton Beckett) "as a kind of bazaar stuffed full of things, [the] idea being that consumer products represented one of the areas in which we were most effective, as well as one in which the Russians . . . were more interested."
> 3 An introductory film by the Eameses, since the team felt that the "80,000 square feet of exhibition space was not enough to communicate more than a small fraction of what we wanted to say."[11] 375 376 377

In addition, the USIA had already contracted for the inclusion of Disney's "Circarama," a 360-degree motion picture that offered a twenty-minute tour of American cities and tourist attractions and which played to about one thousand

Russians an hour;[12] an architecture exhibit curated by Peter Blake; a RCA Whirlpool "Miracle Kitchen"; 378 379 380 a fashion show curated by Eleanor Lambert; a packaging exhibition by the Museum of Modern Art's associate curator of design, Mildred Constantine; and Edward Steichen's famous photographic exhibit The Family of Man.[13] The exhibition also included a full-scale ranch-style suburban house, put up by a Long Island builder and furnished by Macy's. 93 94 362 It was in the kitchen of this fourteen-thousand-dollar, six-room house filled with appliances that the Kitchen Debate began, with an argument over automatic washers.

The multiscreen performance turned out to be one of the most popular exhibits at the fair (second only to the cars and color televisions).[14] *Time* magazine called it the exposition's "smash hit,"[15] the *Wall Street Journal* described it as the "real bomb shell," and US officials believed it was "the real pile-driver of the fair."[16] Groups of five thousand people were brought into the dome every forty-five minutes, sixteen times a day.[17] 384 Close to three million people saw the show, and the floor had to be resurfaced three or four times during the six-week exhibition.[18]

The Eameses were not just popular entertainers in an official exhibition, and *Glimpses of the USA* was not just a series of images inside a dome. The huge

---

9 Box 202, The Work of Charles and Ray Eames, Manuscript Division, Library of Congress, Washington, DC.
10 Stanley Abercrombie, *George Nelson: The Design of Modern Design* (Cambridge, MA: MIT Press, 1995), 163.
11 Ibid, 164.
12 Max Frankel, "Image of America at Issue in Soviet," *New York Times*, August 23, 1959. "Circarama" had already been shown at the 1958 World's Fair in Brussels.
13 Abercrombie, *George Nelson*, 167.
14 "The seven-screen quickie is intended as a general introduction to the fair. According to the votes of Russians, however, it is the most popular exhibit after the automobiles and the color television." Max Frankel, "Image of America."
15 "Watching the thousands of colorful glimpses of the U.S. and its people, the Russians were entranced, and the slides are the smash hit of the fair." "The U.S. in Moscow: Russia Comes to the Fair," *Time*, August 3, 1959, 14.
16 "And Mr. Khrushchev watched unsmilingly as the real bomb-shell exploded—a huge exhibit of typical American scenes flashed on seven huge ceiling screens. Each screen shows a different scene but all seven at each moment are on the same general subject—housing, transportation, jazz and so forth. U.S. officials believe this is the real pile-driver of the fair, and the premier's phlegmatic attitude—not even smiling when seven huge Marilyn Monroes dashed on the screen or when Mr. Nixon pointed out golfing scenes—showed his unhappiness with the display." Otten, "Russians Eagerly Tour."
17 Frankel, "Dust from Floor."
18 Pat Kirkham, *Charles and Ray Eames: Designers of the Twentieth Century* (Cambridge, MA: MIT Press, 1995), 324. From an interview with Wilder by Kirkham in 1993.

array of suspended screens defined a space within a space. The Eameses were self-consciously architects of a new kind of space. The film breaks with the fixed perspectival view of the world. In fact, we find ourselves in a space that can be apprehended only with the high technology of telescopes, zoom lenses, airplanes, night-vision cameras, and so on and where there is no privileged point of view. It is not simply that many of the individual images that make up *Glimpses* have been taken with these instruments. More important, the relationship between the images reenacts the operation of the technologies.

The film starts with images from outer space on all the screens—stars across the sky, seven constellations, seven star clusters, nebulae—then moves through aerial views of the city at night, from higher up to closer in, until city lights from the air fill the screens. **382** The early morning comes with aerial views of landscapes from different parts of the country: deserts, mountains, hills, seas, farms, suburban developments, urban neighborhoods. When the camera eyes finally descend to the ground, we see close-ups of newspapers and milk bottles at doors—but still no people, only traces of their existence on earth.

Not by chance, the first signs of human life are centered on the house and domestic space. From the stars at night and the aerial views, the cameras zoom to the most intimate scenes: "people having breakfast at home, men leaving for work, kissing their wives, kissing the baby, being given lunchboxes, getting into cars, waving good-bye, children leaving for school, being given lunchboxes, saying good-bye to dog, piling into station wagons and cars, getting into school buses, baby crying."[19] As with the Eameses' later and much better-known film *Powers of Ten* (1968),[20] which, incidentally, reused images of the night sky from *Glimpses of the USA*,[21] the film moves from outer space to the close-up details of everyday life. **385** **386** **387** As the working script of the film indicates, the close-ups are of "last sips of coffee" of men before leaving for work, "children washing hands before dinner," "housewives on the phone with clerks (supermarket food shelves in b.g.),"[22] and so on. In *Powers of Ten*, the movement would be set in reverse, beginning in the domestic space of a picnic spread with a man asleep beside a woman in a park in Chicago and moving out into the atmosphere and then back down inside the body through the skin of the man's wrist to microscopic cells and to the atomic level. **388** Even if *Powers of Ten*, initially produced for the Commission on College Physics, was a more scientific, more advanced film in which space was measured in seconds, the logic of the two films (*Glimpses* and *Powers of Ten*) was the same. Intimate domesticity was suspended within an entirely new spatial system—a system that was the product of esoteric scientific-military research but that had entered the everyday public imagination with the launching of Sputnik in 1957. **364** Fantasies that had long circulated in science fiction had become reality. This shift from research and fantasy to tangible fact made new forms of communicating to a mass audience possible.[23] The Eameses' innovative technique did not simply present the audience with a new way of seeing things. Rather, it gave form to a new mode of perception that was already in everybody's mind.

---

19 Charles and Ray Eames, *Glimpses of the USA*, working script, box 202, The Work of Charles and Ray Eames, Manuscript Division, Library of Congress, Washington, DC.

20 *Powers of Ten* was based on a 1957 book by Kees Boeke, *Cosmic View: The Universe in Forty Jumps*. The film was produced for the Commission on College Physics. An updated and more developed version was produced in 1977. In the second version the starting point is still a picnic scene, but it takes place in a park bordering Lake Michigan in Chicago. See Neuhart, Neuhart, and Eames, *Eames Design*, 336–37 and 440–41.

21 See handwritten notes on the manuscript of the first version of *Powers of Ten*. Box 207, The Work of Charles and Ray Eames, Manuscript Division, Library of Congress, Washington, DC. The film is still referred to as *Cosmic View*.

22 *Glimpses*, working script.

23 In 1970, in the context of Charles Eames's third Charles Eliot Norton Lecture at Harvard University, where he once again insisted on the need to incorporate media into the classroom, he still spoke of changing forms of communications with reference to Sputnik: "In post-Sputnik panic, a great demand for taping science lectures; when they were shown on television, distribution cost ended up as 100:1 of production cost; no way to run a railroad." Box 217, folder 10, The Work of Charles and Ray Eames, Manuscript Division, Library of Congress, Washington, DC.

Glimpses breaks with the linear narrative of film to bring snippets of information, an ever-changing mosaic image of American life. **382** And yet the message of the film is linear and eerily consistent with the official message represented by the Kitchen Debate. From the stars in the sky at the beginning of the film—which the narrative insists are the same in the Soviet Union as they are in the USA— to the people kissing their good-nights and the forget-me-not flowers in the last image, the film emphasized universal emotions while at the same time unambiguously reinforcing the material abundance of one country.[24] From the parking lots of factories, which the narrative describes as filled with the cars of workers, to the aerial views of suburban houses with a blue swimming pool in each yard, to the close-ups of shopping carts and supermarket shelves full of goodies and housewives cooking dinner in kitchens equipped with every imaginable appliance, the message of the film was clear: We are the same as you, but, on the material level, we have more.

Glimpses, like the "Splitnik" house, displaced the USA-USSR debate from the arms-and-space race to the battle of the appliances. And yet the overall effect of the film is that of an extraordinarily powerful viewing technology, a hyperviewing mechanism that is hard to imagine outside the very space program the exhibition was trying to downplay. In fact, this extreme mode of viewing goes beyond the old fantasy of the eye in the sky. If *Glimpses* simulates the operation of satellite surveillance, it exposes more than the details of life in the streets: it penetrates the most intimate spaces and reveals every secret. Domestic life itself becomes the target, the source of pride or insecurity. The Americans, made insecure by the thought of a Russian eye looking down on them, countered by exposing more than that eye could ever see (or at least pretending to, since "a day in the life of the USA" became an image of the good life, without ghettos, poverty, domestic violence, or depression).

Glimpses simply intensified an existing mode of perception. In fact, it synthesized several already existing modes that were manifest in television, space programs, and military operations. As is typical of all the Eameses' work, it was the simplicity and clarity of this synthesis that made it immediately accessible to all.[25]

2.

What kind of genealogy can one make of the Eameses' development of this astonishingly successful technique?

It was not the first time they had deployed multiple screens. In fact, the Eameses were involved in one of the first multimedia presentations on record, if not the first. Again it was George Nelson who set up the commission. In 1952 he had been asked to prepare a study for the Department of Fine Arts at the University of Georgia in Athens, and he brought along Ray and Charles Eames and Alexander Girard. Instead of writing a report, they decided to collaborate on a "show for a typical class" of fifty-five minutes. Nelson referred to it as "Art X," while the Eameses called it "A Rough Sketch for a Sample Lesson for a Hypothetical Course." **390** The subject of the lesson was "communications,"[26] and the stated goals included "the breaking down of barriers between fields of learning ... making people a little more intuitive ... [and] increasing communication between people and things."[27] The performance included a live narrator, multiple images (both still and moving), sound (in the form of music and narration), and even "a collection of bottled synthetic odors

---

24 Apparently even the forget-me-nots were understood in precisely the intended way, as symbols of friendship and loyalty. According to the Eameses, the audience could be heard saying "nezabutki," "forget-me-not," as the flowers appeared on the screen as the last image of the film. Neuhart, Neuhart, and Eames, *Eames Design*, 241.

25 For example, *Powers of Ten* was a "sketch film" to be presented at an "assembly of one thousand of America's top physicists," but the Eameses decided that it should "appeal to a ten-year-old as well as a physicist." Paul Schrader, "Poetry of Ideas: The Films of Charles Eames," *Film Quarterly* 23, no. 3 (Spring 1970): 10.

26 "Grist for Atlanta paper version," manuscript, box 217, folder 15, The Work of Charles and Ray Eames, Manuscript Division, Library of Congress, Washington, DC.

27 Neuhart, Neuhart, and Eames, *Eames Design*, 177.

that were to be fed into the auditorium during the show through the air-conditioning ducts."[28] Charles Eames later said, "We used a lot of sound, sometimes carried to a very high volume so you would actually feel the vibrations."[29] The idea was to produce an intense sensory environment so as to "heighten awareness." The effect was so convincing that apparently some people even believed they smelled things (for example, the smell of oil in the machinery) when no smell had been introduced, only a suggestion in an image or a sound.[30]

It was a major production. Nelson described the team arriving in Athens "burdened with only slightly less equipment than Ringling Brothers. This included a movie projector, three slide projectors, three screens, three or four tape recorders, cans of films, boxes of slides, and reels of magnetic tape."[31] The reference to the circus was not accidental. Speaking with a reporter for *Vogue*, Charles later argued that "'Sample Lesson' was a blast on all senses, a super-saturated three-ring circus. Simultaneously the students were assaulted by three sets of slides, two tape recorders, a motion picture with sound, and peripheral panels for further distraction."[32]

The circus was one of the Eameses' lifetime fascinations[33]—so much so that in the '40s, when they were out of work and money, they were about to audition for one. They would have been clowns, but ultimately a contract to make plywood furniture allowed them to continue as designers. And from the mid-1940s on, they took hundreds and hundreds of photographs of the circus, which they used in many contexts, including *Circus* (their 180-slide, three-screen slide show accompanied by a sound track featuring circus music and other sounds recorded at the circus), [129] presented as part of the Charles Eliot Norton Lectures at Harvard University that Charles delivered in 1970, and the film *Clown Face* (1971), a training film about "the precise and classical art of applying makeup" made for

Bill Ballentine, director of the Clown College of Ringling Brothers Barnum & Bailey Circus. **391** The Eameses had been friends with the Ballentines since the late '40s, when the Eameses had photographed the circus's behind-the-scenes activities during an engagement in Los Angeles.[34] Charles was on the board of the Ringling Brothers College and often referred to the circus as an example of what design and art should be, not self-expression but precise discipline:

> Everything in the circus is pushing the possible beyond the limit—bears do not really ride on bicycles, people do not really execute three and a half turn somersaults in the air from a board to a ball, and until recently no one dressed the way fliers do. . . . Yet within this apparent freewheeling license, we find a discipline which is almost unbelievable. . . . The circus may look like the epitome of pleasure, but the person flying on a high wire, or executing a balancing act, or being shot from a cannon must take his pleasure very, very seriously. In the same vein, the scientist, in his laboratory, is pushing the possible beyond the limit and he too must take his pleasure very seriously.[35]

The circus, as an event that offered a multiplicity of simultaneous experiences that could not be taken in entirely by the viewer, was the Eameses' model for their design of multimedia exhibitions and the fast-cutting technique of their films and slide shows, where the objective was always to communicate the maximum amount of information in a way that was both pleasurable and effective.[36]

---

28 George Nelson, "The Georgia Experiment: An Industrial Approach to Problems of Education," manuscript, October 1954, quoted in Abercrombie, *George Nelson*, 145.
29 Owen Gingerich, "A Conversation with Charles Eames," *American Scholar* 46, no. 3 (Summer 1977): 331.
30 Ibid.
31 Nelson, "Georgia Experiment."
32 Allene Talmey, "Eames," *Vogue*, August 15, 1959, 144.
33 Beatriz Colomina, "Reflections on the Eames House" in Albrecht, *The Work of Charles and Ray Eames*, 128. See also chapter 3.
34 Neuhart, Neuhart, and Eames, *Eames Design*, 373; Bill Ballentine, *Clown Alley* (Boston: Little, Brown, 1982).
35 Charles Eames, "Language of Vision: The Nuts and Bolts," *Bulletin of the American Academy of Arts and Sciences*, October 1974, 17–18.
36 Neuhart, Neuhart, and Eames, *Eames Design*, 91.

But the technological model for multiscreen, multimedia presentations may have been provided by the war-situation room, which was designed in those same years to bring information in simultaneously from numerous sources around the world so that the president and military commanders could make critical decisions. **357** It is not without irony, in that sense, that the Eameses read the organization of the circus as a form of crisis control. In a circus, Charles said, "there is a strict hierarchy of events, and an elimination of choice under stress, so that one event can automatically follow another... There is a recognized mission for everyone involved. In a crisis there can be no question as to what needs to be done."[37] A number of the Eameses' friends were involved in the secret military project of the war rooms, including Buckminster Fuller, Eero Saarinen, and Henry Dreyfuss, whose unrealized design involved a wall of parallel projected images of different kinds of information.[38] **358** It is not clear that the Eameses knew anything about the project during the war years, but it is very likely, given their friendship with Fuller, Saarinen, and Dreyfuss, that they would have found out after the war. In 1970, in the context of his second Norton Lecture, Charles referred to the war room as a model for city management:

> In the management of a city, linear discourse certainly can't cope. We imagine a City Room or a World Health Room (rather like a War Room) where all the information from satellite monitors and other sources could be monitored; [Fuller's World Game is an example.] ... The city problem involves conflicting interest and points of view. So the place where information is correlated also has to be a place where each group can try out plans for its own changing needs.[39]

The overall subject of the Norton Lectures was announced as "Problems Relating to Visual Communication and the Visual Environment," and a consistent theme was the "necessity to devise visual models for matters of practical concern where linear description isn't enough." Kepes's *Language of Vision* was a constant reference point for the Eameses. The "language of vision" was seen as a "real threat to the discontinuity" (between the arts, between university departments, between art and everyday life, and so on) that the Eameses were always fighting.[40] Architecture ("a most non-discontinuous art") was seen as both the ultimate model for discontinuity and the discipline where the new technologies should be implemented.

A number of wartime research projects, including work on communications, ballistics, and experimental computers, had quickly developed after the war into a full-fledged theory of information flow, most famously with the publication of Claude Shannon's *Mathematical Theory of Communication* in 1949, which formalized the idea of an information channel from sender to recipient whose efficiency could be measured in terms of speed and noise. This sense of information flow organized the "Sample Lesson" performance. The Eameses said they "were trying to cram into a short time, a class hour, the most background material possible."[41] As part of the project, they produced *A Communication Primer*, a film that presented the theory of information, explaining Shannon's famous diagram of the passage of information, and was subsequently developed in an effort to present current ideas in communication theory to architects and planners and to encourage them to use these ideas in their work. **392** The basic idea was to

---

37 Charles Eames, "Language of Vision," 17–18. See also the typescript of the actual lecture in box 217, folder 12, The Work of Charles and Ray Eames, Manuscript Division, Library of Congress, Washington, DC.

38 Barry Katz, "The Arts of War: 'Visual Presentation' and National Intelligence," *Design Issues* 12, no. 2 (Summer 1996): 3–21. I am grateful to Dennis Doordan for pointing out this article to me.

39 Partial transcript of Norton Lectures. Box 217, folder 10, The Work of Charles and Ray Eames, Manuscript Division, Library of Congress, Washington, DC. Square brackets appear in the original.

40 See, for example, Charles Eames, "On Reducing Discontinuity" (talk given at the American Academy of Arts and Sciences, 1976), manuscript, box 217, folder 17, The Work of Charles and Ray Eames, Manuscript Division, Library of Congress, Washington, DC: "My wife and I had made a commitment to disregard the sacred enclosure around a special set of phenomena called art; in our view preoccupation with respecting that boundary leads to an unfortunate and unwarranted limitation on the aesthetic experience."

41 Gingerich, "Conversation with Charles Eames," 332.

integrate architecture and information flow. **393** If the great heroes of the Renaissance were, for the Eameses, "people concerned with ways of modeling/imaging, . . . not with self-expression or bravura . . . . Brunelleschi, but not Michelangelo,"[42] the great architects of our time would be the ones concerned with the new forms of communication, particularly computers:

> It appeared to us that the real current problems for architects now—the problems that a Brunelleschi, say, would gravitate to—are problems of *organization of information*. For city planning, for regional planning, the first need is clear, accessible models of current states-of-affairs, drawn from a data base that only a computer can handle for you.[43]

The logic of information flow was further developed in the Eameses' 1955 film *House: After Five Years of Living*. The film was made entirely from thousands of color slides the Eameses had been taking of their home over the first five years of its life,[44] **407** **21** shown in quick succession (a technique called "fast cutting" for which the Eameses won an Emmy Award in 1960[45]) and accompanied by music composed by Elmer Bernstein. As Michael Braune wrote in 1966:

> The interesting point about this method of film making is not only that it is relatively simple to produce and that rather more information can be conveyed than when there is movement on the screen, but that it corresponds surprisingly closely with the way in which the brain normally records the images it receives. I would assume that it also corresponds rather closely with the way Eames's own thought processes tend to work. I think it symptomatic, for instance, that he is extremely interested in computers, . . . and that one of the essential characteristics of computers is their need to separate information into components before being able to assemble them into a large number of different wholes.[46]

This technique was developed even further in *Glimpses*, which is organized around a strict logic of information transmission. The role of the designer is to orchestrate a particular flow of information. **393** The central principle is one of compression. At the end of the design meeting at the Eames House in preparation for the American Exhibition in Moscow, the idea of the film emerged precisely "as a way of compressing into a small volume the tremendous quantity of information" they wanted to present, which would have been impossible to do in the eighty thousand square feet of the exhibition.[47] The space of the multiscreen film, like the space of the computer, compresses physical space. Each screen shows a different scene, but all seven at each moment are on the same general subject—housing, transportation, jazz, and so forth. As the *New York Times* described it, "Perhaps fifty clover-leaf highway intersections are shown in just a few seconds. So are dozens of housing projects, bridges, skyscrapers scenes, supermarkets, universities, museums, theatres, churches, farms, laboratories and much more."[48] **372**

According to the Eameses, repetition was employed for credibility. They said, "If, for example, we were to show a freeway interchange, somebody would look at it and say, 'We have one at Smolensk and one at Minsk; we have two, they have one'—that kind of thing. So we conceived the idea of having the imagery come on in multiple forms, as in the *Rough Sketch for a Sample Lesson*."[49] But the issue was much more than one of efficiency of communication or the polemical need to have multiple examples. The idea was, as with the "Sample

---

42 Notes for second Norton lecture, box 217, folder 10, The Work of Charles and Ray Eames, Manuscript Division, Library of Congress, Washington, DC. Eames is referring here to "Professor Lawrence Hill's Renaissance."

43 "'Communication Primer' was a recommendation to architects to recognize the need for more complex information . . . for new kinds of *models of information*." Eames, "Grist for Atlanta."

44 Colomina, "Reflections," passim. See also chapter 3.

45 Charles and Ray Eames won an Emmy Award for graphics for their rapid cutting experiments on *The Fabulous Fifties*, a television program broadcast on January 22, 1960, on the CBS network. It included six film segments made by the Eames Office. Schrader, "Poetry of Ideas," 3.

46 Michael Braune, "The Wit of Technology," *Architectural Design*, September 1966, 452.

47 See Abercrombie, *George Nelson*, 163–64.

48 Frankel, "Image of America."

49 Gingerich, "Conversation with Charles Eames," 332–33.

Lesson," to produce sensory overload. As the Eameses had suggested to *Vogue*, "Sample Lesson" tried to provide many forms of "distraction" instead of asking students to concentrate on a singular message. The audience drifted through a multimedia space that exceeded their capacity to absorb it. The Eames-Nelson team thought that the most important thing to communicate to undergraduates was a sense of what the Eameses would later call "connections" among seemingly unrelated phenomena. Arguing that awareness of these relationships was achieved by "high-speed techniques," Nelson and the Eameses produced an excessive input from different directions that had to be synthesized by the audience. Likewise, Charles said of *Glimpses*:

> We wanted to have a credible number of images, but not so many that they couldn't be scanned in the time allotted. At the same time, the number of images had to be large enough so that people wouldn't be exactly sure how many they have seen. We arrived at the number seven. With four images, you always knew there were four, but by the time you got up to eight images you weren't quite sure. They were very big images—the width across four of them was half the length of a football field.[50]

One journalist described it as "information overload—an avalanche of related data that comes at a viewer too fast for him to cull and reject it . . . a twelve-minute blitz."[51] The viewer is overwhelmed. More than anything, the Eameses wanted an emotional response, produced as much by the excess of images as by their content. They said:

> At the Moscow World's Fair in 1959—when we used seven screens over an area that was over half the length of a football field—that was just a desperate

attempt to make a credible statement to a group of people in Moscow when words had almost ceased to have meaning. We were telling the story straight, and we wanted to do it in 12 minutes, with images; but we found that we couldn't really give credibility to it in a linear way. However when we could put 50 images on the screen for a certain subject in a matter of 10 seconds, we got a kind of breadth which we felt we couldn't get any other way.[51]

The multiscreen technique went through one more significant development at the 1964 World's Fair in New York. In the IBM Ovoid Theater, designed by the Saarinen office, visitors boarded the "people wall" and were greeted by a "host" dressed in coattails who slowly dropped down from the IBM ovoid; the seated five-hundred-person audience was then lifted up hydraulically from the ground level into the dark interior of the egg, where they were surrounded by fourteen screens on which the Eameses projected the film *Think*.[52] **394 395 396 398 425** To enter the theater was no longer to cross the threshold, to pass through the ceremonial space of the entrance, as in a traditional public building. To *enter* here was to be lifted in front of a multiplicity of screens. The screens wrapped the audience in a way reminiscent of Herbert Bayer's 1930 "diagram of the field of vision," produced as a sketch for the installation of an architecture and furniture exhibition.[53] **399** The eye could not escape the screens, and each screen was bordered by other screens. Unlike the screens in Moscow, those in the IBM building were of different sizes and shapes. But once again, the eye had to jump from image to image and

50 Ibid., 333.
51 Digby Diehl, "West Q&A: Charles Eames," transcript, box 24, folder 4–5, The Work of Charles and Ray Eames, Manuscript Division, Library of Congress, Washington, DC. Published as "Q&A: Charles Eames," *Los Angeles Times WEST Magazine*, October 8, 1972, reprinted in Digby Diehl, *Supertalk* (New York: Doubleday, 1974).

52 Mina Hamilton, "Films at the Fair II," *Industrial Design*, May 1964, 37–41.
53 Arthur A. Cohen, *Herbert Bayer: The Complete Work* (Cambridge, MA: MIT Press, 1994), 292. Mary Anne Staniszewski, *The Power of Display: A History of Exhibition Installations at the Museum of Modern Art* (Cambridge, MA: MIT Press, 1998), 25–28.

could never fully catch up with all of them and their diverse contents. Fragments were presented to be momentarily linked together before the connections between them were replaced with others. The film is organized by the same logic of compression, its speed intended to be the speed of the mind.

A "host" welcomed the audience to "the IBM Information Machine," "a machine designed to help me give you a lot of information in a very short time. . . . The machine brings you information in much the same way as your mind gets it—in fragments and glimpses—sometimes relating to the same idea or incident. Like making toast in the morning."[54] **395** Already in 1959, the design team (Nelson, the Eameses, et al.) had used exactly the same term—"information machine"—to describe the role of Fuller's dome in Moscow, taking it from the title of a 1957 film the Eameses had prepared for the 1958 Brussels World's Fair. In addition to the multiscreens, the dome housed a huge RAMAC 305 computer, an "electronic brain" that offered written replies to 3,500 questions about life in the United States.[55] **400** **401** The architecture was conceived from the very start as a combination of structure, multiscreen film, and computer. Each technology created an architecture in which inside/outside, entering/leaving, meant something entirely different, and yet they all coexisted. All were housed by the same physical structure, Fuller's dome, but each defined a different kind of space to be explored in different ways. From the "Sample Lesson" in 1953 to IBM in 1964, the Eameses treated architecture as a multichannel information machine—and, equally, multimedia installations as a kind of architecture.

3.

All of the Eameses' designs can be understood as multiscreen performances: they provide a framework in which objects can be placed and replaced. Even the parts of their furniture can be rearranged. Spaces are defined as arrays of information collected and constantly changed by their users. 402 403 404 405

This is the space of the media. The space of a newspaper or an illustrated magazine is a grid in which information is arranged and rearranged as it comes in: a space the reader navigates in his or her own way, at a glance, or by fully entering a particular story. The reader, viewer, consumer, constructs the space, participating actively in the design. It is a space where continuities are made through "cutting." The same is true of the space of newsreels and television. The logic of the Eameses' multiscreens is simply the logic of the mass media.

It is not by chance that Charles Eames was always nostalgic for his time as a set designer for MGM in the early 1940s, continually arranging and rearranging existing props on short notice.[56] All Eames architecture can be understood as set design. The Eameses even presented themselves like Hollywood figures, as if in a movie or an advertisement, always so happy, with the ever-changing array of objects as their backdrop.

This logic of architecture as a set for staging the good life was central to the design of the Moscow exhibition. Even the famous kitchen, for example, was cut in half not only to allow viewing by visitors but, most important, to turn it into a photo op for the Kitchen Debate. Photographers and journalists knew already the night before that they had to be there, choosing their angle. Architecture was reorganized to produce a certain image. Charles had already spoken, in 1950, of our time as the era of communication. He was acutely aware that the new media were displacing the old role of architecture. And yet everything for the Eameses, in this world of communication that they were embracing so happily,

54 Script of the IBM film *View from the People Wall for the Ovoid Theater*, New York World's Fair, 1964, The Work of Charles and Ray Eames, Manuscript Division, Library of Congress, Washington, DC.

55 "U.S. Gives Soviet Glittering Show," *New York Times*, July 25, 1959.
56 Colomina, "Reflections," 129.

was architecture: "The chairs are architecture, the films—they have a structure, just as the front page of a newspaper has a structure. The chairs are literally like architecture in miniature . . . architecture you can get your hands on."[57] In the notes for a letter to Italian architect Vittorio Gregotti accompanying a copy of *Powers of Ten*, they write: "In the past fifty years the world has gradually been finding out something that architects have always known, that is, that *everything* is architecture. The problems of environment have become more and more interrelated. This is a sketch for a film that shows something of how large— and small—our environment is."[58]

In every sense, Eames architecture is all about the space of information. Perhaps we can talk no longer about "space" but, rather, about "structure" or, more precisely, about time. Structure, for the Eameses, was organization in time. The details that were central to Mies van der Rohe's architecture were replaced by "connections." As Charles said in a film about a storage system he and Ray had designed: "The details are not details. They make the product. The connections, the connections, the connections."[59] But, as Ralph Caplan pointed out, the connections in their work were not only between such "disparate materials as wood and steel" or between "seemingly alien disciplines" like physics and the circus but also between ideas. Their technique of information overload, used in films and multimedia presentations as well as in their trademark "information wall" in exhibitions, was used not to "overtax the viewer's brain" but precisely to offer a "broad menu of options" and to create an "impulse to make connections."[60] **406**

For the Eameses, structure was not linear. They often reflected on the impossibility of linear discourse. The structure of their exhibitions has been compared to that of a scholarly paper, loaded with footnotes, where "the highest level of participation consists in getting fascinated by the pieces and connecting them for oneself."⁶¹ Seemingly static structures like the frames of their buildings or of their plywood cabinets were but frameworks for positioning ever-changing objects. And the frame itself was, anyway, meant to be changed all the time. These changes, this fluctuating movement, could never be pinned down.

Mies van der Rohe's exhibition of his work at the Museum of Modern Art in 1947 was significant, according to the Eameses, not because of the individual objects on display but because of the organizational system the architect had devised to present them,⁶² which communicated, in their view, the idea of Mies's architecture better than any single model, drawing, or photograph could. When Charles published his photographs of the exhibition in *Arts & Architecture*, he wrote: "The significant thing seems to be the way in which he [Mies] has taken documents of his architecture and furniture and used them as elements in creating a space that says, 'this is what its all about.'"⁶³ **178** The multiscreen presentations, the exhibition technique, and the Eameses' films are likewise significant not because of the individual factoids they offer or even the story they tell but because of the way the factoids are used as elements in creating a space that says, "This is what the space of information is all about."

Like all architects, the Eameses controlled the space they produced. The most important factor was to regulate the flow of information. They prepared extremely detailed technical instructions for the running of even their simplest

---

57 Gingerich, "Conversation with Charles Eames," 327. See also Chapter 3.

58 "Powers of Ten—Gregotti," handwritten notes, box 217, folder 11, The Work of Charles and Ray Eames, Manuscript Division, Library of Congress, Washington, DC.

59 Charles Eames, in a film about a storage system the Eameses had designed, quoted in Ralph Caplan, "Making Connections: The Work of Charles and Ray Eames," *Connections: The Work of Charles and Ray Eames*, catalog of an exhibition at the University of California, Los Angeles (Los Angeles: University of California, 1976), 15.

60 Caplan, "Making Connections," 43.

61 Ibid., 45.

62 Colomina, "Reflections," 146. See also chapter 3.

63 Charles Eames, "Mies van der Rohe" (photographs by Charles Eames taken at the MoMA exhibition), *Arts & Architecture*, December 1947, 27.

three-screen slide show.[64] Performances were carefully planned to appear as effortless as a circus act. Timing and the elimination of "noise" were the major considerations. Their office produced masses of documents, even drawings showing the rise and fall of intensity through the course of a film, literally defining the space they wanted to produce or, more precisely, the existing space of the media that they wanted to intensify. With *Glimpses*, the Eameses retained complete control over their work by turning up in Moscow only forty-eight hours before the opening, as Peter Blake recalls it, "dressed like a boy scout and a girl scout," clutching the reels of the film.[65] A photograph shows the smiling couple descending from the plane, reels in Charles's hands, posing for the camera. As he later put it, "Theoretically, it was a statement made by our State Department, and yet we did it entirely here and it was never seen by anyone from our government until they saw it in Moscow. . . . If you ask for criticism, you get it. If you don't, there is a chance everyone will be too busy to worry about it."[66]

The experience for the audience in Moscow was almost overwhelming. Journalists speak of too many images, too much information, too fast. For the MTV and the Internet generation watching the film today, it would not be fast enough, and yet we do not seem to have come that far either. The logic of the Internet was already spelled out in the Eameses' multiscreen projects. Coming out of the war mentality, the Eameses' innovations in the world of communication, their exhibitions, films, and multiscreen performances transformed the status of architecture. Their highly controlled flows of simultaneous images provided a space, an enclosure—the kind of space we now occupy continuously without thinking.

64 "To show a 3-Screen slide show," manuscript detailing the necessary preparations for an "Eames 3 screen 6 projectors slide show" with "sound" and "picture operation procedure," illustrated with multiple drawings, 14 pp., box 211, folder 10, The Work of Charles and Ray Eames, Manuscript Division, Library of Congress, Washington, DC.

65 Peter Blake, in *An Eames Celebration: The Several Worlds of Charles and Ray Eames*, WNET Television, New York, February 3, 1975, quoted in Kirkham, *Charles and Ray Eames*, 320.

66 Eames in Gingerich, "Conversation with Charles Eames," 333.

273

＃ Chapter 8
The Underground House

1964, two years after the Cuban Missile Crisis. The New York World's Fair. Its architecture is dismissed at the time as "too commercial," "too vulgar," and lacking "architectural unity"; perhaps most symptomatic, the masters are missing: "Where are Kahn, Neutra, Mies, Gropius, Yamasaki, Buckminster Fuller, Kiesler, ... ?" asks *Interiors*.[1] And the noted architectural historian Vincent Scully writes "If This is Architecture, God Help Us," an article in *Life* where he states: "The Fair is nothing but the concentrated essence of motel, gas station, shopping center and suburbs. Why go to New York to find it when we have it all at home?"[2] While the institutions of high culture (if one could consider *Interiors*, *Progressive Architecture*, and *Architectural Record* as such) lament their inability to comprehend the fair, only a reporter for *Holiday,* a popular travel magazine, seems able to provide an adequate answer when he writes: "Most of these charges are true; none of them matters. . . . Too commercial? As I see it, commerce is the point of any fair. . . . It is precisely the chaos of architectural styles that lends to Flushing Meadows the nightmare quality any proper world's fair should strive for. . . . As for the vulgarity and the triviality I would grieve to see an iota of them blotted or canceled out, and I include even the frightful neon sign, advertising A&P's baked foods, that glares down upon the fairground from beyond its walls, notwithstanding an edict issued by Mr. Moses himself."[3]

The refined moves of the best modern architects of the time had been replaced by the generic forms of the American commercial landscape, the Pop world that would be recognized a few years later in architectural circles as a vernacular source of inspiration as rich to postmodern architects as the American industrial vernacular and the machine object had been to modern architects since the 1920s. Not only was there Pop art displayed at the 1964/65 fair (including works of Andy Warhol, Roy Lichtenstein, James Rosenquist, and Robert Rauschenberg), but many cultural critics saw the fair itself as a gigantic work of Pop art, and others pointed to the Pop quality of some of its exhibits.[4] **411**

The critics' accusations of commercialism, vulgarity, disunity, and the absence of mastery were not simply a rejection of mass culture. The attack on the kitsch of the fair, the bad taste of its forms of mass culture, constituted an elaborate defense (with antiquated artillery) of a major disruption of the traditional status of architecture against the direct threat posed by new technologies. Architectural magazines were defending themselves against a threat to their own foundations.

It was the dawn of the space age, and the fair introduced a whole new world. Its official theme was "Man in a Shrinking Globe in an Expanding Universe," and its symbol was the Unisphere, a 900,000-pound stainless steel model of the earth 140 feet high and 120 feet in diameter. **408** Dedicated to "Peace through Understanding," the sphere was covered with representations of the continents, with the capital of each nation marked by a light, and encircled by three giant rings representing the first satellites that had launched the space age (Sputnik 1 had been launched by the Soviet Union on October 4, 1957, and Explorer 1 had been launched by the United States on January 31, 1958). Seen from the edge of the pool, the Unisphere showed the dimensions of the earth as it would appear from six thousand miles in space, putting the visitor

---

[1] "Razzmatazz at Flushing Meadow," *Interiors*, March 1964, 98. Other reviews of the fair by professional journals include "The Busy Architect's Guide to the World's Fair," *Progressive Architecture*, October 1964; "Queen of the Fair," *Progressive Architecture*, December 1964; "Best of the Fair," *Interiors*, October 1964; "The House of Good Taste," *Interior Design*, August 1964. See also Rosemarie Haag Bletter, "The 'Laissez-Fair,' Good Taste, and Money Trees: Architecture at the Fair," *Remembering the Future: The New York World's Fair From 1939 to 1964* (New York: Queens Museum and Rizzoli International, 1989).

[2] Vincent J. Scully Jr., "If This Is Architecture, God Help Us," *Life*, July 31, 1964.

[3] Peter Lyon, "A Glorious Nightmare," *Holiday*, July 1964.

[4] In an exception to his negative view of the fair, Vincent Scully enthusiastically embraced the Chrysler exhibit, designed by George Nelson, as the "surprise of the Fair": "It is pop art at its best, and presents Detroit with welcome wit and irony. There is a 'working' engine you can walk into and a demented mock-up of a car of the future you examine from below—the bucket seats are buckets. There is also a zoo of rickety and noisy animals made out of auto parts, some of them looking like the Port Authority helicopter clattering about next door. Scully, "If This Is Architecture," 9. It would seem that Scully is able to embrace the Pop of the fair only when it is the work not of an architect but of a designer.

in the position of an astronaut. On October 21, 1957, the cover of *Life* had featured a model of a globe with a couple of scientists sitting below it scrutinizing computer printouts and another at the top of a ladder setting a cord around the globe to plot the orbit of a planned US satellite. The headline reads, "The Satellite: Why Reds Got It First, What Happens Next." **409** Inside, in an article alarmingly entitled "The Feat That Shook the Earth," there is an image of the pattern of orbits traced by the Sputnik in a typical twenty-four-hour period with a red bulb circling a model of the globe. **410** By May 1, 1964, a remarkably similar image appeared on the cover of *Life*, that of the Unisphere, under the headline "The Worlds Fair Opens." **408** The image that symbolized terror in 1957 had already been assimilated. The Unisphere was the largest spherical structure ever made, and it required calculations so complex that without the aid of high-speed computers it would have been impossible to build.[5] The fair tried to domesticate both the new, frighteningly transformed world and the technologies responsible for that transformation.

The whole fair presented to the viewer, in the words of the Peter Lyon, the *Holiday* reporter, "a world computerized to the teeth, a push button world purveying instant fact and instant wisdom": **412** **413**

> At the Better Living Center there is a computer to tell you what colors to use in decorating your home. . . . At the National Cash Register pavilion a computer feeds out facts to help children with their homework. At the Parker Pen pavilion, a computer will find you a pen pal somewhere in the world . . . and at the Clairol pavilion, a computer advised my wife what color she should dye her hair: "Don't be a sissy," a soft, electronic female voice whispered in her ear, "go ahead, do it!"[6]

Not only were the computers (descendants of the first computer developed to decode enemy messages during World War II) concerned exclusively with domestic issues (displacing into themselves traditional forms of domestic relations in areas as crucial as homework, decoration, companionship, and advising), but, moreover, domestic space itself was deeply disturbed. Within the popular kitsch of the 1964 fair, very elaborate propositions about the status of the modern interior were being made, something that could not be recognized by architectural magazines.

One such proposition was the Underground Home, a traditional suburban ranch-style house buried as protection from the new threat of nuclear fallout.[7] **414** **415** **416** **417** It was the project of Jay Swayze, a Texas military instructor–turned–building contractor of luxury homes who during the Cuban Missile Crisis of 1962 had been commissioned by the Plainview (Texas) City Council to build a demonstration fallout shelter to specifications by the Department of Civil Defense. In a promotional book for underground homes and gardens published in 1980, he discussed the project in the following terms:

> I saw the merit of utilizing the earth as protection against radioactive fallout. As a former military instructor in chemical warfare, I knew that the three ways man could destroy himself were by nuclear fission, nerve gas or germ warfare. Despite President Kennedy's assurance that the threat of war was only temporary, one thing was clear. The nuclear age was upon us, and long-range planning was necessary to protect humanity from possible ill effects.[8]

---

5 *Official Guide New York World's Fair 1964–1965* (New York: Time-Life Books, 1964), 180.

6 Lyon, "Glorious Nightmare,"

7 The Underground Home was constructed by the Underground World Home Corporation (whose president was Jay Swayze), which also proposed underground shopping centers, underground motels, and underground restaurants and nightclubs. See also Bletter, "The 'Laissez-Fair.'" I would like to thank Bletter for directing my attention to the house and Marc Miller for providing original material from the World's Fair archives.

8 Jay Swayze, *Underground Gardens and Homes: The Best of Two Worlds—Above and Below* (Hereford, TX: Geobuilding Systems, 1980), 19.

Swayze quickly turned the military project for a shelter into a domestic project for a house:

> It seemed more logical to make the home and its surroundings a safe harbor where the family would be protected in comfortable, familiar surroundings. . . . Armed with these ideas I moved to the drafting table. . . . Because we can not live in constant fear of war, storms or uncomfortable temperatures, the "better way" must offer protection from such.[9]

The equation of war with weather was symptomatic. The "better way"—Swayze's slogan for the Underground Home—rested on two "obvious advantages": "constant temperature" and "security from natural or man-made hazards." The house offered a controlled environment in which one could create one's own climate by "dialing" temperature and humidity settings: "the breeze of a mountain top, the exhilarating high pressure feeling of a Spring day can be created at will. . . . The clamor of traffic, jets, noisy neighbors—all are gone with a turn of a switch and you are free to rest in silence, or experience for the first time the full range of sensations that today's sensitive stereo systems are able to produce."[10] The house was no longer simply a physical shelter, admitting some parts of the outside world and excluding others. It was a machine that created its own weather, its own outside.

As "windows to the outside world seemed impossible" in an underground shelter, Swayze developed a survey "to learn how much value people placed actually upon windows." He concluded that although windows might be psychologically important, they were, in fact, rarely looked through. Moreover, "with traditional homes we must take what we get for views. After looking outside, I decided an artist could do a thousand times better."[11] In the Underground Home at the 1964/65 fair, traditional windows were superimposed on "dial-a-view" murals, and every room in the house looked out onto a panoramic landscape that could be changed at will. **417** In the prototype of this house, completed in Colorado before the fair, the outside views spanned a continent with San Francisco's Golden Gate Bridge to the west and the New York skyline to the east. The time of day or night could also be "dialed" to fit any mood or occasion. A publicity brochure for the Underground Home at the fair noted that rheostats "permit a rising sun effect in the kitchen, while a star-filled night blankets the 'outdoor' patio." That is, simultaneously!

The displacement of time and space produced within this house problematized traditional spatial distinctions such as that between inside and outside. But these distinctions were not simply abandoned here: they were made strange. Inside the "protective shell," a clear division was maintained between "interior" and "exterior" areas. The definition of terms at the beginning of Swayze's book clarifies that "out-of-doors, backyard, front yard, patio, courtyard, garden, swimming pool" are "all areas *inside* the shell." "Outer/outside" is "anything *not* enclosed in the shell."[12] **422** By internalizing even the inside/outside distinction, the Underground Home offered, again in the words of the *Holiday* reporter, "greater security—peace of mind—the ultimate in true privacy!"[13] And the publicity brochure for the Underground Home read: "A few feet underground can give man an island unto himself; a place where he controls his own world—a world of total ease and comfort, of security, safety and above all, privacy."[14]

"Peace" is achieved in this war by environmental control, control over "the exterior": temperature, noise, air, light, view. The publicity insists not so much on nuclear danger as on intruders, dangers of the street, insects, impurities of the air.

9   Swayze, *Underground Gardens*, 20.
10 *The Underground Home: New York World's Fair 1964–1965*, publicity brochure, Underground World Home Corporation.
11 Swayze, *Underground Gardens*, 20.
12 Swayze, *Underground Gardens*, 10.
13 Lyon, "Glorious Nightmare," 62.
14 *Underground Home*.

In the 1970s, with the oil crisis, the emphasis would turn toward energy saving, and in the 1980s toward ecological concerns. The description of the battlefield changes. The traditional domestic ideal of "peace and quiet" could be produced only by engaging the house in combat, as a weapon: counterdomesticity.

The sponsor of the Underground Home was General Electric, who also commissioned Walt Disney to produce the Carousel of Progress, a series of theatrical sets that exhibited the history of the interior from 1880 to 1964 by tracing the transformations of the house through electricity. In the General Electric pavilion, a demonstration of thermonuclear fusion reaction—"similar to H-bomb"—took place every fifteen minutes under a translucent dome. **419** **420** **421** Nuclear power, a by-product of military technology, was presented both as a mass spectacle and as a transformation of the interior, a new kind of house for a bleak future. **418** Books on a shelf in the Underground Home included *Journey into a Fog* and *The U.S. Air Force Report on the Ballistic Missile*. The fallout-shelter program was presented at the fair by the US Office of Civil Defense and the US Atomic Energy Commission in their "Atomsville, U.S.A." exhibit, which also presented an explanation of nuclear energy for children.[15] In the cold-war mentality, the house of the future would be both nuclear powered and a defense against nuclear attack.

The idea of the house of the future goes back to the beginning of the twentieth century, and its development is tied up with the emergence of new media and new technologies: electricity, telephone, radio, car, airplane, steel frame, concrete, glass, plastic, air-conditioning, television, video, surveillance systems, computer, internet, broadband, wireless networks . . . The dream of the future is technological, and the house is its the laboratory.

The Underground Home, presented at the 1964 fair as "something different in housing" and "the forerunner of dwellings," was part of this tradition of houses of the future, the exacerbation of an existing trend, since houses of the future have always been all about staying inside and keeping the outdoors away. Throughout the twentieth century, images, models and prototypes of elaborate kitchens presented housewives with the illusion of a world at their command, full of push-button-operated, self-cleaning, self-monitoring, labor-saving, automated technological wizardry. But they also presupposed that we were all eating in, not out—as a logical future with a clearly established division of labor may suggest. The inside, like the housewife herself, was immaculately put together, glamorous, irresistible, with appliances taking the shape of objects to admire—to watch, even, as with the introduction of "windows" in ovens and washing machines. The interior became all-absorbing, fascinating, captivating. Why ever go out? Air-conditioning ensured that the outside air was cleansed of all dust, impurities, pathogens. Materials such as steel, aluminum, glass, and plastic were presented as hygienic, dust proof, and self-cleaning. Even visitors and deliverymen were carefully screened or totally kept away, as with fantasies of refrigerators accessible from the outside of the house or hatches for dropping packages, mail, groceries, and so on. Not even the inhabitants of the house crossed the threshold. They seemed never to leave.

Houses of the future were all hyperinteriorized spaces. The house steadily excluded more and more of the outside world as the twentieth century proceeded. In the Underground Home, there was no outside in the end: the house was just an idealized inside. If the basic idea of a house is that it divides an inside from an outside, houses of the future radicalized that division, giving a primitive, even archaic quality to their high-tech fantasies. The Underground Home was a cave in which any image of the outside could be constructed and inhabited, domesticating fear by inhabiting an idealized version to the exterior.

15 *Official Guide*, 206.

Such radical transformations of interior/exterior were not isolated moments within the 1964 fair but its main theme. The IBM pavilion, designed by Eero Saarinen and Associates in collaboration with Charles and Ray Eames, included an egg-shaped theater ninety feet high and covered with the letters IBM repeated one thousand times.[16] **394** **424** The grandstand seats that made up the "People Wall" **396** moved up hydraulically, lifting an audience of five hundred into the theater where they could see "Information Machine," a twelve-minute show created by the Eameses. **425** **398** In the words of *Holiday* reporter Lyon, "fourteen synchronized projectors use nine screens to show you how lucky you are to have a brain, how your brain works, and how a computer does its mechanical best to emulate your cerebration. It is sharp, it is wise, it is funny. . . . Charles Eames . . . is to be thanked for never having condescend to his mass audience and so is IBM."[17] Even Vincent Scully approves of this pavilion in exuberant terms when he describes how visitors were "cheered on by a splendid fellow who began the whole business by appearing before you high on a platform let down from the egg—like a jolly young god, triumphant over gravity. . . . In this punctual *deus ex machina* the designers have hit a Dionysian button, calling up emotions of awe, terror, recognition and joy that are far more religious than those which Michelangelo's *Pietà* evokes in its present shameful setting."[18] **395** The Vatican had lent Michelangelo's *Pietà* to the Fair, and the statue was shown behind a bulletproof plastic shield, with viewers passing by on a moving ramp. The IBM pavilion, on the other hand, showed no objects. It was nothing but a media machine with its occupants lifted into an enveloping array of images, an interior space defined by images illustrating the way the computer thinks: its binary logic, for example, was translated into everyday life—young twins holding hands, a small child blowing out two candles on his birthday cake, a couple of lovers, the number 2, a pair of hands, two apples, and so on. Likewise, the Bell pavilion exhibited the "picturephone": "the televised telephone, or the teletelephone or the videophone or whatever it may be called when eventually it is among us, slaughtering forever such folkways as the blind date, always in the name of Progress."[19] And the Coca-Cola pavilion echoed the Underground Home's environmental simulation by providing simulations of countries: "The visitor experiences not only the sights and sounds of five foreign countries but also their smells and their temperature changes. He goes from a crowded street in Hong Kong (past a fish store whose smell was so overpoweringly authentic that it had to be deodorized before opening day), to the Taj Mahal, to a perfumed rain forest in Cambodia, to a bracing ski resort in the Bavarian Alps, to the slowly canting deck of a cruise ship just off Rio de Janeiro. It is an amusing journey."[20] At the Kodak pavilion the visitor could see, outside, the largest color prints then possible and, inside, the means by which the day's news pictures came in by wire, just as they were being received by newspapers and television stations all over the country. **426** The Kodak pavilion also offered itself as a stage set to take pictures of oneself and one's family in the background of the fair or in such unthinkable places as the moon (there was a "moondeck" on the roof). **427** Everywhere at the fair, new media were seen to make possible new environmental experiences, not simply representing the world, but reconstructing it, media becoming the environment.

Kodak, for example, introduced its new Instamatic camera at the 1964 fair. With it, the camera, this window onto the world, which at the 1939 fair had still

---

16 Saarinen died in 1961, and the building was completed by Kevin Roche and John Dinkeloo.

17 Lyon, "Glorious Nightmare," 57.

18 Vincent Scully, quoted in Bletter, "The 'Laissez-Fair,'" 112. Bletter refers to John E. T. Van Duyl, "The Unforgettable IBM Pavilion at the New York World's Fair of 1964," *World's Fair*, Fall 1987, 9–11. *IBM Fair*, souvenir book, IBM corporation.

19 Lyon, "Glorious Nightmare," 56.

20 Ibid., 57.

been contemplated (like the television) with amazement, as a technological object, had become a mass-consumption object. **428** Moreover, these objects were no longer seen as discrete. The television was everywhere, part of every space. The Instamatic was no longer even a technological object but a cheap piece of plastic: eight dollars, with a built-in flash. With the mass consumption of the camera came the "privatization" of the view, that is, of the "exterior." People could construct their own histories in photographs, in snapshots, just as they could construct the "exterior" of their (underground) houses as images of cities to be seen on the inside.

This is consistent with the idea of the city presented by the 1964 World's Fair in the Futurama exhibits. Whereas the first Futurama, at the 1939 fair, could still present the viewer with a coherent, unified image of the city, a modernist proposal of steel-and-glass towers, an object over which the visitor, a detached, amazed viewer, had no control, Futurama 2 offered a collection of "improbable" places where people were to live in the future: on the moon, in the jungle, below ice, under the sea, and in the desert.[21] **429** **430** **431** **432** **433** Houses had turned into a wide range of spacecrafts, science fiction about to be inhabited. **434** **435** **437**

The visitor of 1964 could achieve "unity" only through a "frame," a collage of images assembled as he or she moved through the fair. This visitor, unlike that of 1939, was given the illusion of control (control over the images both "inside" the house and "outside" on the fairgrounds). This "frame" became that of the television screen. Television was everywhere. Virtually every exhibit in the fair involved television. Indeed, the fair itself was read at the time as "the biggest television set in the world," in the words of one reporter. "It will have everything on the 'screen' except the Beverly Hillbillies, the top rated network show."[22]

But in fact the 1964 fair never had the appeal of the 1939 installment, which is now said to have been "the last fair on earth." By 1964, television itself was more appealing, and the time of the fairs had passed: the mechanism of the World's Fair, the capturing of everything in one place, was no longer operating outside, in the traditional public space, on the fairgrounds, but within the domestic interior. The public domain had been displaced indoors. Or as Patricia Phillips has written:

> Just as the public space has become diminished as a civic site, the home has become in many senses, a more public, open forum. The public world comes into each home as it never has before through television, radio and personal computer. So that rituals that were once shared conspicuously in a group are now still shared—but in isolation. An example of this ambiguous condition is the annual celebration of the New Years' Eve in Times Square. Which is the more public event—the throng of people gathering at 42nd Street to watch a lighted apple drop or the millions of people at home, each watching this congregation on TV?[23]

One thinks also of the televised spectacles of the 1960s: Kennedy's assassination and funeral (in fact, many Americans bought their first television set to "attend" the president's funeral), the moon landing, the Vietnam War, and so on. The home theater of television established a new drama ranging from the collective euphoria of the moon landing to the collective trauma of Vietnam, emphatically removing any division between local private domestic life and international, or even interplanetary, public events. Life and death in the living room.

---

21 While Futurama presented also a "City of the Future" at the 1964 Fair, General Motors declared: "The city, which long strove for growth, is imperiled by its own excesses." Quoted in Bletter, "The 'Laissez-Fair,'" 121. If GM had given up on the city, so did most visitors.

22 "A TV View of the Fair," *New York Sunday News*, April 12, 1964, World's Fair section, 26.

23 Patricia C. Phillips, "Out of Order: The Public Art Machine," *Artforum*, December 1988, 96.

Martha Rosler's "Bringing the War Home: House Beautiful," a series of photomontages realized between 1967 and 1972, ruthlessly exposed the phenomenon by combining generic images of modern suburban interiors from architectural and design magazines with news ad images from the battlefields of Vietnam taken from newspapers and popular magazines like *Life*. 438 439 In these remarkable works, the image on the TV screen becomes the image in the picture window. The house is placed on the battlefield. Rosler removes the division between what is conveyed by the television and domesticity itself. The suburban American house becomes an inhabited television set.

If the glass walls of the postwar suburban house operated as a form of media, literally a way of seeing the world, the prototypical media of the period, television, produced a new kind of space. The glowing image of the TV screen has given rise to a new form of architecture in producing what Paul Virilio has called a "new form of visibility":

> I think we are witnessing a new form of visibility. I think that electronic images are replacing the electrification of towns and of the countryside in the late 19th and early 20th century, in a certain way. . . . Automatic cameras and monitors are replacing street lights and neon lights in towns. When you move around in a modern town you notice that everything is concentrated into a video monitor which is not merely the video monitor of the prefecture of police, or of traffic circulation, but the video monitor of supermarkets, the video monitor of interactive blocks of flats in a closed circuit, and so on. And here we are no longer concerned with an image at all in the representational, artistic, illustrative meaning of the term; it is a question of another light, an electronic lighting, and I think that one can no longer conceive of space, whether it's living space, town space or even the space of the entire territory, without this new lighting.[24]

This new "lighting" that is produced by a new desire for control displaces traditional forms of enclosure. A photograph by Len Jenshel in which a security guard in the desert watches television is symptomatic of that condition.[25] **440** The television set has been placed in the trunk of his station wagon. The site is a no-man's-land. There is no traditional enclosure here, only a car, a surrogate enclosure. But the guard is precisely not in the car but outside it, looking in. The television occupies the space. It is the only thing comfortably placed. Its light passes out. The blue glow illuminates the man's face: he is, in fact, bathed in the light of the television. The security man finds security in the television, warming himself by the light of the electronic fire. But in so doing he is alienated, detached from traditional space.

A photograph of an underground house built by Swayze after the 1964 New York fair shows the television and the fireplace occupying the same wall, very close to each other, with a family gathered around them, warming up. **441** But in a house where the temperature is always kept constant, the function of the fireplace is purely visual. Since the chimney takes out not only fumes but also "undesirable scents or moisture" as part of the air-conditioning, the breathing system, it is actually, like the TV, a window.[26] In the Underground Home it is the TV set that makes possible the radical exclusion of the outside. Or, rather, it is the television set that provides the outside in the inside. The very capacity to connect to the wider world is at the same time the means to disconnect the house from the immediate world.

---

24 Paul Virilio, "The Work of Art in the Electronic Age" (translated transcript of an interview conducted on a French television program), *Block* 14 (1988): 4.

25 This photograph was one of the primary references for Diller + Scofidio's project of the Slow House in North Haven, Long Island, 1989. See Beatriz Colomina, "Domesticity at War," *Assemblage* 16 (1991): 14–41.

26 The etymology of the English word "window" reveals that it combines *wind* and *eye*, as Georges Teyssot has noted, "an element of the outside and an aspect of innerness." E. Klein, *A Complete Etymological Dictionary of the English Language* (Amsterdam, London, New York, 1966); cited in Ellen Eve Frank, *Literary Architecture* (Berkeley and Los Angeles: University of California Press, 1979), 263; and in Teyssot, "Water and Gas on All Floors," *Lotus* 44 (1984): 90. Each year at Christmastime, one American television network broadcasts the "Yule Log," which shows a log constantly burning.

Such combinations of bunker and television could be found everywhere at the fair. The underwater motel in the Futurama exhibit, for example, at once served as a bunker protected by the depths of the ocean, an open glass house, and literally took the form of a television set offering its images of domestic life to whoever swam by. 434

The evolution of the postwar American house relentlessly exhibited two trajectories that are represented at the 1964 fair. On the one hand, the house grew lighter and lighter, as if preparing for flight. On the other hand, it never took off but only gained strength, fortifying itself and bunkering farther down into the ground. In fact, these two trajectories are inseparable. The ever-increasing dematerialization of the house and the displacement of its traditional functions by new technologies of information were matched exactly by an increasing rematerialization at its borders and the emergence of ever-more-enclosing security systems. The cold-war house of the future was a stationary escape vehicle; the inhabitant of the future was able to escape without leaving. The house had finally become the whole world.

Epilogue

We are, we seem to be, on the edge of war. At the threshold. A line has been drawn. Literally, a deadline. In crossing that line, we go to war. We go outside. We leave the homeland and do battle on the outside. But there are always lines in the interior, within the apparently safe confines of the house. Even before we step outside, we are engaged in battle. As we all know but rarely publicize, the house is a scene of conflict. The domestic has always been at war. The battle of the family, the battle of sexuality, the battle for cleanliness, for hygiene, and, more recently, the ecological battle. With recycling, even the waste of the house is subjected to classification. Domesticated. People who lived through WWII are reminded of wartime, and not just because that was the last time they had to recycle. That recycling was all about the making of bombs.

"War is no longer identifiable with declared conflict, with battles," wrote Paul Virilio in 1978. "Nonetheless, the old illusion still persists that a state of peace means the absence of open warfare."[1] War can take place today without visible fighting. The battlefield of this new war is the domestic interior. The house is a military weapon, a mechanism within a war where the differences between defense and attack have become blurred.

An instance of this blurring of limits between war and peace was offered by a roundtable discussion on CBS last night, when the question most insistently asked to the multiple "guests" of the program, to the war "experts," was: "What signs should we be looking for in the next two or three days; what signs will indicate to us that we have *really* entered war?" That is, the media, which is supposed to make visible the war, was at a loss in the moment of identifying what would constitute evidence. The guests, who are, after all, guests in the home of the viewer, are unable to anticipate what the image of the war would be. The image therefore might arrive in the house before it is recognized. The house is already mobilized . . .

This is how I began the lecture "Domesticity at War," from which this book takes its title, delivered at the School of Architecture at the University of Illinois at Chicago on the evening of January 16, 1991. During the lecture, the bombing of Baghdad began. And now, as we go to press, the second war in Iraq continues. The book was written between the two wars. In fact, the manuscript for the book was already completed by September 11, 2001. The events stopped me short. It was not just that the World Trade Center was so close to my home in New York, barely two hundred meters away (the engine of the second plane landed on the roof of the building next door), or that I witnessed it from our roof, so close that you could see deep inside the hole made by the first plane, or that we were evacuated for what seemed an excruciatingly long period of time. What I had written about the myriad effects of the militarization of domesticity in postwar America didn't seem historical anymore. We were now living it. Far too close to write about it. During the first war in Iraq, CNN literally advertised itself with "CNN brings you the frontline to your living room," that is, to what we used to call "front room." Not only do we have the collapse of the "outside" space into this line, this front; but also, since this line is unclear, what the war speaks about is the difficulty of establishing the limits of domestic space. Television not only brings the public indoors, the front line into our living rooms, but also sends the private into the public domain. The various battle lines are multiplied, disseminated, and juxtaposed. The war that is the domestic both occupies and is about this complex space.

This became very clear during the 1991 war in the Gulf, when most of the images we received by newspapers or television were making a spectacle of either

---

1 Paul Virilio, *Popular Defense & Ecological Struggles*, trans. Mark Polizzotti (New York: Semiotext(e), 1990), 36. Originally published as *Défense populaire et Luttes écologiques* (Paris: Editions Galilée, 1978).

military technology, the smart bombs, the stealth bombers, and the missiles (the bombing of Baghdad on January 16, 1991, was compared by a CNN reporter to a July 4 fireworks display 444) or, alternatively, images of the interior—the hotel room from which the CNN journalists reported the first evening of the war by literally describing the view out their windows; Saudis with gas masks on heeding the ancient call to prayer in a bomb shelter; 445 Israelis wearing masks carrying on their domestic lives in shelters or in plastic-lined, gas-proofed rooms in their homes; or Americans at home in front of their television sets. All eyes everywhere were on the screen. And on the screen were other eyes and other screens. The domestic interior at the end of the twentieth century, broadcasting and receiving, live.

While the interior of the end of the nineteenth century offered a refuge from the outside, from the city, from the public, now the public has invaded the interior; it is already inside. Refuge is no longer a viable strategy. Perhaps there is no such thing as refuge anymore. The enemy is always within. So the only form of defense is counterattack; the only form of domesticity is counterdomesticity.

The relationship between architecture and war is not new. We build defensively. Cities were once fortifications built as defense against war, and new wars generate new kinds of thinking about space. In the twentieth century, this is most obvious in the development of new media. Twentieth-century wars were all media wars. During World War I, the telephone and the radio played a crucial role on the battlefields. Battles are said to have been won by *coups de téléphone*.[2] After the war, the technologies deployed by the military were domesticated. In the '20s, airplane service was established throughout Europe, and radios and telephones were widely introduced into the domestic space, radically transforming the relationships between inside and outside, private and public. Modern architecture was in many ways a product of World War I. New media had created a new sense of space in which the distinctions between inside and outside, near and far, had collapsed. Architects responded by creating an architecture where little distinction between inside and outside remained. The inside became a landscape without rooms, and the outside started to be understood as an interior. As Le Corbusier put it: "*Le dehors est toujours un dedans*" (The outside is always an inside).

World War II also had a decisive impact on architecture, and with the new form of war inaugurated by 9/11, new attitudes to space emerge, new understandings of construction, surveillance, air quality, and so on. And again our sensitivity is raised to the complex interactions of architecture and media that transform the relationship between public and private. Take the key role played by the Internet in the planning and execution of the World Trade Center attacks. Money, instruction, and ideas were moved through that space, using public libraries and other public institutions as facades for ultraprivate, ultrasecretive exchanges.

Many people throughout the world were working at their computers, connected through the Internet, and it was in that space where they found out about the attack on the WTC. Others encountered it on television. But perhaps most extraordinary, for the first time in the history of a catastrophe, the families and loved ones of many of the victims were among the first to know when they received cellphone calls made from hijacked airplanes and from inside the World Trade Center towers. In the heart of the spectacular nightmare, covered continuously by every single channel of television, the most intimate exchanges were taking place.

If, during World War II, soldiers used to carry with them good-bye letters to be delivered to their wives, girlfriends, children, or parents in the event of their deaths—letters that were written and rewritten between battles so that they

---

2 Marious-Ary Leblond, *Galliéni parle* (Paris, 1920), 53.

would be updated as close to the end as possible—during 9/11 we had civilians reaching out by cell phone to the people they cared most about in their last seconds of existence. The most human of contacts was enabled by portable phones.

In the aftermath of the events, the desperate attempts on the part of cellphone companies to deliver the last messages that had not gone through attested to the importance of such messages. In a situation in which there were very few bodies recovered, or even fragments of bodies, those messages were all that was left, the very thing that is always missing in tragic accidents. No longer simply a fragile substitute for real people, the digital record became the most solid reality.

Any traditional sense of public and private space became obsolete on 9/11. There was a new sense of space constructed by the unrelenting bombardment of repetitive images through TV and the Internet and the simultaneous exchange of the most intimate and unique, one-on-one communications via cell phones.

9/11 was a hypersaturated media event and a hyperphysical event too. We were suspended within communication, or the lack of it, hanging from our telephones, cell phones, e-mails, TVs, radios, and the Internet. But the closer you were to the World Trade Center site, the more the event was also intensely physical, defined by sensations undetected by the media: the extremely loud, unrecognizable noise of the first airplane crash into the World Trade Center (a bomb, we thought); the trembling of the buildings we occupied (an earthquake, a neighbor thought); cars crashing into each other in the streets below us (perhaps mesmerized at the sight, or suddenly braking in the shock of the sound); the thump of the airplane engine hitting the roof next door, then falling to the sidewalk; the screams of the throngs of people running from the site; the smells, an acrid mix of burning fuel, plastic, and rubber; our apartment going completely dark as it became engulfed in a dense cloud of falling debris as each tower collapsed; the spongy feel of the thick layer of dust and paper at the end of the day, when we were finally forced to evacuate and the National Guard had taken over; the streets filled with unpaired shoes and bags abandoned or lost in the stampede; a big fireman with his safety boots on sitting on the sidewalk at the corner, his back against a building, his hands holding his head, crying inconsolably. Nothing or little of all of this was on the news, which repeated with numbing regularity the planes going into the buildings and the collapse of the two towers. And yet even those who experienced it close by needed the media to make some sense of it.

The Rodney King riots in Los Angeles in 1992 had shown that private video cameras were playing a crucial role in the city—a role never anticipated by manufacturers—as tools of civilian defense, of control of public space by policing the police. If the riots revealed that at any one moment, anywhere, a video camera was already recording, 9/11 showed the role of cell phones in urban space, not as the annoying pieces of equipment that they are, intruding in the few pockets of tranquillity of everyday life, but as emergency tools, tools of civilian defense, not so different from the pieces of battle equipment we have been, in the meantime, encouraged to incorporate into our lives: the gas masks, the wind-up radios and torches, the duct tape, the antiradiation pills, and so on. It is no longer the substance of a fixed building that protects the space of personal life but an array of nomadic technologies. **447**

If the cold-war age was organized around fantasies of the well-stocked concrete bunker, in our age endless catalogs offer survival devices that suggest that the role of the bunker has been taken over by a set of lightweight accessories such that it is even possible to imagine that a thin nylon coat could become a home. The 1995 "Final Home Jacket" by Kosuke Tsumura is a garment "designed to serve as a nomadic 'home' in the event of a disaster. . . . The ample pockets may be filled with newspapers for warmth, or used for storing personal belongings, food, maps and other survival gear. Hand-wash with cold water or dry clean. One size fits all."[3] 447

If 9/11 in New York revealed the cell-phone as the last vestige of domesticity, 3/11 in Madrid revealed the cell-phone as a weapon, triggering the bombs in the trains. Personal defense became public attack. Once again, the intimate relationship between domesticity and war had evolved. If the dilemma for TV analysts in 1991 was how to know that war had begun, the dilemma now is how to know that it has ended. Increasingly, we understand that the so-called war on terror has no end. This, of course, is the lesson of the cold-war years. War does not end. It evolves, and architecture with it.

---

[3] *MoMA Design Store*, catalog, Museum of Modern Art, Spring 2006, 16.

303

Acknowledgments

War and modern architecture: those were the two dominant themes I grew up with. The traumatic experiences of the Spanish civil war, relived again and again in countless stories from all sides, and the immersive day-to-day world of architecture, since our home was essentially an architect's office. It was just a matter of time before I put those two together. This book is dedicated to my mother and to the memory of my father, who both, in so many ways, personify the period I am writing about here. While 1950s and '60s Spain was not postwar America, they were constantly receiving transatlantic signals. The stream of popular magazines and architectural journals that came into the house every day kept pointing to a new kind of modernity. Everything I grew up with, from the chairs to the fashion to the architecture, was modern. And the thought of war never went away.

Preparing a book is like moving through a city that has a curious layout. Certain places become landmarks or temporary homes, and along the way you meet people that help you navigate parts of the territory. I am grateful to the Center for Advanced Studies in the Visual Arts for a Samuel H. Kress Senior Fellowship that allowed me to spend 1995–96 in Washington, DC, doing research in the archives of Charles and Ray Eames at the Library of Congress. Henry Millon and Theresa O'Malley were extraordinary interlocutors and hosts, in the Eamesian sense of creating an atmosphere for exchange. My fellow residents Leah Dickerman, Oskar Batschmann, Dario Gamboni, and William Conklin offered feedback and friendship. The Graham Foundation supported my research on x-ray architecture and invited me to give a series of lectures of the work in progress. I am grateful to the late Richard Solomon for his unique wisdom and personal generosity. I also benefited from a research-support grant from the Resource Collections of the Getty Center for the History of Art and the Humanities. The Princeton University Committee on Research in the Humanities gave several summer research grants and generously contributed to the production of the book.

Writing about the '50s has meant to have, for the first time in my research, the privilege of being able to talk with some of the protagonists and those close to them. It has sometimes also meant seeing them go. I am grateful to Alison and Peter Smithson for many conversations and to their children, Simon, Samantha, and Soraya, who allowed me to continue my research in the Smithsons' archives in Cato Lodge, their house in London, after the death of Peter in March 2003. From Max Risselada, who worked for both the Eameses and the Smithsons, I gained through small details of everyday life revealed in conversation invaluable insights into the world of both couples. Lucia Eames and Eames Dimitrius were kind and helpful. Donald Albrecht opened my eyes to some key documents, and Pat Kirkham generously offered crucial insights. I have also benefited from work in the archives of the Museum of Modern Art in New York, where chief archivist Rona Roob deserves special thanks; the Center for American Architecture, Design and Engineering, in the Library of Congress, where I benefited from Ford Peatross's deep knowledge of the Eameses; the Canadian Centre for Architecture in Montreal; the Victoria and Albert Museum in London; the Queens Museum; the Vitra Design Museum in Weil am Rhein; the Archives of American Art at the Smithsonian Institution; the National Archives in Washington; Harvard University Archives; and the Avery Library at Columbia University. As always, I am especially grateful to Frances Chen, head librarian in the School of Architecture at Princeton University, for making everything seem easy.

Preliminary versions of parts of this book were first published in the journals *Ottagono*, *Assemblage*, *Daidalos*, *ANY*, *Grey Room*, and *In Si(s)tu*, and I am grateful to their respective editors for their support: Alessandra Ponte, K. Michael Hays, Alicia Kennedy, Gerrit Confurius, Cynthia Davidson, Reinhold Martin, Branden Joseph and Felicity Scott, and Joaquim Moreno. Other parts first appeared in *Autonomy and Ideology: Positioning an Avantgarde in America: 1923–4*, edited by Robert E. Somol (Monacelli Press, 1997); *The Work of Charles and Ray Eames: A Legacy of Invention*, edited by Donald Albrecht (Harry N. Abrams, 1997); *The American Lawn: Surface of Everyday Life*, edited by Georges Teyssot (Princeton Architectural Press/Canadian Centre for Architecture, 1999); and *Alison and Peter Smithson: From the House of the Future to a House of Today*, edited by Dirk van Heuvel and Max Risselada (010 Publishers, 2004). Again, many thanks to the editors of these titles for their insights.

My students at Princeton were, as always, the first audience of this work, and I am indebted to their contagious enthusiasm and critical acumen. Many have also worked as assistants at different points, including Susan Nelson, Jennifer Wei Leung, Sergio Lopez-Pineiro, Joaquim Moreno, and Urtzi Grau. I am particularly grateful to Alysa Nahmias, David Allin, and Rosalyne Shieh for their help in the last stages of this book.

Many thanks to the great team at ACTAR, Ramon Prat, Albert Ferré, Michael Kubo, Anna Tetas, Dolors Soriano, and specially Reinhard Steger, whose design so precisely captured the spirit of the work. Beatriz Preciado translated the manuscript for the Spanish edition, and Irene Perez-Porro did the subtle work of copyediting it. Christina Cho copyedited the English edition with great sensitivity and an eagle eye.

Thanks also to all my colleagues in the School of Architecture at Princeton: Star Allen, Christine Boyer, Liz Diller, Ed Eigen, Mario Gandelsonas, Bob Gutman, Ralph Lerner, Paul Lewis, Guy Nordenson, Spyros Papapetros, Jessie Reiser, Carles Valhonrat, Sarah Whitting and Ron Witte, for their companionship, and to my buddies in the Media and Modernity Program, Eduardo Cadava, Brigid Doherty, Hal Foster, Ruben Gallo, Michael Jennings, Thomas Levin, and Anson Rabinbach.

In the end, a book is a collaborative effort, and I am very appreciative of all those around me, particularly my friends who keep a running commentary on one another's work and all things architectural: Liz Diller, Ric Scofidio, Giuliana Bruno, Andrew Fierberg, Tony Vidler, Emily Apter, Rem Koolhaas, Hal Foster, Laura Kurgan, Sylvia Lavin, Tom Keenan, Jeff Kipnis, Felicity Scott, Mark Jarzombek, Reinhold Martin, Mark Cousins, Irene Perez Porro, Benedetta Tagliabue, Txatxo Sabater, Carmen Lopez, Carmen Bonell, Cecilio Sanchez Robles, and my siblings Cristina, Maria, Miguel, and Elena. Above all, I am grateful to my daughter Andrea, who was fascinated by the 1950s way before I was, and to Mark for being there.

Index

1984 see Orwell, George
3/11 302
9/11 297–302

A

Abercrombie, Stanley 251n10, 251n13, 259n28, 263n47
advertisement 6–7, 13, 18, 31, 33–44, 50, 53, 100, 114, 116, 119, 122, 126, 128–137, 149, 160, 171, 194, 202, 218, 230, 231, 244, 269, 276
Aalto, Aino 244
Aalto, Alvar 244
Ain, Gregory 29
    Exhibition *House in the Museum Garden* 8, 47–51, 54, 80–81, 82, 84
Airstream 310
Albinson, Don 250, 161
Albinson, Jon 161
Albrecht, Donald 42n28, 245n8, 259n33, 305, 306
Alteration to a Suburban House see Graham, Dan
American Express 136, 205
An American Family 172
American Academy of Arts and Sciences 88
American National Exhibition in Moscow 54–56, 103, 138, 241, 263–265, 268–269, 272, 92, 93, 94, 359–363, 365, 368–369, 370–377, 379–384
    Kitchen Debate 54–56, 138, 139n73, 241, 251,256, 269, 92, 360, 362–363
    model house 55, see also "Splitnik"
Andrews, Julie 88
A & P 276
Appliance House see Smithson, Alison and Peter
appliances 6, 55, 134–135, 140, 204, 207, 244, 251, 256, 283
archaic 203, 228–229, 283
Archigram 208, see also Chalk, Warren *and* Cook, Peter *and* Greene, David
Architectural Design 93, 159
Architectural Record 23, 42, 276
Arp, Hans 41n22
Arte Ambiente see Celant, Germano
Arts & Architecture 8, 26–28, 53–54, 100, 108, 271, 12, 37–38, 149
Arts Magazine 171
"Art X," see Eames, Charles and Ray, "Sample Lesson . . ."
AS in DS: An Eye on the Road see Smithson, Alison
athletics see gymnastics
atomic bomb 126–127, 136, 140, 228, 282, 149, 211
"Atomsville, U.S.A." 282
automobiles see cars
avant-garde 12, 22–26, 31, 33, 67, 80, 98–100, 102, 108, 149–153, 157, 161–162

B

babies 130–131, 136–137, 252, 199 see also children
Baghdad 297–298
Baker, Josephine 220
Ballentine, Bill 259
Banham, Reyner 26–27, 27n9, 202, 207–208, 229, 232, 317
Barcelona, International Exhibition 170, 176, 182
Barcelona Pavilion see Mies van der Rohe, Ludwig
Barnard College 24
Barr, Alfred 50–53, 51n49, 71, 78, 79n20, 86 see also Museum of Modern Art, New York
barracks 42, 72
Barry, Joseph A. 153n6
Baruch, Bernard 136
Barthes, Roland 206, 211, 244
Bascom, Arthur 210
Bauhaus see Gropius, Walter
Bauhaus Exhibition in Weimar 22
Bayer, Herbert 78, 265, 399
BBC 226
Bearse, P.E. 93
Becket, Welton 250, 377
beetles 120–122, 191, 317
Beetle 207, 207n20, 317 see also Volkswagen
Befreites Wohnen: Licht, Luft, Öffnung see Giedion, Sigfried
Behind the Picture Window see Rudofsky, Bernard
Behrendt, Walter Curt 23n1
Being and Nothingness see Sartre, Jean-Paul
Bell Laboratories 285
Belmont Radio and Television 132
Benjamin, Walter 7, 240
Berko, Ferenc 245
Berlin Building Exhibition see Grosse Berliner Kunstausstellung
Bernier, Rosamond 183n41, 185n46,189n54, 191n55
Bernstein, Elmer 262
Better Homes and Gardens 115, 118, 122, 129, 190
Biennale di Venezia see Venice Biennale
Big Brother 172, 219, 226
Birthday House see Eames, Charles and Ray
Black Mountain College 233
Blake, Peter 50, 51n42, 53n50, 251, 272
Bloomingdale's 50
Boeke, Kees 253n20
bomb shelters 56, 72–73, 75, 80, 138–140, 177, 227–228, 234–235, 279–282, 298, 96–99, 210, 414–418, 422, 441, 445
bombs 72–73, 75–78, 80, 115, 127, 234, 241, 282, 296–298, 300, 302, 149 see also atomic bomb
Bonta, Juan Pablo 171n26

Borg-Warner 128
Borbón, Alfonso de **260**
Braun, Ernst 245
Braune, Michael 262
Brennan, Annemarie 220n53
Breuer House *see* Breuer, Marcel
Breuer, Marcel 25, 40–41, 46–47, 53n50, **90**
  bedroom for Piscator, Berlin 154
  Breuer House, Connecticut 25
  House in the Museum Garden 8, 25, 40–41, 41n19–23, 46–47, 53–54, 80, **14 58 59 60**–**61 66 67 68 78 79 85**
  see also Museum of Modern Art, New York
Brick Country House *see* Mies van der Rohe, Ludwig
Bridge House *see* Eames, Charles and Ray
Bringing the War Home: House Beautiful see Rosler, Martha
Brinkman & Van der Vlugt 149
Brunelleschi, Filippo 262
Buchloch, Benjamin H. D. 172n28
Buch neuer Künstler 67
bugs *see* insects
Buick 133
Building in France, Building in Iron, Building in Ferro-concrete
  see Giedion, Sigfried
Built in the USA: Postwar Architecture see Museum of Modern Art, New York
Built in the USA: Since 1932 see Museum of Modern Art, New York
Bulletin of the Museum of Modern Art see Museum of Modern Art, New York
Business Week 188
bunkers 140, 185, 191, 227–228, 292, 301, **96**–**98 207 210**
  see also bomb shelters
Butler Manufacturing Company 62–63, 71, 74, **100**–**102**
Byvoet and Duiker 154

c

Cabine hôteliers see Schein, Lionel
Cadillac 133, 244
Calder, Alexander 41n22
Camel cigarettes 128
camouflage 72–73, 75, 75n19, 78–79, 219, **120**
Cape Canaveral 240, *see also* space program
Caplan, Ralph 270
caravans 204, **310**
Carousel of Progress *see* Disney
cars 6, 32, 116, 133, 134, 147, 149, 182, 203–209, 218, 233 251,252, 256, 282, 291, **23 186 223 227 312 313 315 316 370 436**
Carson, Johnny 172
Carson, Rachel 122n33, 127, 127n39
Cartwright, Lisa 146, 147n1-2, 149n5

Carville, James 136
Case Study House program 8, 25–29, 108, **12 22 37 48 49 50 122 123 124 125 126**–**127 143 144 169**
caves 228, 235, 283, **339**
CBS 182, 184, 188, 296
Celant, Germano 173
cell phones 300–301
Century of Progress International Exhibition, Chicago 1933-34 182
Chalk, Warren 208
Chareau, Pierre 25, 44, **33 73**
chemicals 122–127, 279
Chenal, Pierre 103, **175 247**
Chermayeff, Serge 46
Chevrolet 133
Chicago International Fair **221**
children 29, 40, 41n19, 72, 93, 97, 115, 126, 130, 132, 139, 153, 155, 206, 208, 218–219, 234, 252–253, 278, 282, 284, **46 84 98**–**99 114 136 137 138 160 161 165 188**–**189 199 200 202**–**204 207 210 228 241 242**–**243 247 332 366 406 425**
Chrysler 133–134
"Circarama" *see* Disney
Circus *see* Eames, Charles and Ray
Citroën DS 204–207, 211, **313 315**
cleanliness 67, 74, 81, 157, 160, 161, 163, 231, 232, 236, 283, 296,
  see also hygiene
clients 27, 46, 54, 97, 156, 160, 162, 184, 185
clothing 205, 208, 209, 210, 211 *see also* fashion
Clown Face see Eames, Charles and Ray
clowns *see* Eames, Charles and Ray, and circus
CNN 297–298
Coca-Cola 116–117, 285
cold war 12, 19, 54–56, 137–142, 177, 191, 241, 282, 292, 301–302
Colquhoun, Alan 18
Colomina, Beatriz, *Privacy and Publicity* 18, 29n13
collage 98, 195, 286
Communication Primer, A see Eames, Charles and Ray
computers 148, 240, 261, 262–263, **353 354**–**355 356 357 380 400 401 406 412 413**
  IBM, RAMAC 268, **400**–**401**
Computer Perspective, A see Eames, Charles and Ray
Concrete Country House *see* Mies van der Rohe, Ludwig
Concrete Office Building *see* Mies van der Rohe, Ludwig
Constantine, Mildred 251
consumer 8, 12, 55, 91, 107, 133–135, 171, 194, 197, 200, 202, 206, 250, 269
control room *see* situation room
Cook, Peter 208–209
Corbett, Mario 45
Corney, Kenneth 216
credit cards 136, *see also* American Express

Crystal House *see* Keck, George Fred
Cuban Missile Crisis 276, 279
cure cottages 161

D

Daily Mail 210, 214, 228, **321 325 332**
    Ideal Home Exhibition 194, 214–221, 235, **292 306**
Davos 154, **238 239** *see also* Thomas Mann
DDT 126–128, **194 196 198**
de Duve, Thierry 68
Defense House *see* Fuller, R. Buckminster, Dymaxion Deployment Unit (DDU) *and* Museum of Modern Art, New York
Delco Appliance 135
DeMars, Vernon 45–46
department stores 8, 55, 148–149, 245 *see also* Bloomingdale's *and* Gimbel's *and* Macy's
Design for Postwar Living Competition 28, 54, **38 90**
De Stijl exhibition in Paris 22
De Stijl 67
Diagram of the Field of Vision *see* Bayer, Herbert
Diehl, Digby 33n17–18, 87n4, 91, 265n51
Diller + Scofidio 291n25
Dinkeloo, John 287n16
disease *see* illness
Disney
    Carousel of Progress 282
    Circarama 138, 250
divorce 165, 207
Döcker, Richard
    sanatorium in Waiblingen 154, **237**
    Terrassentyp 154, **235–239**
    Weissenhof Siedlung, Stuttgart 155, **186 235**
Dodge 133
Drake, Gordon 29n7
Draper, Ruth 45n30
Drexler, Arthur 191
Dreyfuss, Henry 260, **357 358**
DS *see* Citroën DS
Duchamp, Marcel 68–70, 71n1, 81, 218
Duckett, Edward 172
Duiker, Jan **240**
DuMont 184, **283**
Dunlopillo 196
Dunne, Philip **165**
Dunne, Philippa and Miranda **165**
Dymaxion bathroom *see* Fuller, R. Buckminster
Dymaxion car *see* Fuller, R. Buckminster
Dymaxion Deployment Unit (DDU) *see* Fuller, R. Buckminster
Dymaxion House *see* Fuller, R. Buckminster

E

Eames, Charles and Ray 6–8, 18–19, 26–29, 30–33, 40, 80, 83–109, 202–203, 241, 245, 250–272, 284, **47 50 124 125 126–127 131 134 159 185 372 385 404**
    Birthday House 96
    Bridge House 32, 100–101, **12 50 144 169**
    Charles 29–33, 80, 87, 89–91, 93, 97, 100–101, 106, 245–246, 258–260, 264, 269–271, **13 21 44–45 52–53 132 146 153 154–155 176 177 178 179 407**
    Charles Eliot Norton Lectures 87–88, 106, 253n23, 258–260, **129**
    and Christmas 26, 29, 86, 88, 96, **36 47 131**
    and circus 87–89, 258–260, 270, 272, **129 130 389**
    Circus 258, **129**
    and clothes 19, 32, 88–89, **126 131 134**
    Clown Face 258, **391**
    Communication Primer, A 261, 263n43, **392**
    Computer Perspective, A **406**
    Computers at Work **413**
    Eames House (Case Study House 8) 6–8, 24, 26, 29–32, 83–109, 250, 263, **5 11 12 21 30–31 36 49 122–127 135 142 145–148 154–158 167 170–174 176–177 182–183 186–187 402–404 407**
    Eames Office 89, **10 21 407**
    Entenza House (Case Study House 9) 30, 90, **48 143 144**
    on *The Fabulous Fifties* (TV program) 263n45
    fiberglass chairs 197
    and film 19, 31–33, 96, 100–103, 245, 250–272
    and gifts 6–7, 86, 93–97, 108
    Glimpses of the USA (1959) 96, 103, 245, 251–257, 263–264, 272, **372–373 382 383–384 393**
    Herman Miller Showroom, Los Angeles 107, **184–185**
    House: After Five Years of Living 19, 102–103, 262, 21, 135, 158, 176–177, 407
    House of Cards 90, 93, **138**
    IBM pavilion *see* Saarinen, Eero
    Information Machine 268, 284, *see also* IBM pavilion
    Kwikset House 90, **140–141**
    and masks 88, 93, **132 160 164**
    Mathematica Exhibition **134 108–109**
    and Mies van der Rohe 100–102, 106–109, 178–181
    in photographs 29, 32, 86–88, 97, 101, 108–109, 273, **124–127 131 134 159 164 187 374**
    and photography 86–88, 97–98, 101–102, 106–107, 258–259, 271
    plywood animals 29, **46**
    plywood cabinets 29, **43 405**
    plywood children's furniture 29, **46 161 163**
    plywood furniture 29–30, 90, 92, 96, 258, 271, **43–44 152 161 405**
    plywood lounge chair 29, **44**

plywood splint   29, **40**–**42**, **45**
Powers of Ten   252–253, 270 , 385–389
Ray   86, 88, 90, 92, 96, 98, 102, **10**, **20**, **38**, **47**, **150**, **164**, **404**, **405**
Revell Toy House   90, 96, **139**
Sample Lesson for a Hypothetical Course   257–264, 268, **390**
Think   265, **398**, **425** *see also* IBM pavilion
toys   29, 90, 93, 96–97, **46**, **136**–**139**, **160**
What Is a House?   **153**
Wilder House   32–33, 96, **54**–**57**
Eames House   *see* Eames, Charles and Ray
Eastman Kodak pavilion   *see* Kahn and Jacobs
Eigen, Edward   41n20
Eisenman, Peter   185n48
Electromotive   133
émigrés   12, 26, 162
Entenza House   *see* Eames, Charles and Ray
Entenza, John   8, 12, 27, 29–30, 96, 108, **13**, **126**
Errazuris House   *see* Le Corbusier
exercise   155–157, **234**, **235** *see also* gymnastics
exhibition houses   202, 217, 219–220, 251 *see also* model houses
Exhibition House in the Museum Garden   *see* Ain, Gregory
    also see Museum of Modern Art, New York
expanded cinema   241
eyes   *see* vision, eyes

F
Fagus Work building   *see* Gropius, Walter
fallout shelters   *see* bomb shelters
fallout suit   **211**
Family Fallout Shelter   *see* United States Department of Defense
Family of Man, The   *see* Steichen, Edward
families   28, 32, 40, 42, 56, 62, 63, 71, 116, 130–132, 135–140, 163–164, 172, 184, 280, 285, 291, 296, **84**, **98**–**99**, **114**, **202**–**204**
Farnsworth, Edith   153, 155n7, 165
Farnsworth House   *see* Mies van der Rohe, Ludwig
fashion   79, 88, 108, 134, 163, 244, 251, **11**, **88**, **121**, **186**, **321**, **322**–**323**, **324**, **325**, **334**, **336**–**337**, **343**, **447** *see also* clothing
Faust, Christopher   **354**–**355**
Fibromold   196
Friedrichstrasse Skyscraper   *see* Mies van der Rohe, Ludwig
Fields, Gracie   45n30
film, architecture and   31, 62, 100, 103, 147 *see also* Eames, Charles y Ray, and film
FLIT   122, 126, **193**
food   6, 56, 126, 134, 196, 202, 216, 228, 253, 276, 302, **6**, **85**, **96**–**98**, **135**, **196**, **302**
Ford   133
Ford Motor Company pavilion   **436**
Fortune   245

Frampton, Kenneth   46, 229
Friedman, Alice   155n7, 165
Frank Brothers   *see* Eames, Charles and Ray, plywood cabinets
Friedrich, Caspar David   109
Frigidaire   133
Fujikawa, Joseph   172
Fuller, R. Buckminster   41, 62–81, 103, 184, 232–233, 250, 260, 276, **110**, **346**
    Defense House   *see* Dymaxion Deployment Unit
    Dymaxion bathroom   232
    Dymaxion car   182, **221**
    Dymaxion Company   63
    Dymaxion Deployment Unit (DDU)   41, 42, 54, 62–81, 232, **69**, **101**–**109**, **112**–**119**, **121**
    Dymaxion House   81, 184, 232, **346**
    Dymaxion Shelter prototype   **226**
    geodesic dome   103, 245, 250, 268, **368**–**369**, **372**–**373**, **384**
        see also American National Exhibition in Moscow
    Wichita House   73–74, 233, **110**, **111**
    World Game   260
Funk, John   46
Futurama   286
    Futurama 1 (1939 World's Fair)   286, **429**, **430**, **431**, **432**, **433**
    Futurama 2 (1964 World's Fair)   286, 287n21, 292, **414**, **434**, **437**

G
G (Gestaltung)   22, 106, **24**
Galassi, Peter   42
gardens *see* lawns and gardens
Garden of Paradise, The   235, **306**, **349**
Garnier, Tony
    Industrial City   155
gas masks   298, **301**, **446**
gaze   32, 146, 165, 168, 240, **446** *see also* surveillance *and* voyeurism
gender   132, 221, 244, **212**–**215**, **254**–**255** *see also* sex, sexuality
General Electric   132, 134, 147, 282, **200**, **419**–**421**
General Motors   133–134, **201** *see also* Futurama
Giedion, Sigfried   148, 154–156
    Befreites Wohnen: Licht, Luft, Öffnung   154, **232**–**234**
    Building in France, Building in Iron, Building in Ferro-concrete   155
geodesic dome   *see* Fuller, R. Buckminster
gifts   *see* Eames, Charles and Ray, and gifts
Gimbel's   46
Girard, Alexander   250, 257
Glasarchitektur   *see* Scheerbart, Paul
Glasshaus   *see* Taut, Bruno
Glass House   *see* Johnson, Philip
Glass House on a Hillside   *see* Mies van der Rohe, Ludwig

glass house   146, 164, 165, 173, 177, 182, 189, 190, 192
Glassraum, Glass Industry Exhibit of Stuttgart   see Mies van der Rohe, Ludwig and Reich, Lilly
Glass Skyscraper   see Le Corbusier and Mies van der Rohe, Ludwig
Glimpses of the USA   see Eames, Charles and Ray
Good Design   see Museum of Modern Art, New York
good life   6, 91, 256, 269, **202**–**203**
Goodyear   134
Goldsholl, Morton   **65**
Gräff, Werner   22
Graham, Dan   169–182
   Alteration to a Suburban House   169–173, **258**–**159**
   and Mies van der Rohe   170–176
   "Homes for America"   171, **262**–**263**
   Public Space/Two Audiences   173, **270**
   Video Projection Outside Home   171, **264**
grain bins, silos   41, 62–72, 80–81, **100**–**101**
Graves, Michael   188
Greene, David   208
Greenwald, Herb   172, **266**
Gregotti, Vittorio   270
Gris, Juan   41n22
Gropius, Alma   18, **18**–**19**
Gropius, Ise   13, **16**–**17**
Gropius, Walter   13–18, 53n50, 67, 276, **17 19**
   Bauhaus   149
   Fagus Work building   149
   Werkbund Exhibition, Paris   202, **220**
Grosse Berliner Kunstausstellung   22, 25n4, 154
Gulf, Persian   74
Gulf War   296–297
gymnastics   154–155, **242**–**243** *see also* exercise

H

Haag Bletter, Rosemarie   277n1
Häfeli, Max
   house in Zurich   154, **233**
Häfeli and Pfleghard, Max
   Sanatorium in Davos   **238 239**
Hamilton, Richard   195, see also Independent Group
Happenings   241
Harvard, Graduate School of Design   13, 26, 46
Hays, Michael   23n3
Hedrich-Blessing   **29 272**
health   128–129, 132, 146–147, 155–156, 161–165, 231–232
   see also medicine *and* mental health
Healy Guest House   see Rudolph, Paul
Hefner, Hugh   330, see also Playboy
Henderson, Nigel   203, **308**–**309** *see also* Independent Group

Henriksen, Margot A.   119n19, 139n75,79, 165n20
Herdeg, Klaus   53n52
Herman Miller   97n18
Herman Miller Showroom   see Eames, Charles and Ray
Hermès   54, **91**
Highlights and Shadows   see Kodak Research laboratories
Hine, Thomas   170
Hitchcock, Henry-Russell   23–24, 25n4, 51, 53n50, 189
Hodgson House   see Johnson, Philip
Hofmann, Hans   102, 108, **172 173**
Holiday   245, 276, 278, 281, 284
Hollywood   31, 269
"Homes for America"   see Graham, Dan
Hotpoint kitchens   **366**
House: After Five Years of Living   see Eames, Charles and Ray
House & Garden   **188**–**189 287**
House Beautiful   114–117, 119, 153, 165, 188, 196, 290, **190**
House in the Museum Garden   see Breuer, Marcel
House of Cards   see Eames, Charles and Ray
House of the Future   see Monsanto *and* Smithson, Alison and Peter
House of Tomorrow   see Keck, George Fred
Houses for Good Living   see Wills, Royal Barry
housewives   55, 138, 218–219, 244, 253, 256, 283, **254**–**255**
hygiene   129, 156, 232, 296, *see also* cleanliness

I

IBM   268, 284
   Computers at Work   see Eames, Charles and Ray
   IBM pavilion   see Saarinen, Eero
   RAMAC   305, see computers
Ideal Home Exhibition   see Daily Mail and Scottish Daily Mail
illness   128–129, 146, 163, *see also* mental health *and* tuberculosis
Illness as Metaphor   see Sontag, Susan
Independent Group (IG)   7, 7n2, *see also* Hamilton, Richard *and* Henderson, Nigel *and* Smithson, Alison and Peter
   Parallel of Life and Art   203, **308**
   Patio and Pavilion   195n3, 203, 208, 229, 234–235, **309 319**
Industrial City   see Garnier, Tony
information   68, 240–241, 256, 259–264, 268–272, 284, 292
   information overload   264
insects   103, 117–122, 126–128, 134, 207, 281, **191 193 197**–**198 317**
   see also beetles *and* Japanese beetle
insecticides   119, 122, 127, 134, 140, **194**–**196 198**
Inspectoscope   148
Institute of Contemporary Arts, London (ICA)   7n2
Interiors   191, 276
International Style   see Museum of Modern Art
   Modern Architecture: International Style

Internet   272, 282, 299–300
Iraq war   297
Izvestia   245

J

Japanese beetle, as pests   119–122, 147–148, **191**
Jahrbuch des Deutschen Werkbundes   67
Jeanneret, Pierre
    L'Esprit Nouveau Pavilion   202
    Nestlé Pavilion   202
    Villa Stein-De Monzie   312
jeans   205, 211
Jeep   50, 149
Jeepster   50
Jenkins, Dorothy   88, **133**
Jenshel, Len   291, **440**
Johnson, Philip   22, 24–25, 28, 45–46, 50–53, 130, 170, 177–185, 188–191, **274 276–277 285**
    Glass House   24–25, 171, 177, 182–188, 190, **28 273–274 278–279 281 284 287 290–291**
    Hodgson House   184
    This Is Philip Johnson (TV program)   182, 189
    and television   177–191
Journal of the American Institute of Architects   23
Journal of the American Medical Association   147
Josephine Baker House   *see* Loos, Adolf

K

Kahn, Albert   **429** *see also* Futurama
Kahn, Louis   177, 276
Kahn and Jacobs   285, **426 427**
Kaufmann, Edgar   40, 51, 53n50, **64 150**
Keck, George Fred   45
    Crystal House   149, 182, **223**
    House of Tomorrow   182
Kelvinator   134–135
Kennedy, John F.   56n57, 139, 279, 287
Kepes, Gyorgy   261
Kessel, Dmitri
Khrushchev, Nikita   55, 138, 241, 244, **92 360 362–363**
Kiesler, Frederick   276
    Space House   214, **327**
Kim, Jeannie   219n53
King, Rodney, riots   301
Kipnis, Jeffrey   189n49
Kirkham, Pat   89n10, 91n12, 98n25, 103n27, 251n18, 272n65, 305
kits of parts   90
Kitchen Debate   *see* American National Exhibition in Moscow
kitchens   41n19, 50, 55, 71, 125, 153, 163, 164, 196, 206, 226, 227, 233n80, 241, 251, 256, 269, 281, 283, **84 85 92 254–256 302–303 366 378 379 380–381** *see also* Whirpool Miracle Kitchen
Klearflax   53, **87**
Klee, Paul   98
Klein, Stanley H.   **93**
Knox, Doris   **152**
Koch, Carl   45
Koch, Robert   156
Kodak Research Laboratories   285
    Instamatic camera   285–286
Kodak pavilion   *see* Kahn and Jacobs
    Highlights and Shadows   146, 153, 164–165, **212–213**
    Supermatic Shutter   **428**
Koenig, Pierre   **22**
Krausse, Joachim   235n82
Kwick-dry   **344**
Kwikset House   *see* Eames, Charles and Ray

L

Lacan, Jacques   168, 169n21
Ladies' Home Journal   6, 44, 188
Lake Shore Drive apartments 860–880   *see* Mies van der Rohe, Ludwig
Lambert, Eleanor   251
Language of Vision see Kepes, Gyorgy
L'architecture d'aujourd'hui   13, 25–26, 27n7, 44, **32**
L'architecture d'aujourd'hui (film)   *see* Le Corbusier *and* Chenal, Pierre
Lasdun, Denys   221n61
Laszlo, Paul   25
Laver, James   209
La Ville Radieuse   *see* Le Corbusier
Lavin, Sylvia   162, 163n15
lawns and gardens   6, 114–140, 157, 169, 171, 190, 197, 197n9, 200, 228–235, 281, **190 194–195 201 206–209**
    as therapy   117, 119, 128
    victory gardens   115–116, 133–134, **201**
lawn mowers   45, 128, 130, 132, 134, 136, 140, 244
Le Corbusier   13, 18, 22–23, 28, 30–31, 46, 54, 67, 103, 148, 155–157, 188, 204–206, 234, 299, **19 26**
    Errazuris House   53
    Fondation Le Corbusier, Paris   18
    Glass Skyscraper   149
    L'architecture d'aujourd'hui (film)   31, 103, **175 247**
    L'art decoratif d'aujourd'hui   157
    La Ville radieuse   156–157, **221 245 246**
    Les Maisons Voisin   28, **39**
    L'Esprit nouveau   30, 54, 67, **25 39 91**
    L'Esprit Nouveau Pavilion   202
    Maison Citrohan   204
    Nestlé Pavilion   202

Ozenfant House   24
Vers une architecture   22, **24**
Villa d'Avray   103
Villa Savoye   103
Villa Stein-De Monzie   **312**
Villa Stein in Garches   103
Ville Contemporaine   18
Weissenhof Siedlung   **186 235**
Léger, Fernand   41n22
Leisurama House   *see* Lowey, Ramond
L'Esprit nouveau   22, 30, 54, 67, **25 39 91**
L'Esprit Nouveau Pavilion   *see* Le Corbusier and Jeanneret, Pierre
Levitt, William   137,
Levittown   184, **209**
Lichtenstein, Roy   276
Life   56, 96, 108, 114–115, 117, 120–121, 126–128, 130, 133, 135–136, 138, 149, 188, 200, 244–245, 276, 278, 290, **211 365 408–409**
L'Illustration   54
Lipstadt, Hélène   245n8
Lissitkzy, El   22
   Proun rooms   22
Look   188, 245
Loos, Adolf   148
   Josephine Baker House   220
Louds family   *see* An American Family
Lovell Beach House   *see* Schindler, R. M.
Lovell "Health" House   *see* Neutra, Richard
Lowey, Ramond   55
   Leisurama House   55, **95**
L. Teweles Seed Co.   132
Lurcat, André   154
Lyon, Peter   278, 284

M
MA   67
Maalox   134
machine aesthetic   100
Macy's   55, 251
Magic Mountain, The   *see* Mann, Thomas
Magnum Photos   245
Maison Citrohan   *see* Le Corbusier
maison plastique   *see* Schein, Lionel
malathion   127
Mallet-Stevens, Robert   31
   Villa Noailles   155
Mann, Thomas   154, 161
Market in Moscow   *see* Melnikov, Konstantin
Marling, Karal Ann   55n54, 139n73, 245n1
masks   130–131, 298, *see also* Eames, Charles and Ray, and masks

gas masks   298, 301
masque   *see* Smithsons, Alison and Peter
mass production   26, 28–29, 40, 42, 46, 54, 62–63, 68, 70, 73–74, 184, 197, 204, 211
Masey, Jack   250
Matalin, Mary   136
Mathematical Theory of Communication   *see* Shannon, Claude
Matter, Alexander (Pundy)   **46**
Matter, Herbert   108, **15 37 152**
McAndrew, John   40, 51
McCall's Book of Modern Houses   163
McCall's   85
McCoy, Esther   27n11, 92, 93n5
Meccano set   29
medicine   118, 122, 127–131, 134, 136, 146–149, 153–157, 160, 162–163, 169, 176, *see also* health
Melnikov, Konstantin
   Market in Moscow   202
   USSR Pavilion in Paris   202
Mendelsohn, Erich   149, **222**
mental health   118, 161, 164–165, **254–255**
   psychoanalysis   162, 164
   psychology   117–118, 138, 162–164, 280
Mercedes-Benz   **186**
Merchandise Mart   51, **63**
Mercury   133
Mertins, Detlef   23n3
Metro Goldwyn Mayer (MGM)   31, 62, 90, 269
Michelangelo   262, 284
Mies van der Rohe, Ludwig   22–24, 32, 46, 86, 98–102, 106–109, 153, 155, 170–173, 176–183, 188–190, 194, 202, 270–271, **51 266**
   860-880 Lake Shore Drive apartments   172–173, **267–269**
   Barcelona Pavilion   106, 170, 176, 182, 201, 234, **260**
   Brick Country House   23, 24
   Concrete Country House   22–23
   Concrete Office Building   22
   Farnsworth House   24, 32, 101, 109, 153–154, 165, 171, 177–183, 189, 194, **29 51 187 229 257 272 275 280 288 289**
   G (Gestaltung)   22, 106, **24**
   Glass House on a Hillside   100, 182, **168**
   Glass Room, Glass Industry Exhibit of Stuttgart   23, 182
      see also Lilly Reich
   Glass Skyscraper   22–23, 98, 153, **24 231**
   Museum for a Small City   98
   Office Building on Friedrichstrasse   23, 153, **230**
   Resor House   98
   Seagram Building   188–189
   Tugendhat House   81, 155, **241–243**
   Velvet and Silk Café   106, 202 *see also* Reich

Miracle Kitchen *see* Whirlpool
Mirrors 169–171, 173
missiles 8, 73, 241, 282, 298 *see also* Cuban Missile Crisis
Mock, Elizabeth B. 44
model houses 55, 185
Model Housekeeping 210
Monsanto House of the Future 197, **304**
Moore, James 31n16
Moses, Robert 276
Morley, Chris 62–63
Moscow *see* American National Exhibition
Motherwell House *see* Chareau, Pierre
Motherwell, Robert 44
Motor Wheel Corporation 130
MTV 272
Müller, Paul 126
Mumford, Lewis 47, 47n40, 53
Museum for a Small City *see* Mies van der Rohe, Ludwig
Museum of Modern Art, New York 6, 8, 24–25, 32, 40–55, 70–71, 75–81, 92, 101, 106, 170, 189, 251, 271
   Bulletin of the Museum of Modern Art 42–45, 71–72, 75, **70 74 76 103 118**
   Department of Architecture and Design 46, 50–51
   exhibition houses program 8, 25, 40–47, 50–51, 54, 80
   exhibitions:
      Art in Progress 53, **89**
      Britain at War 75n19, 78
      Built in USA: Post-War Architecture 50
      Built in the USA: Since 1932 51
      Camouflage for Civilian Defense 75, 75n19, 78, **120**
      Defense House *see* Fuller, R. Buckminster, Dymaxion Deployment Unit
      Exhibition House in the Museum Garden *see* Ain, Gregory
      Family of Man *see* Steichen, Edward
      Good Design 40, 51, **62–65 150**
      House in the Museum Garden *see* Breuer, Marcel
      Mies van der Rohe 32, 101, 106, 170, 189, 271, **51 178–181**
      Modern Architecture: International Style 6, 24, 45, 51, **4 27**
      National Defense Poster Competition 78
      New Furniture Designed by Charles Eames 92
      Power in the Pacific *see* Steichen, Edward
      Road to Victory *see* Steichen, Edward
      Tomorrow's Small House 44–47, 54, **76–77**
      Useful Objects in Wartime 40, 54
      Useful Objects under $10 40, 54, 79
      Wartime Housing 44–45, 54, 78
   publications:
      Museum of Modern Art: The History and the Collection,
      The 41n25, 80
   parties for the army 44, 45n30, 78, **75**
   symposia/lectures
      "Apropos of 'Readymades'" 70
      "What Is Happening to Modern Architecture?" 51, 81

N

NASA **356**
National Committee on the Housing Emergency 44
National Guard 301
National Housing Administration (NHA) 45
Nautilus 214, 230, *see* Verne, Jules
Nelson, George 81, 250, 257–258, 264, 268, **376–377**
"Art X" *see* Eames, "Sample Lesson . . ."
Nelson, Paul 149
Nestlé Pavilion *see* Le Corbusier *and* Jeanneret, Pierre
Neuhart, John and Marilyn 87n3, 89n8, 91n11, 245n8, 253n20, 257n24, 259n3–6
Neutra, Richard 162, 171, 276, **253**
   Case Study House 25
   Hinch House **261**
   Kahn House **252**
   Lovell "Health" House 162
   Rainer Apartment **253**
   Scioberetti Residence 162
   Tremaine Residence 25
New Deal Program 62
Newsweek 188
New York **350 351**
New Yorker, The 53
New York Times 148, 263
New York Times Magazine 188
Night of the Iguana 88
Nimmons, George C. 23n1
Nixon, Pat 244, **365**
Nixon, Richard 54–55, 138, 164, 241, 244, **92 360 361 362–363**
Noyes, Eliot 250
nuclear fallout 279

O

Office Building on Friedrichstrasse *see* Mies van der Rohe, Ludwig
Oldsmobile 133
Orwell, George 219
Osler, William 160
Ozenfant, Amédée 22, 30, **26**
Ozenfant House *see* Le Corbusier
Paimio Sanatorium *see* Aalto, Alvar

P

Paolozzi, Eduardo 203, **6** see also Independent Group
Parallel of Life and Art see Independent Group
Parathion 127
Parke, Davis 129
Parker, William Stanley 23
Patio and Pavilion see Independent Group
Pearl Harbor 75, 120
Pepsi-Cola 244
Perspex 196
Peutz, Fritz 149, **224**–**225**
Pevsner, Nikolaus 148
Pfleghard and Häfeli **238 239**
Philco 41n23
Phillips, Patricia 287
photo-collage see collage
photography 42, 78, 97, 98, 115, 205, 234, 286
  aerial photography 115
Picasso, Pablo 98
picture windows see windows
Piscator see Breuer, Marcel
plan, open 153, 165
Plan-Tech Associates 45
plastics 63, 67, 196–201, 203, 228, 232–233, 235–236, 282–284, 286, **166 204 210 305**
play 80, 87, 97, 115, 136, 153, 155, 206, 218–220
Playboy 218, 226–227, **330 331**
Plymouth 133
Plywood 63, 70, 200, see also Eames, Charles and Ray, plywood furniture
Pogo chair see Smithson, Alison and Peter
Poll Parrot **200**
Polly Ester 197n4
Pontiac 133
Pop art 208, 276, 277
  British Pop 195
porches, sleeping 161–163
Power in the Pacific see Steichen, Edward
Powers of Ten see Eames, Charles and Ray
prefabrication 18, 32, 41–42, 45, 47, 62, 68, 134, 184, 200, 208
privacy 41n19, 164–165, 172, 218, 228, 233, 236, 281, **256**
Privacy and Publicity: Modern Architecture as Mass Media
  see Colomina, Beatriz
Progressive Architecture 276
Proun rooms see Lissitkzy, El
psychoanalysis see mental health
psychology see mental health
Public Space/Two Audiences see Graham, Dan

Pupin, Michael **214**
Put Away House see Smithson, Alison and Peter
Pyrex 149

Q

Quetglas, José 171n25
Quonset hut 42–44, **72 73**

R

Radiant City, The see Le Corbusier, *La Ville radieuse*
Rainer, Louise **253**
RAMAC see computers and IBM
Rapson, Ralph 27n7
Rauschenberg, Robert 276
RCA 184, 251, **379**–**380**
readymade 68–71, 81
reality television see television
Red Cross 136
Reed, Peter S. 42n28
reflections 88, 92, 101, 107, 169, 170, 203, **131 154**–**155 182**–**183**
Reich, Lilly 23, 25n4, 106, 182, 202
  Glass Room, Glass Industry Exhibit of Stuttgart 23, 182, see also Mies van der Rohe
  Velvet and Silk Café 106, 202, see also Mies van der Rohe
Renaissance 201, 262
Resor House see Mies van der Rohe, Ludwig
Revell Toy House see Eames, Charles and Ray
Revere Copper and Brass 132–133, **114 201**
Richter, Hans 22
Riley, Terence 41n20
Ringling Brothers Barnum & Bailey Circus 258–259
Road to Victory see Steichen, Edward
Robbins, David 7n2
Roche, Kevin 285n16
Rockefeller, John 47
Rodney King riots 301
roof gardens see terraces
Roosevelt, Eleanor 47, **83**
Roosevelt, Franklin D. 44
Rose, Charlie 188
Rosenquist, James 276
Rosler, Martha
  Bringing the War Home: House Beautiful 290, **438**–**439**
  In the Place of the Public: Observations of a Frequent Flyer **352**
Röntgen, Bertha **214**
Röntgen, Victor **215**
Rudofsky, Bernard 164, 165n21
Rudolph, Paul 13, 26, **34 35**

S

Saarinen, Eero 30, 33n17, 53n50, 90–91, 101, 250, 260, 265, 284, 285n16
  Entenza House 30, 90, **48 143**
  fiberglass chairs 197
  IBM pavilion 265, 268, 284, **394–398 424–425**
  Womb chair **331**
"Sample Lesson for a Hypothetical Course" see Eames, Charles and Ray
sanatoriums 146, 154, 160–161, **237–239 244**
Sandeen, Erik J. 139n73
Sanders, Walter **113**
Saran Wrap 149
Saranac 161, **247**
Sartre, Jean-Paul 168
satellites 241, 256, 260, 277–278, see also Sputnik
Saturday Evening Post 245
Scheerbart, Paul 182
Schein, Lionel 197
Schindler-Chase House see Schindler, R. M.
Schindler, R. M.
  Lovell Beach House 162, **251**
  Schindler-Chase House 162
Schinkel, Karl Friedrich 25n4
Schocken department store see Mendelsohn, Erich
Schrader, Gerhard 127
Schulze, Franz 173n31
Schunck Glass Palace see Peutz, Fritz
science fiction 177, 184, 211, 214, 230, 253, 286
Scioberetti Residence see Neutra, Richard
ScotTissue see toilet paper
Scott Jenkins, Virginia 116, 117n9, 130
Scottish Daily Mail Ideal Home Exhibition 194
Scully, Vincent 276, 284
Screening the Body see Cartwright, Lisa
Seagram Building see Mies van der Rohe, Ludwig
Sears, Roebuck 90
sex, sexuality 121, 217–218, 220, 296, see also gender
Shannon, Claude 261
Shell 129
Show Magazine 188
Shreve, Lamb & Harman Associates **411**
Shulman, Julius 245, **22 142 172 183**
Silent Spring see Carson, Rachel
Silk Exhibition see Mies van der Rohe, Ludwig *and* Reich, Lilly
silos see grain bins, silos
situation room 240, 260, **357 358**
  control room 206, 240, **353 354–357**
Sky House see Smithson, Alison and Peter

Smith, Elizabeth 8n3, 27n9, 87n3
Smithson, Alison and Peter 6–7, 13, 26–27, 86, 92–97, 100, 194–236, **159 315 318–319 342**
  Alison 6, 194, 197, 204–206, 209, 220–221, 234
  AS in DS: An Eye on the Road 205, **313–315**
  mat-cluster 195n3, 197, 197n9
  on Mies 194
  Tulip chair **299**
  Appliance House 195n3
  "But Today We Collect Ads" 7
  on cars 204–208
  on clothing 205, 208–211, 216, 226
  "Eames Celebration" 93, 97
  on the Eameses 6, 93–97, 100
  Egg chair 196
  Fonthill see Upper Lawn pavilion
  Heroic Period of Modern Architecture, The 13, 194
  House of the Future (H.O.F) 194–236, **292–298 300–303 306–307 320–326 328–329 333 335–338 340–343 345 348**
  Independent Group see Independent Group
  masque 200–201
  on Mies 201–202
  Ordinariness and Light **310–311**
  Parallel of Life and Art see Independent Group
  Patio and Pavilion see Independent Group
  Petal chair 196
  Peter 26, 86, 100, 200, 205–207, 209–210, 217, 220–221, 227n63, 229, 235, **307 316 337**
  and photography 205, 206
  Pogo chair 196
  Put Away House 195n3
  Saddle chair 196
  Sky House 195n3
  This Is Tomorrow 195n3
  Team 10 195n3
  Upper Lawn Pavilion, Fonthill 205, **313**
Snyder, Robert 63n1
Some Like It Hot see Wilder, Billy
Somol, R. E. 163n15
Sontag, Susan 156, 157n9–10
Sound of Music 88
South African Architectural Record 23
South Pacific 88
Soviet Exhibition in New York 241
space
  outer space 234, 252, **426 427**
  space program 214, 216, 257, 277, see also Cape Canaveral *and* Sputnik

spacecraft 68, 177, 211–214, 226–228, 286
Space House *see* Kiesler, Frederic
Splitnik 241, 256, **93 94** *see also* American National Exhibition in Moscow, model house
Sports Illustrated 245
Sputnik 234, 241, 253, 277–278, **364 409 410**
standardization 18, 29–30
Staples, Robert 250
Steichen, Edward 42, 78
    Family of Man 251
    Power in the Pacific 42, **76**
    Road to Victory 42, 78, **70–71**
Stewart, Martha 184-185
Stoller, Ezra 245, **209 273 284–285**
Stubbins, Hugh 45
Stum & Walter seed company 116
submarines 211, 214, 226–228, 230, *see also* Nautilus
suburbs 40, 44, 46–47, 50, 55, 72, 80, 114–115, 122, 132, 135, 137–140, 148, 153, 165, 168–173, 177, 184, 191, 229, 241, 244, 251–252, 256, 276, 279, 290
Suburban Documentation Project *see* Faust, Christopher
Sunset 245
surveillance 146–148, 153, 168, 177, 219, 256, 282, 290, 299, **216–219 265** *see also* Orwell, George
Suspended House *see* Nelson, Paul
Swayze, Jay 279–281, 291, *see also* Underground Home

T

Taft, Robert 136
Target TB 147
Taut, Bruno 182, **277**
Team 10 195n3
tear gas 140
television 40, 41, 41n23, 96, 103, 132, 135, 165, 171–172, 177, 182–184, 188, 191, 214, 218–221, 226, 240, 244, 251, 257, 269, 272, 282, 285–292, 297–299, 300, 302, **67 68 268–269 282 283**
    Big Brother 172, 226
    reality television 191, **265**
    see also An American Family
Ten Commandments, The 88
tents **248–249**
terraces 154–157, **233 235–9 241 244 247 251–252**
Terrassentyp *see* Döcker, Richard
terror 146, 164–165, 278, 284, 302
terrorism 148, 297–302
Teyssot, Georges 291n26
Thermoplastics Ltd. 196
Think *see* Eames, Charles and Ray
This Is Tomorrow *see* Smithson, Alison and Peter

Thonet chair 202
Time 139, 251
Times Square 287
Tinling, Teddy 209, 216
toilet paper 129–131, **199**
Tomorrow's Small House *see* Museum of Modern Art, New York
Tonight Show, The 172
toys 6, 72, 93, 97, 218, *see also* Eames, Charles and Ray, toys
tranquilizers 138, 164
transparency 170, 172, 177
trauma 56, 91, 168, 287
Tredick, Ann **116**
Tremaine Residence *see* Neutra, Richard
Trudeau, Edward Livingston 161, **249**
Tsumura, Kosuke 301, **447**
tuberculosis 146–148, 153–157, 160–164, **233 248–249**
Tugendhat House *see* Mies van der Rohe, Ludwig
Tupperware 197, **305**
Twindow **228**
twins 173, 284, **228**
Twitchell, Ralph 25–26, **34–35**
Tyler-May, Elaine 55n54, 135n61, 245n1, 241

U

Underground Home 279–283, 285, 286, 291, **414–418 422–423 441**
Unisphere 277–278, **408**
United Nations Atomic Energy Commission 136
United States Information Agency (USIA) 250
United States Department of Agriculture 62, 121
United States Department of Defense 139
United States Office of Civil Defense 278, 282
University of Georgia, Department of Fine Arts 257
University of Illinois at Chicago, School of Architecture 297
US Air Force Report on the Ballistic Missile, The 282
US Plywood Association 28, **38**
US Public Service 147
US Rubber Ferris Wheel *see* Shreve, Lamb & Harman Associates
USSR pavilion *see* Melnikov, Konstantin

V

van der Meulen, John 27n7
van Nelle factory *see* Brinkman & Van der Vlugt
Venice Biennale 173, **270**
ventilation 156, 233
Verne, Jules 211, 230
Vers une Architecture *see* Le Corbusier
veterans 117–118, 138
victory 53

victory carpets 53, **87**
victory dresses 53, **88**
victory gardens *see* lawns and gardens
video cameras 148, 171, 282, 290, 301, **354**–**355**
Video-Architecture-Television: Writings on Video and Video Works 1970–1978 *see* Graham, Dan
Video Projection Outside Home *see* Graham, Dan
Vietnam War 287, 290
Vigoro 114
Villa d'Avray *see* Le Corbusier
Villa Noailles *see* Mallet-Stevens, Robert
Villa Savoye *see* Le Corbusier
Villa Stein-De Monzie *see* Jeanneret, Pierre *and* Le Corbusier
Villa Stein in Garches *see* Le Corbusier
Virilio, Paul 290, 296
vision, eyes 97, 100, 102–103, 107, 146, 153, 155, 157, 165, 168, 176, 182, 202–204, 217, 219–220, 252–253, 256, 261, 265, 290, 298, **399**
see also gaze, *and* voyeurism
visiting nurses 160
Vogue 79, 108, 258, 264
Voisin, Gabriel 28, 30, **39**
Volkswagen 207–209
voyeurism 32, 217, 219–220, **263**

W

Wall Street Journal 245, 251
Wachsman, Konrad **164**
Waiblingen, sanatorium in *see* Döcker, Richard
Ward, James 63n3
war *see* Gulf War, Iraq war, Vietnam War, World War I *and* World War II
Warerite 196
Warhol, Andy 172, 276, **442**–**443**
war room *see* situation room
War Time Housing *see* Museum of Modern Art, New York
Wasson-Tucker, Susanne 46
weapons 28, 45, 55, 74–75, 119, 121–122, 125–128, 134, 138, 140, 302
Weedone **192**
Weissenhof Siedlung 155, **186 235** *see also* Döcker, Richard *and* Le Corbusier
Wells, H. G. 196
Werkbund exhibition, Cologne 182
Westinghouse 134
What Is a House? *see* Charles Eames
Whirlpool Miracle kitchen 251, **378 379 380**–**381 378**–**379**
white, whiteness 156, 160–161
Whitney, David 189n49
Wichita House *see* Fuller, R. Buckminster

Wide World Photos 139
Wilder, Audrey 32, **52**–**53 57**
Wilder, Billy 31–32, 96, 108, 245, 250, **52**–**53 57 162**
 Some Like It Hot 245
Wilder House *see* Eames, Charles and Ray
Wills, Royal Barry 163
windows 63, 67, 73, 148, 149, 156, 157, 160, 161, 188, 217, 219, 220, 226, 231, 233, 240, 280, 283, 291, 298, **268**–**269**
 picture windows 164, 165, 168, 170–173, 182, 184, 191, 221, 290, **228 261 438**–**439**
Whitfiled, Stephen J. 135n62, 137n65,71
Winkler, Allan M 139 n79
Wizard of Oz, The 62
woman, women 47, 87, 114–119, 126, 128, 130–132, 135, 137, 137n66, 139, 146, 160–161, 164–165, 210, 216–217, 244, **196 365 368**–**369 366**–**367** *see also* gender *and* sex, sexuality
Woman's Home Companion 6, 47, 50, **82**
World Game *see* Fuller, R. Buckminster
World's Fair
 Brussels 268
 Chicago 149
 Moscow *see* American National Exhibition
 New York (1939) 285–287, **429 430 431 432 436**
 New York (1964) 228, 265, 276–287, 291–292, **394 395 395 408**–**421 424**–**427 434**–**435 437 442 443**
World Trade Center 297, 299, 300
World War I 12, 28, 42, 53, 54, 298–299
World War II 6, 12, 28, 42, 54, 114, 122, 138, 140, 163, 194, 227, 240, 279, 296, 299
Wright, Edward 195n2
Wright, Frank Lloyd 45–46, 171
Wright, Gwendolyn 161
Wurster & Bernardi 46
Wyeth medical products 129

X

x-rays 145–191, 217, 231, **212**–**214 216**–**219 227**

Y

Yamasaki, Minoru 276

Z

Zenith **367**
Zimbel, George 245
Zonnestraal *see* Byvoet and Duiker

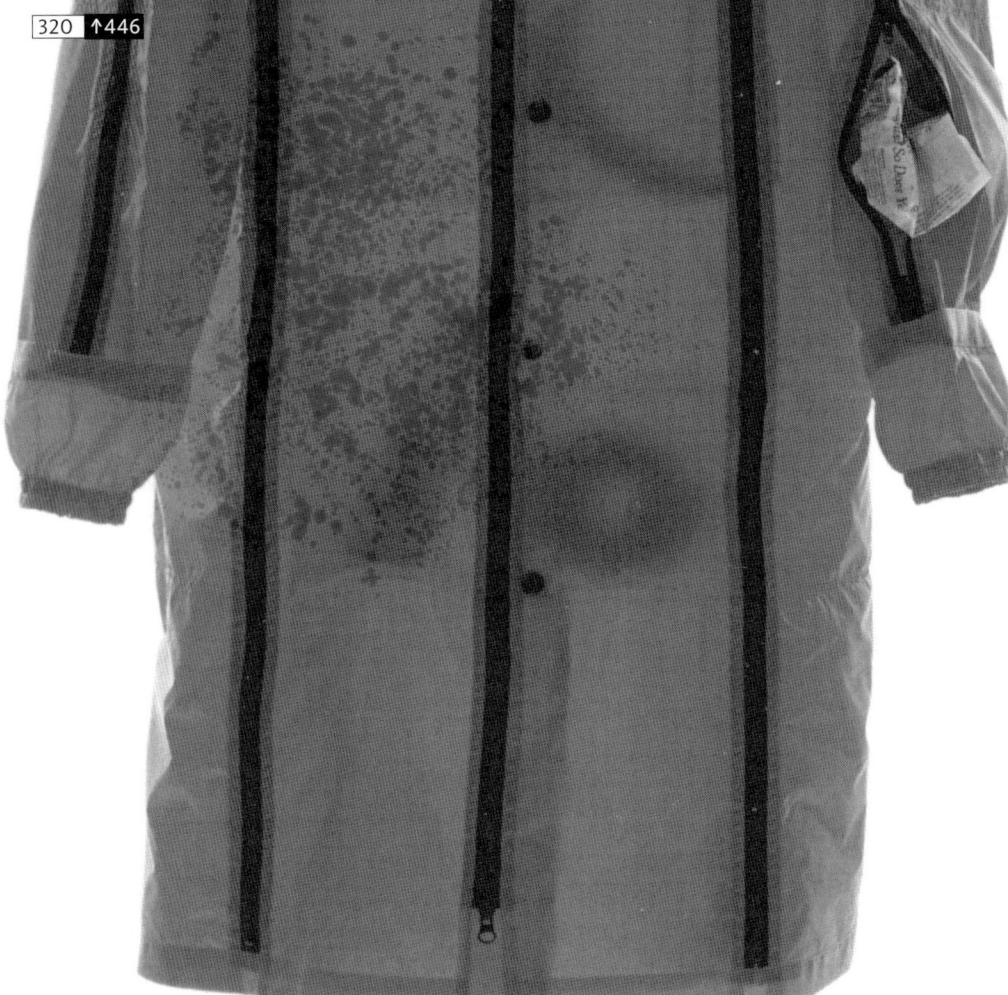